CHRISTIAN FAITH
& OTHER FAITHS

STEPHEN NEILL

INTERVARSITY PRESS
DOWNERS GROVE, ILLINOIS 60515

Other books by Stephen Neill

The Interpretation of the New Testament
A History of Christian Missions
The Church and Christian Union
Jesus through Many Eyes
The Supremacy of Jesus

© *1984 by Stephen Neill. Published in England under the title* Crises of Belief.

Published in the United States of America by InterVarsity Press, Downers Grove, Illinois, with permission from Hodder and Stoughton Limited, England.

InterVarsity Press is the book-publishing division of Inter-Varsity Christian Fellowship, a student movement active on campus at hundreds of universities, colleges and schools of nursing. For information about local and regional activities, write IVCF, 233 Langdon St., Madison, WI 53703.

Superior figures after dates of publication in footnotes indicate the edition referred to.

Cover illustration: Roberta Polfus

ISBN 0-87784-337-6

Printed in the United States of America

Library of Congress Cataloging in Publication Data
Neill, Stephen, 1900-
    Christian faith and other faiths.

    Bibliography: p.
    Includes index.
    1. Christianity and other religions.   2. Religions.
I. Title.
BR127.N37   1984   261.2   84-19193
ISBN 0-87784-337-6

19	18	17	16	15	14	13	12	11	10	9	8	7	6	5	4	3	2
98	97	96	95	94	93	92	91	90	89	88	87						

Preface —— *8*

I The Problem Set ———— 9

II The King of the Jews ———— 34

III Islam in Crisis ———— 57

IV Renascent Hinduism ———— 91

V The Doctrine of the Lotus ———— 125

VI The Primal World ———— 159

VII No Faith and Faith Implicit ———— 189

VIII A Search for Light ———— 220

IX Christendom ———— 257

Select Bibliography —— *289*

Index —— *299*

Preface

I was pleased when I received a request that I should provide a replacement for a book *Christian Faith and Other Faiths* (OUP) which is no longer available. I know that the earlier work proved useful to a number of readers; I hope that in its new form it may continue to be useful to a younger generation.

When I set to work on the necessary revision, I found that I should have to work much harder and in more detail than I had expected. For this there were two simple reasons: a great deal has happened in recent years in the world of the non-Christian religions, and I myself know a great deal more about these religions than I did when the lectures on which the book is based were first delivered in Melbourne in 1960. So each chapter has had to be carefully revised, and several have been extensively or almost completely rewritten. As a result, a reader who is familiar with the older book will find much in the revision that will be familiar, in as much as my attitude to the non-Christian religions and to the way in which they ought to be approached by the Christian has not greatly changed; but I have tried to do justice to each of the religions as it is in the year 1983, and in this sense the book is new. I have tried to be like the wise scribe of whom Jesus spoke, who brings forth out of his treasure-house things new and old.

I have to express my indebtedness to many friends who have helped me by criticism and advice; to publishers who have graciously given permission for the use of quotations from works of which the copyright belongs to them; to the staff of Hodder and Stoughton, and in particular to Pauline McCandlish who produced a complete typescript of the book as it now appears, dexterously weaving together new and old into what I hope will appear as an almost seamless robe.

S.N.
Oxford
May 1983

CHAPTER I

The Problem Set

Rather more than a century ago (1860), the first international missionary conference of modern times was held at Liverpool. Full records were kept. If we read today the lectures and discussions, we have almost the feeling of being listeners in on those proceedings of long ago. Much of what passed strikes a surprisingly modern note; many of the concerns expressed and the problems faced are almost the same as those to which expression would be given at a similar conference today. And yet we discover that those godly Christians of the nineteenth century were living in a very different world from ours.

They were in two respects denizens of a world that was very soon to pass away. In the first place, very little space was accorded in their discussions to the non-Christian religions by which they were surrounded all the time in their missionary work. Secondly, to them 'missions' were something that were carried on in strange and far distant lands. On one side was Christendom, with its more than a millennium of Christian culture, its political dominance, its immense and rapidly increasing wealth; on the other was the non-Christian world that had waited so long for the diffusion of the light of Christian truth.

For their disregard of the non-Christian faiths those pious Christians must not be too severely blamed. There had been notable pioneers in the study of those faiths, but the general attitude of Christians through the centuries had been one of suspicion, if not of active dislike. Even the noblest of the medieval missionaries had seen in the worship of the 'heathen' nothing more acceptable than detestable idolatry; their prayers were no better than abomination. Ignorance was widespread; attention to the non-Christian systems could be brushed on one side as a mere waste of time.

Though the fathers and brethren of 1860 did not know it, the

study of religions was just about to break through into an
entirely new phase. In the very next year, the distinguished
Indian civilian, later Principal of the University of Edinburgh, Sir
William Muir, completed his life of the Prophet Muhammad
based on original sources, and thus rescued the figure of the
founder of Islam from the glosses and confusions of a century. In
1871 E. B. Tylor published his pioneer work *Primitive Culture*, and
opened the mind of the west to the idea that the manners and
religious ideas of those long despised as barbarians could be both
interesting and a worthy subject of academic study. In 1875 the
German professor turned Oxford man, Max Müller, published
the first of the great series of *Sacred Books of the East*, in the fifty
volumes of which the major classics of all the great religions of
Asia were made accessible to readers acquainted with English. In
1890 Sir J. G. Frazer, with *The Golden Bough*, put religious
anthropology on the map.

As these 'treasures of darkness' penetrated the consciousness
of educated men and women, something like a gasp of
astonishment arose. Surprise was followed by appreciation, and
even by admiration. There was an element of exaggeration in
this new approach; inevitably Saṁkara and Rāmānuja came to be
compared with Plato and Aristotle, the hymns of the Rig Veda
with the Psalms of David, and so on. But the interest was
genuine, and became widespread; it came to be generally
understood that, though Christianity might stand supreme, it
did not stand alone among the great religions of the world.

Christians, because of the intensity of their convictions, were
perhaps rather slower than others to join in the chorus of
adulation for the contemporary discoveries of the past, though
they too made notable contributions to the positive work of
scholarship. Then, not quite a century after the Liverpool
Conference, the unexpected happened – Pope John XXIII startled
the Roman cardinals by saying 'We will have a Council.' Before
long it became clear that what had started as a purely Roman
Catholic project would grow and spread itself in unforeseen
directions; in addition to much that was of only local interest it
would find many things to say about the non-Christian religions
of the world.

For an understanding of the change that has taken place in the
Christian attitude towards these non-Christian religions,
nothing can be more strongly recommended than the study of

the document of Vatican II called *Lumen Gentium*, the light of the Gentiles. The Fathers assembled in council go very far in their appreciation of these other forms of faith, not hesitating to give expression to the view that God has revealed himself in many ways, and that even in the forms of religion that seem farthest removed from the Christian way, there may be men and women who in sincerity and humility follow such light as they have, and so may be found acceptable by the Father of all. This does not absolve the church from the duty of proclaiming the truth of Christ to all men everywhere, since that truth is of universal application, and all human beings have the right to know of the One in whom the full salvation of mankind has been revealed.

Some feel that the Council went too far, and did not adequately safeguard the uniqueness of the Christian revelation. The use of the word 'salvific', conveying salvation, in a number of Roman Catholic writings on these non-Christian faiths, seems to imply a view of salvation which would not be everywhere acceptable. But the generosity of the approach of Vatican II has called forth wide response both in the Christian and in the non-Christian worlds. It is perhaps better to go too far than not to go far enough. Wherever human beings in any way at all are seeking the unseen Father of our spirits, it is good that they should be approached with reverence and the desire to understand.

In 1860 missionaries were not mistaken in regarding themselves as pioneers in the contacts between the nominally Christian west and the rest of the world.

To be a missionary was an adventurous and rather hazardous occupation. Three years before the Liverpool Conference was held a number of missionaries had fallen victims to the violence which accompanied the great Indian uprising. Ten years later the heroic Bishop John Coleridge Patteson was killed by islanders in Melanesia, apparently in revenge for other islanders kidnapped and carried off by 'blackbirders' (white kidnappers).

The end of the century was marked by the Boxer riots in China, in which more than a hundred missionaries lost their lives. In the first week of the new century the veteran James Chalmers with a young companion was killed and eaten by the inhabitants of the Fly River in Papua New Guinea. Hazards continue up to the present day, but they are now shared with indigenous Christians and with other foreigners; the Christian mission is simply part of the blending of the life of the west with that of the east and south.

By 1860 the missionary cause was well established in many great centres of population, but pioneers lived under conditions of almost unimaginable isolation. Until well on in the twentieth century those assigned to posts in inland China took with them as much sugar as they reckoned they would need in a seven-year period of service, knowing that none would be available from any local source of supply. A well-known Anglican missionary to the Eskimo, E. J. Peck, knew that one ship would pay him one visit a year in his lonely outpost. He arranged that the ship should bring him *The Times* of London for a whole year. Every day he solemnly read *The Times*: it made no difference that the paper was a year out of date; Peck kept up his sense of being part of a great world, and even in his isolation being part of the affairs of that world.

A century later we were living in what is perhaps the greatest mixing of populations that the world has ever seen.

When C. M. Doughty made the sensational journey (1876–8) that he has recorded in his great book *Travels in Arabia Deserta*, his life was constantly in danger; no Christian could live with safety in inner Arabia. Now the oil industry has brought in thousands of technicians from Europe, America and Asia to live in the midst of an Arab and Muslim population. In Saudi Arabia Christians still have to walk very warily; permission has been given for the holding of Christian services, but no Christian symbol such as a cross may be displayed, and the Christian presence may not be thrust on the senses of Muslims. In the neighbouring state of Kuwait, by contrast, full religious liberty prevails. There are a few Kuwaiti Christians of ancient lineage, a very small group of converts from Islam; but Christian churches exist and flourish, and Christian services are held in no less than nine languages. Foreigners and nationals live in considerable isolation from one another; but the Christian is aware the whole time that he is living in a land stamped by a culture very different from his own, the texture of which is determined through and through by the Islamic faith.

Migration has not flowed in one direction only. In the United States one of the most successful of the minority communities is that of the Koreans, to be followed now in tragic circumstances by the Vietnamese. For the first time in history, Great Britain is facing the problem of considerable ethnic minorities, the great majority of whom are non-Christian. The size of these minorities has been much exaggerated; they still number less than 5 per cent of the population. Nevertheless, it is a somewhat daunting experience for the vicar of an English parish to realise that the majority of those committed to his care are Hindus, Sikhs or Muslims. The study of these religions was not included in the curriculum of the institution in which he learned his theology, and he becomes painfully aware that he is almost wholly ignorant of these peoples, of what they believe and how they live. Whether we like it or not, mission is no longer a vague and romantic idea; it has washed up on our very shores and has become part of our existence.

Mutual ignorance is still to a large extent the rule – we know little of them, and they know little of us. But there is a new factor in the situation. In the nineteenth century, when the Christian bore witness to the non-Christians around him, he had in most cases the advantage of superior knowledge. Today this is very far from being invariably the case. Among our neighbours from other races and cultures, there will be a small minority who have studied the Christian faith in detail, have compared it with the inheritance that they have received in their own tradition, and have found no reason to change their ancient religion for another. This does not mean that Christian witness is not to be borne; but it must be borne with circumspection, and with a deep regard for the feelings of those who have not accepted the Christian faith.

During the period of the mutual discovery of the various religious faiths of mankind, what was at the time called 'comparative religion', but should more correctly be called 'the comparative study of religions', was highly popular. At its most superficial, this led to an almost deliberate vagueness, and to the belief, still commonly held by those who have given little attention to the subject, that there is a basic reality called 'religion' which is common to all mankind, that all religions say essentially the same things, and that the great religious leaders of mankind have spoken with essentially the same voice. Such a conclusion can be reached only by disregarding the very real differences which exist between different types of religion, by reducing religion to the night in which all cats are grey. Comparison of one religion with others is legitimate and valuable; but it can prove profitable only if there has been general agreement about the objects between which comparison is to be made, the criteria which are to be employed, and the result it is hoped to establish.

The first problem, naturally, relates to the meaning to be attached to the word 'religion'. No finally satisfactory definition has ever been found. If the definition is too broad, this may result in including all systems of thought to which men have given unconditional loyalty; this would make it impossible to exclude Marxism, though most Marxists would declare themselves to be uncompromising opponents of religion in all its forms. In another direction, too wide a definition might be found to include all human beings activated by feelings of goodwill towards others; but, if the definition is so wide, there will be little on which disagreement or agreement will be possible, and the points of comparison will to a large extent be lost. On the other hand, if the definition is too narrow, some forms of association or activity that are generally accounted as religious would be excluded. Eighteenth-century definitions usually included belief in God and in immortality. But Buddhism has no formulated belief in God, and excludes everything which in common parlance would be called immortality. Yet almost all would agree that this system which has survived for more than two thousand years has an unmistakably religious quality.

So, between the too broad and the too narrow, where are we? It may be impossible to arrive at an entirely satisfactory definition, or to state exactly what we mean when we use the word 'faith'. Yet we must start somewhere, if we are to set any boundaries to our study. One statement of the nature of religion which has been found valuable is that it is based on a refusal to believe that the visible universe is ultimately self-explanatory in purely three-dimensional terms. This would exclude systems which are resolutely materialistic and believe that nothing exists which cannot be measured, numbered and weighed. It would include all systems, however simple, which reckon with the possibility of a fourth dimension, invisible, mysterious, yet not unrelated to the capacity of man to look beyond himself, to ask questions and not be discouraged if no finally satisfactory answer to his questions can be found. If this rather broad basis is accepted, comparison between religions can be profitably considered in a variety of different ways.

If we are agreed that comparative study is possible, one

approach which has been found to be practically useful is that of discrimination between different types of religion. Not every religious system will fit into whatever principle of classification may be adopted, and there will be a certain amount of overlap, some systems fitting into more than one of the indicated slots.

One rather clear distinction is that between the prophetic and the mystical types of religion – between those in which there is emphasis on active proclamation and those in which religion is understood principally in terms of inner apprehension. Some religions look back to a historical and identifiable founder (Islam, Christianity); the origin of others is lost in the mists of time; Hinduism has had great teachers, but no founder who can be named, in contrast to the Sikh religion which looks back to Guru Nānak (1469–1539). In some religions, doctrine and practice are determined in relation to a recognised and acknowledged sacred book; in others, the traditions are unwritten and are handed down by word of mouth from generation to generation. The religions of nature reflect the unchanging sequence of the seasons of the year and look for the return of all things to that which they were originally; religions of history believe that the processes which we observe in the universe had a beginning, and look forward to a consummation in the future (Judaism). To tribal religions admission is usually by birth alone – adoption from one tribe to another is in certain cases possible but is rare. (In this sense Hinduism is a tribal religion.) Some religions have from the start claimed universal validity (Buddhism, Christianity, Islam), and recognise various forms and processes of initiation, usually associated with some particular profession of faith or obedience.

One method of comparison which has proved its worth is in an area described in the title of the famous book by Professor G. van der Leeuw, *Religion in Essence and Manifestation*.[1] Religion may be regarded as something simply interior, the relationship between the human being and the object of trust or worship. But all religions, except those which are purely mystical, have activities which are visible and tangible; these can be used as the key to the inner mysteries, but also as a means of comparison with other religions which are marked by similar activities. These rites and

---

[1] *Religion in Essence and Manifestation* (London, 1938).

activities can conveniently be summed up under the headings: holy places, holy people, holy objects, and holy words.

The ancient Roman religion had all these four elements. Most of us can remember from our school-days the Vestal virgins. They served in the temple of Vesta; they were specially selected people; they had the task of caring for a very holy object, the sacred fire which must never be allowed to go out; they carried out rituals accompanied by holy words, couched in such ancient Latin as to be hardly intelligible, in ceremonial formulae the validity of which depended on their being recited with perfect accuracy. The Christian churches have almost all retained in one form or another these four common elements. They have holy places – churches or sanctuaries which are kept separate from all common use. They have holy objects – the elements of sacraments which traditionally may be touched only by holy people – the priests who are specially ordained to minister in holy things, and to carry out ceremonies accompanied by ancient words which must be recited exactly in the prescribed form.

These manifestations of holiness are, as we have said, keys to help us unlock the mysteries of religion. Simple people may well be content if the ritual is carried on in the ancient and accustomed way and go no further. But sooner or later some enquiring soul is going to ask, 'What do these things *mean*?' It then becomes clear that the outward manifestations are valuable, and valid, because in them are enshrined religious ideas in which are expressed, or which are coloured by, the understanding which a people has of the universe by which its members are surrounded and in which they have to live out their lives.

Every religion is to some extent a religion of ideas. Comparison of the ideas expressed or implicit in one religious system with the corresponding ideas in another is thus possible.

We can work out more or less accurately the Christian idea of God, and compare with this the idea of God as it is found in Islam. But, when we engage in comparisons of this kind, we must not forget that, in doing so, we are dealing with abstractions. In order to make comparison possible, we have detached certain ideas or theories or doctrines from the experience that gave rise to them; but, when we have done so, they are no longer living realities. Such study has the same value as the dissection of a specimen in the laboratory, and this must not be underestimated. But we must not be surprised if it tells us little about the religions in question, as these are lived out and experienced by those who profess them.

More and more we are coming to realise that faith is experienced as a whole, and cannot be experienced in any other way.

This has come home to us forcibly in recent years in ecumenical debate between adherents of different forms of the Christian creed. Even when we appear to agree on a doctrine or a certain form of words, our agreement is conditioned and limited by the rest of the system to which we adhere. The result is that emphases are different, perspectives are not the same, and even the apparent agreement is encompassed by the net of disagreement about other things. If this is true even within the varieties of Christian faith, how much more must it be true when we try to compare Christian faith in God with that which in some way comes near to it, the Muslim faith in God. Those things which are experienced as wholes are in fact not commensurable, any more than one scent is really comparable with any other. Genetic or historical connections may be traced; it is just the fact that a knowledge of the Bible and of Christian faith underlies certain parts of the Koran. An understanding of such connections is useful in the study of religion as it is in the study of music. But, when we have said that the young Beethoven was at certain points influenced by Mozart, we have not really said anything very important about either of them; the music of each has to be felt and appreciated in terms of itself and of nothing else. Even when, as can happen, one musician has actually stolen a phrase or a melody from another, what he does with it is so idiosyncratic that the connection has little more importance than that of a historic accident. The greater the composer, the less is it possible to think or speak of him in terms other than those of his own achievement.

The musical parallel is perhaps that which will help us most to understand the shift that has taken place in the modern approach to the study of religions. The only method which promises results is that of self-exposure, as complete as possible, to the impact of a religion as a whole. The attitude is not that of *theoria*, the dispassionate contemplation which was the ideal of the Greek; this leads to apprehension without involvement. The new approach is that of engagement, personal involvement in something which is of deep concern to us because it is of deep concern to millions of our fellow human beings.

For this modern attitude to 'comparative religion' it has become common to use the not very attractive contemporary word 'empathy' – the attempt to enter as far as is possible into the thoughts and experiences of others without losing the integrity of one's own independence. Thus a Christian expert in Buddhism, who has lived many years in Japan, has given to a recently published book the title *Buddhist Christian Empathy*.[2] It is clear what he means by this choice of title – he has done his utmost to *feel* Buddhism as the Buddhist feels it, to understand Buddhism as the Buddhist understands it, yet not to abandon his stance as a *Christian* friend of Buddhists.

This is an exacting, indeed almost a terrifying, approach. Can one launch oneself into the heart and spirit of another religion without disloyalty to one's own? Does not such an approach involve a measure of detachment incompatible with deep adherence to any system of religious belief? Oddly enough, experience seems to show that anxiety to be groundless. It is those who have the deepest and most confident faith who have the courage to launch out on this adventure of the human spirit; and their own commitment renders them more, not less, sensitive to the commitment of others whose faith finds a different object and a different form of expression. This way does call for sympathy and discrimination. It does demand patience and a willingness to suspend judgment. It does not involve indifference to truth or the abandonment of all objective criteria of judgment.

Each religion, as we study it, will be found to be one expression of man's reaction to the total human situation within which he has to live. Our questions concerning each will relate to its adequacy in the context of that total situation. Does it take account of everything, literally everything, in the human situation? Or are there certain areas that are disregarded and ignored? What needs of the human spirit does this system meet? Are there legitimate needs of the human spirit that it disregards or denies? To what extent does it serve man in the fullest development of his potential? Is it related to the concept of community, of the city in which man can dwell at peace and in

---

[2] J. Spae: *Buddhist Christian Empathy* (Chicago, 1980).

harmony with his neighbours? Does it point to a fulfilment beyond the limits of time and space?

It may be objected that this is a man-centred way of approaching the subject. The answer to this objection is that, if we are to study man's religious experience as a whole, we must have some starting point. The only starting point which commends itself is that of establishing certain *concerns* which seem to be common to all human beings, and using these concerns as a basis for comparing one set of answers with others. This means that for the moment we shall be postponing the question of *truth* in religion. This is defensible in practice. But the question of truth, which in the field of religion means the question of the validity of the answers given by a particular religion to the questions raised by the situation of man in the totality of his universe, cannot be evaded for ever. In the field of religion, certainty, in the sense of mathematical certainty, is not to be had. But our study will certainly challenge our own answers, tentative and approximate as they may be, to this central and all-important question of ultimate truth.

We are engaging in this study frankly as Christians. We do not pretend to stand on any Olympian height of detachment from which we can survey all forms of human religion with splendid impartiality. We know now that that cannot be done. In all investigation – even in the most austere researches of the nuclear physicist – the personal equation is involved. In the study of religion the personal equation is at its highest, and it would be unscientific to pretend that this is not so. We shall speak and question as those who live within one particular system, one particular understanding of the world. But this does not necessarily mean that our approach will be prejudiced, and that we shall distort everything we see by looking at it through our own spectacles, though this is a danger that must be borne in mind. It does mean that our study can be carried on only by way of dialogue. We shall question others as to their beliefs. But this means that we must expose ourselves, honestly and without protection, to the questions that they may ask of us.

If we meet some intellectually acute and competent adherents of the other religions, we shall find that the questions they put to us will be relevant, searching and at times embarrassing. They will not be satisfied by trivial or superficial answers. It follows that today the comparative study of religions is not for those of timid spirits and queasy stomachs. It is a stern and relentless business. But, if it is the incomparable privilege of Christians to stand at or near the centre of truth, we shall have everything to gain and nothing to lose by exposing ourselves to questioning. The questions should help to elucidate our own faith, to open up aspects of it that were previously hidden from us, perhaps to rid us of some illusions, and in the end to strengthen our hold on that which, or rather him whom, we have believed.

How, then, are we to prepare ourselves for an open-minded approach to the non-Christian religions? Our dialogue with our non-Christian friends will be conditioned by certain pre-suppositions, common to almost all Christians, as to the way in which Christians think, as to the questions which in their opinion must be raised if useful discussion is to be possible, and as to the area within which they think it possible for answers to these questions to be found.

To start with we may lay down three categories within which Christians find themselves thinking all the time, and without the use of which they cannot think as Christians at all. These are not yet beliefs or doctrines; they lie behind all doctrines and make possible the formulation of doctrines when the appropriate time comes.

1. The first is the principle of contingency, or contingent being.

Human thought has swayed over the centuries between the extreme of realism, the belief that the visible world is all that exists; and the extreme of idealism, the belief that the visible world does not really exist at all except in so far as our minds give it a certain brief and illusory reality. Christian thought rejects both these extremes. The world, and man within it, has reality, has existence. But this is a wholly dependent reality and existence. Nothing in the world, and least of all man himself, can be explained in terms of forces and principles solely within this world. There is a beyond, in dependence on which the world exists and man can find his freedom.

If we wish to go a step farther and put the matter theologically, we cannot think as Christians without the concept of creation. We take our stand on the first verse of the Bible: 'In the beginning God created the heavens and the earth.' In quite recent times the doctrine of creation has become the centre of some very cogent Christian thinking.

2. Secondly, we can think only in terms of purpose.

The most significant thing about human beings is that they are creatures which can form purposes. It is probably true that man alone among living beings has the capacity for conceptual thought – his universal use of articulate speech suggests it – but we know so little of the mental processes of animals that this is hard to prove. We do see traces of purpose even among the animals. But these are rudimentary, and seem to depend more on instinctive response than on conscious planning. Man has the faculty of forming purposes, such as the purpose of writing a book, which may involve years of effort, the co-ordination of innumerable subsidiary purposes, the co-operation of a great many other minds, which can be adhered to in the face of frustration, disappointment and partial failure, and in the carrying out of which a writer may feel that he is most truly living.

The purpose of God is one of the postulates of Christian thinking. This is very different from the old argument of design. That argument was too simple; it broke down in face of the all too evident fact that the universe considered as a machine does not work nearly so well as a machine designed by infinite intelligence and maintained by infinite power ought to do. It took far too little account of imperfection, failure and tragedy. Very different from this is the idea of purpose. We are accustomed to working out our own purposes slowly, patiently, and by the use of materials that are always more or less refractory. An observer might find it extremely difficult to guess what the purpose is, as he sees an author sitting surrounded by an apparently shapeless and hopeless chaos of notes. But, given the necessary resolution, conviction and patience, the shape of the purpose will eventually emerge. If, then, there is a divine purpose in the universe, and if it emerges only slowly, through many set-backs and apparent failures, if at times it is evident to faith rather than to sight, we shall be neither surprised nor disturbed. Such a method cannot be stigmatised as either irrational or unworthy of a God who is prepared to respect the freedom of the human creatures with whom he has to deal.

3. The third conviction is that events really happen, and that once they have happened, no power in heaven or on earth can cause them not to have happened.

History is the sphere in which we have to operate and in which God also is pleased to operate. Now history is always the scene of the unexpected, the unpredictable, the irrevocable, the unalterable and the unrepeatable. The forces that operate in history are so manifold and complex that the historian who is unwise enough to prophesy the future is almost certain to be proved wrong. In one sense there is no new thing under the sun. But, when human wills operate, they do produce situations which have never existed before. And history never repeats itself. There are similarities between one period and another but there is no exact repetition; the elements of flexibility and uncertainty are always present. Some religions are based on the idea of the everlasting return, that all things in the end will come back to exactly that which they have been before. (This was the view, among others, of the ancient Stoics.) This is not the view of the Christian. To him the past is unalterable because it has already happened; the present is the moment of risk and adventure; the future holds out the possibility of glorious fulfilment, influenced but not precisely determined by the past.

All this should prepare us to recognise that man is extremely important in the Christian scheme of things. It is an exaggeration, but perhaps a helpful exaggeration, to say that Christian doctrine can be reduced to a doctrine of man. But, of course, this means man in dependence on God, and no sense at all can be made of Christian thought unless full attention is paid to both poles of the ellipse.

More perhaps than any other form of religion or philosophy Christian faith takes the human situation seriously. It never doubts for a moment that it is a great and glorious thing to be a human being. Faith can find a place, though not without criticism, for all the wonderful achievements of the human race in society, in culture, in art, even in the somewhat tarnished glories of technical civilisation. But at the same time it looks with wide-open and dispassionate eyes on the squalor, the contradictions, the self-destroying absurdity of human existence. By our ingenuity we have built up a brave new world of our own invention, and now, like a child tired of its toys, we seem to be set on destroying it, and with it the whole race of which we are a part. In vision and aspiration man's head touches the heavens, but his feet still stand firmly in the ooze and slime of primeval chaos. As Pascal saw clearly, we cannot understand man unless we consider him in both his greatness and his misery. But, having made an exhaustive inventory of the misery, Christian faith still affirms that it is a good thing to be a human being.

This being so, it should come as no surprise that Christianity is the religion of a Man. We shall encounter other religions which have historical founders, but in none of them is the relation between the adherent of that religion and its founder similar to that which the Christian believer supposes to exist between himself and Christ. The old saying 'Christianity is Christ' is almost exactly true. The historical figure of Jesus of Nazareth is the criterion by which every Christian affirmation has to be judged, and in the light of which it stands or falls.

Jesus came to show what human life really is. The characteristic dimension of human existence is freedom. On this narrow sand-bank between existence and non-existence, between coercion and chaos, God has withdrawn his hand so far as to make a space in which we can be really, though not unconditionally, free. In Jesus we see what a free man looks like. We could hardly have guessed in advance that this is what the picture would be.

The first paradox in this freedom is that it means complete acceptance of a situation as it is given without man's own choice, the situation into which man is thrown without his knowledge or consent. Jesus was born a Jew and lived under Roman oppression. At no point does he show resentment against this situation or regard it as a hindrance to the fulfilment of his task. These are the raw materials given him by God; with these materials and no others is he to work out the perfect pattern of human liberty. What is true of him is true also of us all. Within the limits of the given material a great variety of choice is open to us, but there are certain unalterable structures of our life; if we resent these or kick against them, we merely reduce our capacity to make the best of what may in itself be a rather unpromising situation.

The second paradox is that this freedom can be lived out only in a state of total dependence upon God. This element in the life of Jesus is made plain in all the Gospels. At first sight, surprisingly, it is more deeply stressed in the fourth Gospel, the Gospel of the glory of Christ, than in the other three. Again and again in this Gospel Jesus affirms that of himself he can do nothing, that he does only what he sees the Father doing, that he speaks only the words that the Father has given him to speak. He cannot act until his hour has come – and this means always the *kairos*, the moment appointed by the Father. To the lusty spirit of independence which is characteristic of our highly independent age, such dependence might seem to resemble slavery rather than freedom. It is not immediately self-evident that the richest freedom is enjoyed in perfect co-operation, as when pianist and violinist each finds his perfect complement in the playing of the other.

In the world as it is, this freedom can be exercised only in suffering. This is true of all who would live the life of freedom. It is perfectly exemplified in the life of Jesus. He did live as a Jew. But he could never identify himself completely with any standards other than those which he himself set; his attitude was one of critical loyalty. This independent attitude was bound to draw down on him, as it will on others who live as he lived, the hostility of those who are committed to the status quo, and who through laziness or self-interest are unwilling to listen to a new and challenging voice. But such hostility can never take away from the free man his inner liberty. When as in the case of Jesus it is carried to the extreme limit, has nailed him to a cross and taken away the last vestige of his outward liberty, he still remains sovereign in his inner freedom; he is master of the situation and not they. Across the ages he has affirmed the paradox of his mastery.

The purpose of this exemplary life of freedom was to restore to all men the possibility of true human life as from the beginning it was intended to be. Life as we know it is full of contradictions, and contradictions lead to frustration and weakness. The life of Jesus is life without inner contradiction, and therefore peerless in its strength.

The miracles of Jesus are to serve as signs of the breaking in of the new order. Almost every one of them is concerned with the restoration of human existence to its normal working – the withered hand is quickened with new life, the paralytic takes up his bed and walks, not without a reminder that the paralysis of sin is a graver matter than the paralysis of arms and legs. Even the saying that the poor have the Gospel preached to them (Luke 4: 18), is to be interpreted under this rubric of restoration. The 'poor' are not simply the poor in this world's goods, though this is also included; they are those who in their helplessness have looked up to God in hope and expectation. To them the word is now given that their prayer has been heard – God himself is bringing in his own new order: 'The world's great age begins anew.'

But this renewal cannot be through regression to an imagined past of primitive innocence. Adam and Eve have eaten of the tree of the knowledge of good and evil, and they cannot go back to the garden of Eden. They can only go forward to a new relatedness to God. Jesus is the last Adam; he too is tempted, in just the same way as the first Adam, to assert his independence of God and so to fall away from the true reality of human life. He is accepted because he wins the victory over temptation, and in him human nature is maintained in perfect fellowship with God up to the point of death and beyond it. No other can be accepted in this way since no other is the equal of Jesus in human stature or essential goodness. For all the rest of us the renewal of fellowship can take only the form of forgiveness.

For this reason the affirmation of the forgiveness of sins is the heart of the proclamation of the message of Christ. That is why the new order brought in by Christ is spoken of as the new creation. Forgiveness is always creative; it brings into being a new world, a totally new situation, in which alienation has been taken away and has been replaced by a new and firmer fellowship. This is true even of human forgiveness. Much more is it true of the forgiveness of God. Forgiveness is always a movement in one direction – from the one who has been wronged to the one who has done wrong. It can never spring from any other motive than sheer goodwill, caused by nothing other than the spontaneous generosity of the one who is prepared to forgive. God created one universe in the beginning by the word of his power; now he has created another by the word of his grace offered by God in Christ.

It is often assumed that the word God is univocal, that it means the same to all people at all times. This is certainly not the case. In the preceding pages the word God has been used a number of times without closer definition; but at this point an attempt at definition must be made, if what follows is to be clear. When a Christian uses the word 'God', the meaning is the Father of our Lord Jesus Christ – and nothing else. Until we have seen Jesus, we have not seen God in all the fullness of that which can be known of him. 'He that hath seen me hath seen the Father' says Jesus in the fourth Gospel (14: 9). The converse is true. He who has not seen Jesus has not seen the Father.

Christian theology has at times gone astray by taking as the basis for our understanding of the nature of God other sources – Greek philosophy, natural knowledge – and failing to take as seriously as it should the tremendous assertion of the New Testament that it is in Jesus that we see God. If this assertion is true, then any idea we may previously have had of God must undergo a reconstruction which amounts to rebuilding from the basement to the coping-stone. We need not deny the value of the Old Testament and of all that we can learn from it in order to recognise that even the Old Testament is a preface that gives only hints and glimpses of the glory that is to follow. For, if we see God in Jesus Christ, what is the principal thing that we learn about him? It is that God is a servant, and that, when he most fully makes himself the servant of all, the glory of his power finds its fullest self-expression.

No other interpretation of the being of God is possible, if we take seriously what has been said about freedom as the indispensable dimension of the true life of man. One who respects the freedom of another in a very real sense makes himself the servant of that other. And God respects the freedom of man. He exercises no coercion. When men reject and repudiate his good purposes, apparently he allows himself to be frustrated; he gives himself, as it were, helpless into their hands, just as Jesus suffered himself to be helpless in the hands of those who could do him the utmost wrong. How else can we explain the age-long history of wrong and sorrow on the earth?

For it is a mistake to imagine that this aspect of the being of God dates only from the coming of Jesus into the world. It is true that the Son of God took upon himself the form of a servant. It is true that, though he was rich, for our sakes he became poor. But this could come about only because what was seen in Jesus was there in God from the beginning. The greatest act of God's self-emptying was the creation of a universe on which he would confer existence in a measure independent of himself. God was, and nothing else was. He was unrelated to anything except himself. And then of his own free will he chose to be related to a world existing in space and time. He exchanged his liberty for the servitude of being bound to the created world that he had brought into being. Having made the world he would not forsake it; he had committed himself to the world, to the world including its sorrow and its sin.

All too often the coming of God into the world in Jesus Christ is spoken of almost as though it were a kind of trick, a desperate remedy adopted to put right an almost desperate situation. This travesty of theology can be avoided if we take seriously the revelation that Jesus has given of the Father. The incarnation was inevitable because God is what he is. Love leads to redemptive action. Love entered into time and redeemed time. Love entered into the human race as one of us, and by doing so made all things new.

Jesus Christ is a figure of history. In him is seen the action of God at a particular point of space and in a particular epoch of time. But the writers of the New Testament were right in seeing that this action in history cannot be understood, unless we look both before and after it.

'The same was in the beginning with God.' The doctrine of the pre-existence of Christ is not a theological puzzle intended to make faith difficult: it is our assurance that the mercy which was manifest in Jesus was there from the beginning. What we touch in him is the unchanging love of God our servant.

'And he shall come to be our judge.' God has committed all judgment to him because he is the Son of man. So it is that, while the New Testament looks forward to that day of triumph when the nature of the new creation will finally be revealed, at the same time it tells us that the judgment is going forward day by day. The verdict of the day of judgment will not be some arbitrary sentence imposed upon us from without; it will simply be the manifestation of what we have made of ourselves, and the standard and criterion of judgment will be what we have done with that divine light, the fullness of which is seen in Jesus Christ. Every one is faced with the alternatives of coming to the light, in so far as light has been given, or turning from the light and choosing to remain in darkness. We are our own judges; we pass sentence on ourselves by what we are and do.

The Christian outlook on the future is never separated from Jesus and the continuing reality of what he is. The details of the narratives of the resurrection of Jesus Christ may cause us some perplexity; as to the central truth that they are intended to express there can be no doubt. The most striking feature of the narratives is their homeliness; here is no magnificent theophany in power, but a familiar figure who is prepared to eat a piece of grilled fish, and to stand on the shore of the lake cooking breakfast for his hungry friends. The risen Jesus whom the astonished disciples meet is the same Jesus whom they have known. If we may so put it, the manner of his being is changed, but *he* is not changed. He is the same yesterday, today and for ever. He has not been re-absorbed into God from whom he came; he is for ever Jesus, and no eternity can touch the reality of the mysterious 'taking of the manhood into God'.

This is decisive for all Christian thinking about the future of the individual and of the church. We too shall be changed, but we shall still be ourselves. That is why the creed speaks of the resurrection of the body and not of the immortality of the soul. John Donne (1572–1631), in a famous passage, wrote in terms of a literal resuscitation of the flesh, in which God would gather together every seed-pearl that had been scattered through his wide universe.[3] Some Christians who take the Bible quite literally are likely to express their belief today in terms similar to these. But more accurate study of the Greek language, as used in the period of the New Testament, suggests that here 'body' comes as near as any word available to those ancient writers to what we mean today by personality. We may join with William Temple, who once arrived panting at the top of a steep ascent in the Lake District with the words, 'I am glad that I don't believe in the resurrection of the flesh.' But we are encouraged to believe that, just as Jesus is Jesus for evermore, so it is I myself who will be raised to new life in that other world.

The Bible is the story of God's care for the individual. He holds all the universe in the hollow of his hand; yet the word of God comes to Moses, to Isaiah, to this particular person and to that. It is by God's care for each one of us that we are held in life. There is no reason to suppose that the love of God for you and me is affected by so small an accident as physical death. But, if there is love, there must needs be a lover and a loved one. The mystic may think of the total absorption of the self into God, so that there is no longer any distinction between I and Thou. This is not the Christian picture. God called the I into being, and gave it room to stand against himself, in order that the relationship might become eternal and find its fulfilment in a world exempt from change and chance.

---

[3] Sermon XXII, Easter Day, 1627.

The reality of the individual is in his relatedness to God. But this is never thought of out of connection with the complementary relatedness to other selves. To the mystic the presence of other selves may seem irrelevant or even a disturbing nuisance. The Christian, whether he likes it or not, is bound by the profession of his faith to accept his brother, the brother whom, without his choosing, God has given him in the church.

This is only common sense. If we are destined to live with one another for ever and ever, we had better begin to learn to live with one another now. Thus in Christian faith there is nothing whatever of that 'flight of the alone to the alone', made famous by the closing phrase of the *Enneads* of Plotinus. Every picture, every image, of life in the beyond given to us in scripture is strictly social in character. The book of Revelation culminates in the vision of the city. The mind of the reader who knows the Old Testament goes back to such phrases as 'Jerusalem is built as a city that is at unity within itself' (Ps. 122: 3), and to other words which speak of the earthly Jerusalem as a community of responsible individuals bound together by loyalty to one another and to their God. This is the ideal which finds its consummation and its perfection in the Christian hope for each one of us and for the church. We find the reality of our being not in our loneliness, not in 'what we do with our solitariness', as A.N. Whitehead supposed, but in the fullness of relatedness to other human spirits in whom also God dwells.

Christians have never been able to explain to themselves or others the nature of eternal life as this is experienced by finite spirits. We tend to think of it merely as the prolongation of chronological time without end, without the natural limit of death. The ancient myth of Tithonus warns us that this would be a frightful prospect. Time without end would seem to be also time of endless boredom. On the other hand the Greek concept of a timeless eternity in which nothing happens does not fit well into Christian categories of thinking. The only God we know is God in action; that the same God is also God in repose we may well believe; it is beyond the possibilities of our understanding to bring together the two aspects of his being. This means that, if we speak at all of the other world, we can do so only in terms of apparent paradox and contradiction, and this will always be an offence to those who like everything to fit into the tidy categories of philosophic thought.

The aim of this section of our study has not been to give in tabloid form an outline of Christian doctrine. Its purpose has been to indicate certain perspectives, or perhaps we should call them dimensions, without the use of which it is not possible to speak of Christian faith at all. It has been necessary to make use of such terms as creation, history, personal being, responsibility, forgiveness, relatedness, resurrection. Some of these dimensions are not found in other great religions, and some are found only in order to be violently repudiated. Hence the difficulty of comparative study. What is it that we are really comparing? We shall not insist at every point on these Christian categories while looking at other religions in their contemporary form. But we must constantly bear them in mind; otherwise our study is in danger of being unrealistic, and of leading to apparent reconciliations which are in fact no more than empty and irresponsible truces.

And yet, with all these qualities that distinguish it so sharply from every other form of human religious experience or ideal, Christian faith claims for itself that it is the only form of faith for men. By its own claim to truth it casts the shadow of imperfect truth on every other system. This Christian claim is naturally offensive to the adherents of every other religious system. It is almost as offensive to modern man, brought up in the atmosphere of relativism, in which tolerance is regarded almost as the highest of the virtues. But we must not suppose that this claim to universal validity is something that can quietly be removed from the Gospel without changing it into something entirely different from what it is. The mission of Jesus was limited to the Jews and did not look immediately beyond them; but his life, his methods and his message do not make sense unless they are interpreted in the light of his own conviction that he was in fact the final and decisive word of God to men.

Attempts to demonstrate the 'absoluteness' of Christian faith on rational or philosophic grounds cannot be said to have been entirely successful. As long as faith is interpreted in terms of *understanding*, it is always possible that understanding might be reached in some other way than that of the Gospel of Jesus Christ – indeed that some other form of understanding might prove in the light of modern knowledge to be more complete and more logically self-consistent. It is better, perhaps, to speak rather of the universal relevance of Christianity than of its absolute validity.

Here we are on safer ground. For the Christian Gospel is rooted in event and not in idea. Now every event in history is in itself unique and unrepeatable. It is possible to find parallels to almost every saying of Jesus in the books of the Rabbis; that does not alter the fact that each human life is distinct from every other, and that any system of religious faith which is not centrally concerned with Jesus Christ cannot closely resemble a system which *is* so centrally concerned.

Simply as history the event of Jesus Christ is unique. Christian faith goes a great deal farther in its interpretation of that event. It maintains that in Jesus the one thing that needed to happen has happened in such a way that it need never happen again in the same way. The universe has been reconciled to its God. Through the perfect obedience of one man a new and permanent relationship has been established between God and the whole human race. The bridge has been built. There is room on it for all the needed traffic in both directions, from God to man and from man to God. Why look for any other?

Christian faith is prepared to submit itself to the most radical tests as to its relevance to the life of man now and at all other times. It maintains that in Jesus account has been taken of the whole human situation in every aspect; nothing has been overlooked or ignored. No situation can ever arise in the future which cannot be interpreted in the light of the central event of human history – though the interpretation may demand more sensitiveness, patience and humility than Christians are able always to command.

Making such claims, Christians are bound to affirm that all men need the Gospel. For the human sickness there is one specific remedy, and this is it. There is no other. Therefore the Gospel must be proclaimed to the ends of the earth and to the end of time. The church cannot compromise on its missionary task without ceasing to be the church. If it fails to see and to accept this responsibility, it is changing the Gospel into something other than itself.

Naturally to the non-Christian hearer this must sound like crazy megalomania and religious imperialism of the worst kind. We must recognise these dangers: Christians have on many occasions fallen into both of them. But we are driven back ultimately on the question of truth. It is not crazy megalomania for the science of chemistry to affirm that the physical universe has been built up in one way and not in another; the atomic

weights of the various elements have been worked out and are
printed in a table – that is the way things are and no amount of
wishing will make them any different from what they are. It is
true that new discoveries are being made all the time, and that
the physical universe proves to be far more subtly constructed
and flexible than we had at one time supposed. This does not
invalidate the earlier results, which still stand. The Christian
claim is very close to the claim of the chemist. It states quite
simply that the universe under all its aspects has been made in
one way and not in another, and that the way in which it has been
made has been once for all declared in Jesus Christ. The
statement made in the fourth Gospel (John 14: 6) that Jesus is the
truth does not mean that he was stating a number of good and
true ideas; it means that in him the total structure, the inmost
reality, of the universe was for the first time and for ever
disclosed.[4] But, since this truth is set forth not in propositions, to
which intellectual assent would be the right response, but in
personal form, what it calls for is understanding, but understanding reached by way of personal surrender and not simply by
way of intellectual analysis. The man who has seen Jesus as the
truth of God is thereby pledged 'to do the truth', in a self-
commitment which must become ever more intelligent and ever
more complete until it reaches its consummation beyond the
limits of space and time.

On all this the Christian cannot compromise. Yet his approach
to the other forms of human faith must be marked by the deepest
humility. He must endeavour to meet them at their highest, and
not cheaply to score points off them by comparing the best he
knows in his own faith with their weaknesses, weaknesses such
as are present also in the Christian scheme as it is lived out by
very imperfect Christians. He must, as far as imagination will
permit, expose himself to the full force of these other faiths in all
that they have that is most convincing and most alluring. He
must rejoice in everything that they possess of beauty and high
aspiration. He must put himself to school with them, in readiness

---

[4] 'Reality', in many contexts in the fourth Gospel, is a correct translation for the
word which can also be translated 'truth'. In 1 John 5: 20, the phrase 'the true God'
means the genuine God, in comparison with whom all others will be found to be
counterfeits. For the expression 'to do the truth', see John 3: 21, 1 John 1: 6, and
the penetrating comment by A.E. Brooke in *The Johannine Epistles* (1912), p. 14.

to believe that they may have something to teach him that he has not yet learned. He must sympathise with their earnest efforts to relate themselves to the needs of men in the modern world. He must listen with respectful patience to every criticism that they have to make both of Christian thought and Christian practice.

All this can be done, if the Christian is really humble. Self-assertion is always a sign of lack of inner confidence. If the Christian has really trusted in Christ, he can open himself without fear to any wind that blows from any quarter of the heavens. If by chance some of those winds should blow to him unexpected treasures, he will be convinced that Christ's storehouses are wide enough to gather in those treasures too, in order that in the last day nothing may be lost.

CHAPTER II

The King of the Jews

A great many people have read the notable novel to which the *Prix Goncourt* for 1959 was awarded – *Le Dernier des Justes* by André Schwarz-Bart, translated as *The Last of the Just*.

This is a story of Jewish life. Its first scene is that of the infamous massacre at York on 11 March, 1185, when the archbishop of the day proclaimed a pogrom against the Jews in the name of the God of the Christians. Most of the Jews were caught and killed immediately, but a number, with Rabbi Yom Tov Levy, took refuge in a deserted tower where they were besieged for seven days. On the seventh morning the rabbi said to his companions: 'Brethren, God has given us life; let us ourselves give it back to him.' So each in turn the Jews drew near to the rabbi, to receive from one hand the benediction of God and from the other the knife; and last of all the rabbi turned the knife against his own throat.

Later there grew up a legend among the Jews that God had revealed to Solomon, the son of Rabbi Yom Tov Levy, who had been miraculously saved from the massacre, that in each generation there would be born in his family a righteous man who would receive in his own heart the sorrows and sufferings of the whole race. This would be a terrible vocation, but to the end of time the race of the righteous would not fail.

This legend is not meaningless, expressing as it does the profound conviction in the heart of the Jew that, though God seems to have forgotten, he has not really forgotten; he is still there. In the words of the old chronicler, 'Companions in our age-long exile, as the waves flow into the sea so all our tears flow back into the heart of God.' This accounts for the panic of the small boy, called though he does not know it to be one of the righteous, when he is first brought face to face with the possibility that God may not exist: 'Oh my God, if you do not exist, what becomes of all the suffering? It is just lost, just lost.'

It would be hard to imagine a more dramatic manner of presenting the tragic history of the Jews. Repeatedly in history the Christian sword has been drawn against them. Edward I in 1291 drove them out of England; Ferdinand and Isabella (1492) drove them out of Spain. No Christian nation can claim that in this matter it is free of guilt. And now the twentieth century has seen the most terrible of all the manifestations of this fury, carried this time to the point of a determination to exterminate the race in its entirety. No one knows exactly how many Jews perished in Hitler's Germany and in the conquered countries; sober estimates put the figure at six million, and probably this is not an exaggeration. There has been in history no crime greater than what the Jews appropriately call the 'holocaust'.

And yet the Jew survives. Almost alone among the ancient races of the world he has retained his separate and distinguishable existence.[1] It is hard to say what it is that has kept the Jews together. There has certainly been considerable mixing of the blood. The Jewish people has been scattered over the face of the earth. Jews have become loyal citizens of a variety of countries, and have fought heroically against one another in the alien conflicts of the Christians. The law and the synagogue have done much to hold them together. Even among highly secularised Jews, the family, and the lighting of the sabbath candles at sunset on Friday, have been a continual reminder of their Jewishness. But many Jews have sat loose to both law and synagogue without losing their identity. Hatred, massacre, exile, forcible conversion, have reduced their numbers – and yet there there still are, in almost every country of the world, a mystery and a problem to their neighbours.

Is it perhaps the fact that we Christians have created Jewry? That strange and evil plant anti-Semitism keeps rearing its ugly head; even in civilised societies, where one would have believed such things to be completely impossible, the Jew seems destined to be pointed out as the inevitable victim. Is it this that holds Jews together? Is it that every Jew knows in his heart of hearts that he has been appointed for suffering, and that every Jew carries somewhere deep within him the heart of a martyr? Hundreds of witnesses have described the astonishing dignity with which

---

[1] The nearest parallel is that of the Armenians, also a persecuted race.

Jews of both sexes stripped themselves of their garments, leaving even these poor spoils to their enemies, laid themselves down in Hitler's trenches, and waited for the machine-gun bullets that would add them to the endless roll of Jewish martyrs.

★

There they are. In some areas they present themselves as a political or a social problem. In others they are felt to be a menace. The Christian has a different approach. He believes that the world is ruled by the providence of God. If that is so, has God a purpose in keeping his ancient people in being as a people? If so, what may that purpose be?

This was the problem with which Paul had to wrestle in chapters nine to eleven of his Epistle to the Romans. It has been the habit of commentators to concentrate on the first eight chapters of the Epistle as a great exposition of the foundations of the Christian faith – and such indeed they are – and to pass rather lightly over the other eight chapters. For instance, Bishop Anders Nygren in his deservedly celebrated Commentary on the Epistle (1944) takes 355 pages for the exposition of the first eight chapters, and only 101 for the whole of the rest. In particular there is a tendency to regard the three chapters, nine to eleven as an intrusive body, a parenthesis, which can be neglected by the reader without serious loss.[2]

In reality these three chapters form the very heart of the argument. Older expositors tended to treat the Epistle as a theological treatise – here at last, in contrast to the other Epistles, Paul has consented to set out in systematic form the essentials of his theology. More recent study has come back to chapters fourteen and fifteen as the clue to the interpretation of the whole, and has recognised that here as elsewhere Paul writes his letter in response to problems in the Christian life that simply must be faced. It is true that, as is his way, in order to find an answer to immediately practical questions he has to sound all the depths of the mysteries of God. But it is the practical question that sets him loose on his theological quest. What then was the

---

[2]But the recent commentary (1979) by C.E.B. Cranfield of the University of Durham redresses the balance.

question put to him by fellow Christians in Rome, whom he did not yet know face to face?

There were several different groups in this mainly, or entirely, Gentile Church. There were proselytes, who had become Jews by accepting the rite of circumcision, and were therefore under obligation to keep the whole of the Jewish law. There were those known as 'God-fearers' or 'God-reverers' (Acts 13: 50, 17: 17, etc.), who attended the synagogue and accepted in the main the teachings of the Old Testament, but had not put themselves under the yoke of the Jewish law. There were those who had come straight in from the Gentile world, to whom the Jewish background of the others seemed strange and irrelevant. And, of course, outside the church there were some Jews who had never accepted the revelation in Christ, and still walked in the way of the fathers.[3]

Not much imagination is needed if we are to realise the questions by which such a Christian community was faced. There were all the problems of a Christian fellowship living as a small minority, surrounded by non-Christians who followed other traditions and customs and forms of worship.[4] There were the problems of Christians of varying backgrounds and points of view trying to live together in mutual respect and harmony. Could Christians who observed the Jewish law in whole or in part claim some superiority to those who did not? Or should all Christians be on an equality together? In the background all the time was the continued existence of the Jewish people. Had God cast off this people in favour of the Christians? Who now had the best claim to the title 'Israel'? Was the covenant with Abraham and Moses abrogated, or had it still some validity?

In these difficult chapters Paul has brought us face to face with what is still a problem for the church in the twentieth century. In our century, as in the first, Christians of equal sincerity approach the problem in differing ways, and are satisfied by varying solutions.

The first and simplest view is that Christ, as the end of the law,

---

[3] Since the Emperor Claudius had expelled all Jews from Rome, (Acts 18: 2) probably in AD 49, the number of these continuing Jews may have been rather small when Paul wrote his letter, probably in AD 56.

[4] These are dealt with by Paul more extensively in 1 Corinthians than in Romans.

is the end also of the history of Israel. In its crudest form this finds expression in the bitter traditional attitude that the Jews rejected Jesus and that therefore God has rejected the Jews – a view which runs directly contrary to Paul's affirmation that God has not cast off his people. In more theological form, it has been maintained that the church, as the true Israel, is the heir to all the promises made of old to Israel after the flesh. The survival of the Jews is merely an historical accident, perhaps a warning. Jewry is a sociological phenomenon. But from the point of view of revelation and of the Word of God its day is at an end.

It is possible to quote Paul himself in defence of this understanding of the situation. In a number of contexts he addresses Christians in terms which make no sense unless they are in very truth the Israel of God. He assures them that they are heirs through faith of the promises made to Abraham. The whole concept of 'the people of God', with the remarkable transference in 1 Peter 2: 9 of all the characteristics of the old Israel to the new, strengthens this view. It is through the church that the manifold wisdom of God is to be made manifest to the whole creation. It is within the church that the creator Spirit is at work and that the living Word of God is now spoken.

In sharp contrast to this is the view held by some that the old Israel and the new are both in a real sense the people of God, and that they co-exist for the fulfilment of separate but significant purposes of God. In the Christian camp Dr James Parkes has probably gone farther than anyone else in affirming the continuing validity of the synagogue alongside the church.[5] He writes:

> Judaism was obviously not an incomplete Christianity but a *different kind* of religion. It is almost true to say that every strength in Christianity is a weakness in Judaism, and *vice versa*. Christianity is an orthodoxy and Judaism is an orthopraxis, and each has the special quality of its character... Judaism spoke to man as a social being; Christianity to man as a person, as an ultimate end in himself.[6]

---

[5] See *Frontier*, Winter 1959, pp. 271-7; but also a whole series of books, notably *Judaism and Christianity* (Chicago, 1948), especially ch. 5, 'The Rediscovery that Jews are a Living People and Judaism a Living Religion'.
[6] *Ibid*, p. 273.

Even Christians who do not find it possible to accept all Dr Parkes's affirmations may well find themselves led to believe that the gravest schism within the church took place not in AD 1054, when eastern and western Christendom drew apart, nor in the sixteenth century through the Reformation, but when church and synagogue at the end of the first century irremediably separated themselves from each other. By this separation the church was inevitably cast into the arms of the Hellenistic world, and ever since that time has continued to think in terms which are mainly of Greek and not of Hebraic origin. This may have been a necessary step in the evangelisation of the Graeco-Roman world; some scholars regard it as the moment of the theological downfall of the church. Today we are laboriously learning from our Old Testament experts the meaning of the Hebrew categories and of the Semitic approach to life, which are the background of the Gospel; it may be that we shall not recover the fullness of our inheritance until the Jews come to be our teachers within a restored fellowship of the people of God.

A third view, which found wide acceptance among evangelical Christians in the eighteenth and nineteenth centuries, was that God had preserved his ancient people with a view to some great task to be fulfilled in accordance with his purposes in the last days. Paul had looked forward to the union of Israel with the redeemed community in an experience which he can describe only as life from the dead (Rom. 11: 15). The nineteenth century was a time of intense interest in 'unfulfilled prophecy'. Much of this was based on unscientific methods of biblical interpretation and led to fantastic conclusions. But there was widespread expectation that the second coming of Christ would be preceded by the conversion of the people of Israel, and almost unanimous agreement among those who interested themselves in such things that the Jewish people would return to Palestine 'in unbelief'.

This was indeed to put faith in the highly improbable. Zionism, the hope of a return to the land of their fathers, had never quite died out in the minds of pious Jews. As early as 1852 British writers were urging the creation of a Jewish state in Palestine under British protection. Similar ideas were afoot in western Europe, though not as yet under the title Zionism. Zionism as an organised movement took shape in the terrible year of persecution in Russia, 1882. In the same year Leo Pinsker published his book *Auto-Emancipation*, which for many years served as the textbook for Zionist thinking. From that time on, small groups of Jews did make their way to the Holy Land, but few of these immigrants were suited to the life of agricultural pioneers. The settlements were small and poor, and were saved from extinction only by the generosity of Baron Edmond de Rothschild. By 1914 there were perhaps 100,000 Jews in Palestine, not a large nucleus for the formation of an independent Jewish state. Yet, as so often in history, it was the improbable which actually came about.

Few things in modern history are stranger than the story of the contacts between Arthur James Balfour (1848–1930) and Chaim Weizmann (1874–1952). Balfour, the most experienced statesman in England, was a cool philosopher with a sceptical turn of thinking, religious but not excessively so, and a devout reader of the Old Testament prophets. Weizmann, a brilliant chemist, had rendered a number of services to the British government during the First World War, and for these he may have felt that he deserved some recompense. It seemed unlikely that the enthusiasm of the perfervid Zionist would succeed in persuading the calm aristocrat of the justice of his plea that Jerusalem was as much Jewish as Manchester was British;[7] but so it came about, and the result was the famous Balfour Declaration of 1917:

> His Majesty's Government will view with favour the establishment in Palestine of a national home for the Jewish people, and will use their best endeavours to facilitate the achievement of this object, it being clearly understood that nothing shall be done which may prejudice the civil and religious rights of the existing non-Jewish communities in Palestine, or the rights and political status enjoyed by Jews in any other country.

It is important to note exactly what was said. The British government did not declare in favour of making Palestine *the* national home of the Jewish people. They saw that Palestine was

---

[7] The interview took place in Manchester in 1916. What Weizmann actually said was 'We had Jerusalem when London was a marsh' (*Trial and Error* ch. 8). See the moving and affectionate account of Weizmann in Isaiah Berlin: *Personal Impressions* (Oxford, 1982²).

capable of supporting a much larger population than had been possible under Turkish rule; they hoped that both the Jewish and the Arab elements might increase, and that the two groups might learn to live together in a state of amity and co-operation. What happened was very different from what was intended.

Wide differences in understanding of the Declaration became evident from the start. The attitude of the Jews to Palestine is rather like that of the Afrikaners to South Africa. This is the land which God has given them. Arabs may have been in occupation for a thousand years, and may continue, if they wish, to live in the Jewish state; but they can never claim equality of status with the real owners of the soil, any more than blacks in South Africa can claim equality with the whites. It seems that some at least among the Jews think that their dominion should extend to the limits of the empire of Solomon – from the river of Egypt to the great river Euphrates.

The attitude of the Arabs is naturally entirely different. The more extreme among them claim nothing less than the destruction of the state of Israel and the departure of the last Jew from the land. The most moderate, supported by the Arab nations, claim at least autonomy in the areas in which the majority of the population is Arab.

The experiences of more than a quarter of a century have not brought Jews and Arabs any nearer to a common point of view. The claim that Jerusalem and not Tel-Aviv should be the capital of the country has not found general favour in the world. Many have admired the courage and expertise of Israeli airmen in rescuing the passengers of an aircraft hijacked and stationary at Entebbe airport; but the recent destruction by Israeli raiders of the nuclear installations of Iraq, the annexation of the Golan Heights in Syria and the invasion of Lebanon in 1982, have disturbed the minds of many who cannot be accused of any unfavourable attitude towards the Jews. The existence of the state of Israel and the tensions in that part of the world between Jew and Arab are a source of anxiety to all who care for the peace and well-being of the peoples of that area, and indeed for the peace of the world.[8]

---

[8] For a temperate and profoundly sympathetic analysis of this situation, see Kenneth Cragg: *This Year in Jerusalem* (London, 1982).

On all these subjects there is great diversity of opinion among Christians. The Jewish lobby in America is so strong that many American Christians are inclined to support the Israeli point of view. Christians in a number of other countries feel sympathy with the Arabs, at least in the more moderate of their claims. Many would prefer to remain neutral in matters which do not directly concern them. But the existence of the state of Israel has brought home to Christians all over the world a theological problem which many of them would have preferred to evade, but which now presents itself as inescapable. What are we to think of the Jewish people, of the religion of Judaism, and of the duties of Christians in relation to both?

★

The simplest answer would be to let them go their own way, and have as little to do with them as possible, except in the way of personal friendship if we should happen to meet them. They do not want to convert us, and we should feel under no obligation to try and convert them to our way of thinking.

This point of view received strong support some years ago from an eminent Christian thinker. Professor Reinhold Niebuhr (1892-1971), a Christian friend of many Jewish scholars, has written of Christian attempts to convert Jews:

> Our analysis assumes that these activities are wrong not only because they are futile and have little fruit to boast for their exertions. They are wrong because the two faiths despite differences are sufficiently alike for the Jew to find God more easily in terms of his own religious heritage than by subjecting himself to the hazards of guilty feeling involved in conversion to a faith which, whatever its excellences, must appear to him as a symbol of an oppressive majority culture ... Practically nothing can purify the symbol of Christ as the image of God in the imagination of the Jew from the taint with which ages of Christian oppression in the name of Christ have tainted it.[9]

---

[9] R. Niebuhr: *Pious and Secular America* (New York, 1958), p. 108. Recently a Christian Jew expressed in my hearing the remarkable view that such an abandonment of Christian responsibility in relation to the Jews is in itself a form of anti-Semitism.

A challenge so trenchantly expressed deserves careful consideration.

It is not difficult to show that the Christian approach to Israel has not been quite so infructuous as Niebuhr supposed. In earlier days generations of students of the New Testament were brought up on Dr A. Edersheim's *Life and Times of Jesus the Messiah* (1883), a work which could hardly have been written except by one who was himself a convert from rabbinic Judaism. The American Episcopal Church does well to include in its commemorations (15 October) the noble Bishop Isaac Schereschewsky (1831–1906), who after his conversion to the Christian faith went to China, and though almost completely paralysed for the last twenty-five years of his life completed the translation of the Bible into Wen-li, the classical form of the Chinese language. One of the most eminent converts in England in recent years, Dr Hugh Montefiore now Bishop of Birmingham, has recorded that, as a schoolboy at Rugby, one night he lay down to sleep a Jew and woke in the morning to find himself a Christian.

The idea of conversion – that a Jew should cease to be a Jew and should become a Christian – is detestable to the majority of Jews; the convert is a traitor to his people as well as to his faith, a renegade, a turncoat. It is hard for a Jew to believe that such a conversion is ever genuine, a religious experience that will not be denied. Yet the process of conversion does go on; and an increasing number of Jews, such as those who join the movement called Jews for Jesus, maintain that to have become Christians does not involve the loss of their Jewishness but is in truth its fulfilment.

When this point has been dealt with, we are still left with two profound problems raised by what Niebuhr has written.

Has anyone ever any right to try to convert anyone from one religion to another? A Hindu or a Muslim or a Buddhist who leaves an old faith to find a new home in the Christian church is likely to have to endure the same obloquy, the same rejection by friends and relations, as the Jewish convert. He too has to leave the familiar to launch out on an unknown world. He too may have to accept a faith burdened with traditions of colonialism and oppression which are disagreeable to him. Had he not better stay at home? This question has been decisively answered by Bishop Hassan Dehqani-Tafti of Iran, himself a convert from Islam, whose name has become well known in the west through his almost miraculous escape from assassination in his own country. Of course any convert will be called to bear the cross. But, if he feels that he has been led by God himself to bear the particular cross of public profession of faith in Christ, what right have Christians to forbid him to bear that cross? Of course they must not bring any pressure to bear upon him to do so; it must be his choice. But who are we to attempt to deny him the right to choose?[10]

The second problem arises from Niebuhr's use of the expression 'to find God'. This implies that to find God in Jesus Christ is the same as to find him in the covenant with Moses. But is this so? If we affirm that the Jew can so find God, and the Hindu can find him through his own traditions without the traumatic experience of separation from his culture and traditional ways of living, have we not yielded to the relativism which is so popular today? The Christian is a Christian because he believes that to have encountered God in Jesus Christ as the word of God is an experience entirely different from any other kind of experience. This being so, he cannot do otherwise than desire, not to impose his convictions on others, but to share with all men, Jew and Gentile alike, the unique experience which is his life.

Even when this is admitted, it remains true that the nature of the Christian approach to believers of other traditions needs to be thought out afresh in relation to new situations. The term 'missions to Jews' has fallen under the displeasure which almost everywhere attaches to the words 'mission' and 'missionary'. To the Jew the term speaks of the time when Jews were weak and poor and Christians were rich and strong, of patronage and charity in the bad sense of the term. The Christian Approach to Israel, the Church's Ministry to Israel – these are better terms. Yet perhaps today we have to go even further, and talk only in terms of the dialogue between synagogue and church, between Christian and Jew.

A little definition is needed. In what circumstances does genuine dialogue become possible? Peaceful co-existence, in which neither faith interferes with the other, is acceptable to

---

[10] See his book *Design of my World* (reprint, 1978).

many. Friendly discussion, with a view to mutual enlightenment, has much to commend it. But in neither case is it correct to speak of dialogue. That can arise only in what, in modern terminology, may be called an existential situation, a situation in which all the participants are personally, deeply, and even passionately concerned. Such a situation is reflected in the Platonic dialogue, in which, for all the elegance of style, the wit, the brilliant dialectic, there is a deep underlying seriousness. The aim is not the victory of this or that side in the argument, but the emergence of the truth. If the truth emerges, it may be different from the truth as envisaged by the various participants at the beginning of the argument; each may find himself confronted with an understanding of truth ampler and more compelling than he had ever previously enjoyed, and this may lead him to the abandonment of positions which he had ardently maintained.

If this is true in realms such as that of philosophy, it is still more true when adherents of various forms of faith meet one another in the exercise of genuine dialogue. Believers regard themselves as being in possession of the truth, though, if they engage in dialogue, they must accept the possibility that the truth as they have known it may stand in need of amplification or even of correction. But, if truth is truth, it must be of universal validity no less than the findings of science, in so far as these have been established by experimental verification. It is the fact that all religions, other than those which are purely national or tribal, do make in one form or another a claim to universality.

It is at this point that the Christian believer approaches his Jewish friend with a question; how does a Jew today understand the significance of his faith in a world-wide context?

A theme which runs through many sections of the Old Testament is the argument between rigidly national claims and an outlook of universality as this is found at the highest points of prophetic Judaism. On the one hand is the rigid exclusiveness of the book of Nehemiah, which holds that the 'mixed multitude' must be kept separate from the true stock of Israel; on the other the noble utterances of the second Isaiah: 'It is too light a thing that you should be my servant to raise up the tribes of Jacob and to restore the preserved of Israel; I will give you as a light to the nations, that my salvation may reach to the ends of the earth' (Isa. 49: 6). These words have become familiar to generations of Christians through their New Testament application in the *Nunc*

Dimittis: 'to be a light to lighten the Gentiles, and to be the glory of thy people Israel'. In the days of Jesus Judaism was a proselytising religion, witnessing to the unity of God in a polytheistic world, and drawing many to itself, into full membership or to less perfect adherence, by the simplicity of its theistic faith and by the excellence of its ethical teaching. In the many years of suppression and persecution by Christians, it was almost impossible for Judaism to exercise this function. How does it see its responsibility to the world in these days of restored freedom and political independence?

An elaborate answer to this question has been provided by the most original of Jewish thinkers in the twentieth century, Franz Rosenzweig (1886–1929). Rosenzweig's most important book, *Der Stern der Erlösung* (1921; 3rd edn. 1954), has at last been translated into English,[11] and it is therefore possible for English readers to make the acquaintance of this singularly lovable figure. The book is untidy and ill-organised, full of rather cloudy rhetoric, and not infrequently obscure; but it does bring the reader close to a sincere and gifted Jew wrestling with the problem of what it means to be a Jew in the twentieth century, and how the relationship between church and synagogue is to be understood.

Rosenzweig had many Christian friends and relations. As a young man he was just on the point of becoming a Christian when he found himself drawn to the ceremonies of *Rosh Hashanah*, the Jewish New Year. Moved by the rhythms of the Hebrew language and of the ancient chants by which it is accompanied, he realised that this was his home, and from this conviction he never strayed. But this left him with the duty of explaining to his Christian friends why he had not joined them in the faith which they regarded as the fulfilment of Judaism, and how he now regarded those whom he loved and respected, though they stood on the other side of the divide.

He developed the theology of the two covenants – the covenant in Moses which was given to the Jews, and the covenant in Jesus which has been given to the Christians. These two are complementary, the one to the other, Judaism being the eternal fire and Christianity the eternal rays, and this will be so until the

---

[11] Franz Rosenzweig: *The Star of Redemption* (Boston, 1971).

end of time. The vocation of the Jew is in a sense passive – to stay where he has always been, with God. The vocation of Jesus was to go out into the world to call the Gentiles to himself, so that they might be brought to share in the covenant which is not theirs by right. Jew must not interfere with Christian, and Christian must not interfere with Jew – each must be faithful in the fulfilment of the duty given to him by God, each must respect the integrity of the other. Will the two covenants ever be brought into one? Only in the last days, the days of Messiah; when this will come, and what it will mean when it does come, is known to God alone. Until those days come, the Christian has need of the Jew. The Christian vocation is a very perilous one; as the Christian goes out into the world, he is always in danger of becoming assimilated to it, and so failing to be true to his vocation as a witness to the truth. He needs the Jew, who, in so far as he remains faithful to his vocation of staying with God, reminds the Christian of what he ought to be if he is to remain faithful to his own covenant vocation.

Not all contemporary Jews would declare themselves disciples of Rosenzweig, but many would feel that he has pointed out the way in which they can combine deep regard for the Christian faith with passionate hostility to the idea of conversion and to those of the Jewish faith who have taken the step which Rosenzweig at the last moment refused to take.

The second question with which the Christian comes to the Jew relates to Jesus of Nazareth. If there is a certain validity in the covenant proclaimed in the New Testament, how is the Jew to regard Jesus through whom this new covenant has been made available to men?

Through long centuries the Jews simply evaded this question. In the fourth Gospel, the Jews never refer to Jesus by name, but simply as 'this man';[12] one generation of Jews after another has followed in this path. Two Jewish writers have written movingly of the way in which Jewish children were guarded against contact with the one whom the Jewish people had decided to ignore:

The Jews encountered Jesus once at a single moment in history,

---

[12] This, it is said, is the manner of referring to those who have been formally excommunicated.

encountered Him as a people, and as a people acquiesced in the rejection of Him by their leaders. From that moment in history onward, all that concerned Christ was carefully withheld from following generations, as parents withhold a painful and terrible secret from their children... Of course 'the children' were living in the world and news of this 'secret' was bound to reach them, and reach them it did, not as 'good news', but as 'bad news', not as a message of love but all too often as a message of hate... which was, of course, not an encounter with Christ at all, rather with the devil, who often does his important work under the mask of piety.[13]

Christians have begun, though inadequately, to repent of what they have done to the Jews over the centuries. One encouraging sign of this was the attitude of the second Vatican Council towards the Jewish faith and the Jewish people. The old absurd expression 'deicide', the murder of God, has been abandoned, not without opposition from some Christians of the Arab world. The idea that, because some Jews centuries ago plotted the death of Jesus, all Jews at all times must be judged equally guilty, seems to have been consigned to the rubbish-heap from which it ought never to have emerged. The Council in generous terms recognised all that the Christian church owes to the Jewish people. It affirmed that the 'spiritual patrimony common to Christians and Jews is great... and wishes to foster and recommend that mutual understanding and respect which is the fruit above all of biblical and theological studies and of brotherly dialogues.'[14]

If Christians are beginning to discover Judaism and to look on it with friendlier eyes, the rediscovery of Jesus by the Jews is an even more remarkable phenomenon. Many Jews today would not hesitate to recognise Jesus as the greatest of all the teachers of their race and to claim him as their own.

Scholars have long been familiar with the work on *The Synoptic Gospels* of the eminent liberal Jew, C.G. Montefiore, which

---

[13] Cornelia and Irving Süssman: 'Marc Chagall, Painter of the Crucified' in *The Bridge*, ed. John M. Oesterreicher, vol. I, (New York, 1955), p. 107. The writers quote from a young Jewish scholar the striking words 'The Jews never rejected Christ because they never encountered Him.' Arthur A. Cohen: 'The Encounter of Judaism and Christendom', *Cross Currents* (Spring 1951), pp. 91-2.

[14] *The Documents of Vatican II* (New York, 1966⁹), p. 665.

appeared first in 1909. Montefiore was firmly convinced that it was possible both to remain a loyal Jew, and at the same time to absorb all that is best in the teaching of the New Testament. He does not hesitate to recognise from time to time what is new, original and splendid in the words of Jesus. On the parable of the lost sheep, he writes:

> This direct search for, and appeal to, the sinner, are new and moving notes of high import and significance. The good shepherd who searches for the lost sheep, and reclaims it and rejoices over it, is a new figure, which has never ceased to play its great part in the moral and religious development of the world.[15]

Another and touching witness to this new discovery of Jesus is Victor Gollancz who, in his letters to his grandson Timothy, pours out his interest in the Christian faith: 'I am desperately anxious that you should understand Christianity... there are things in Christianity, I feel certain, that can be better understood for a previous understanding of Orthodox Judaism.' To him the teaching of the Sermon on the Mount is the supreme answer to the sorrows and perplexities of men. He describes his own spiritual pilgrimage in his early days: 'I was on the way to the adoration of Christ... He lives and reigns for me eternally; and whether or not I should hesitate to call Him Lord, I can assuredly call Him Master.' It may seem strange that, having come so far on the way, Gollancz should not have taken the final step in the acknowledgment of Christ as Lord. The answer is probably to be found in his attitude to the resurrection of Jesus: 'In the physical resurrection I was hardly interested at all... I am of the opinion... that no educated man genuinely "believes in" it now... but the spiritual Resurrection is another matter; this is an undeniable fact, and of supreme importance.'[16]

A considerably younger writer, Scholem ben-Chorin (b. 1913) now a resident of the state of Israel, has written of Jesus in terms of affection perhaps even more intense than those used by Gollancz. As a boy in his native Munich, ben-Chorin was sent to a Roman Catholic school, where he had to attend religious

---

[15] Vol. II (1927²), pp. 520-1.
[16] *My Dear Timothy* (London, 1952), pp. 111, 394, 402, 403.

instruction, and listened to what he heard with greater eagerness than the Christian boys. 'So I have never been able to free myself from the book, and from the Jewish man of whom it speaks. They have entered into my very substance, yes, my Jewish substance; I cannot imagine what my life would be like without the dialogue with the elder brother Jesus.' And yet the rejection is as emphatic as the acceptance: 'With great sorrow I have said to him with my whole life: You are not he; you are not the deliverer, the one who brings in the kingdom.'

Geza Vermes, in his book *Jesus the Jew, a Historian's Reading of the Gospels*, has set to work, by his own account, to rescue Jesus from both Christians and Jews, to show 'that this man, so distorted by Christian and Jewish myth alike, was *in fact* neither the Christ of the Church, nor the apostate and bogey-man of Jewish popular tradition'... to make 'the repayment to him of a debt long overdue'.[17]

When Christians want to understand what Jews think of Jesus, there is no one to whom they might turn with greater expectancy than to the venerated teacher Martin Buber (1878–1965). In him too they find the same dichotomy between eager appreciation and decisive rejection at certain points:

I firmly believe that the Jewish community, in the course of its renaissance, will recognize Jesus; and not merely as a great figure in its religious history, but also in the organic context of a messianic development extending over millennia, whose final goal is the Redemption of Israel and of the world. But I believe equally firmly that we will never recognize Jesus as the Messiah Come for this would contradict the deepest meaning of our Messianic passion... In our view, redemption occurs for ever, and none has yet occurred. Standing bound and shackled in the pillory of mankind we demonstrate with the bloody body of our people the unredeemedness of the world.[18]

This does not mean that there is no point at which Jews and Christians can meet. Christians also read the Old Testament; they do not read it quite as Jews read it, nevertheless this is a focal

---

17 *Jesus the Jew* (Collins, London, 1973), p. 17.
18 *Pointing the Way* (New York, 1957), p. 18.

THE KING OF THE JEWS

point of fellowship:

> To you the book is a forecourt; to us it is the sanctuary. But in this place we can dwell together, and together listen to the voice that speaks here... Your expectation is directed toward a second coming, ours to a coming which has not been anticipated by a first. To you the phrasing of world history is determined by one absolute midpoint, the year nought; to us it is an unbroken flow of tones following each other without a pause from their origin to their consummation. But we can wait for the advent of the One together, and there are moments when we may prepare the way before him together.[19]

Every Christian must be delighted by this eirenical utterance. And yet the difference in point of view cannot be concealed. Christians believe that Jesus stood before the world as a messianic figure, and that he was right in doing so; Jews think that he was mistaken, and that this was a disastrous mistake:

> Jesus is the first in the series of men who stepped forth from the seclusion of the servants of God, forth from the real 'messianic secret', and in their hearts and in their speech attributed messiahship to themselves... That this first one... was incomparably the purest, most legitimate of them all, the one most endowed with real messianic power, does not alter the fact of his firstness, rather does it belong to it, belong to the awful and pathetic reality of that entire series of self-appointed Messiahs.[20]

Buber's criticisms of Jesus seem to rest on the assumption that we know what redemption is, or ought to be. The Old Testament picture is fairly clear. It is the picture, dear to the heart of a peasant people, of that paradisal time when peace will rule, and every man will sit under his vine and his fig-tree in the glow of a long summer afternoon. This happy time may be preceded by days of affliction for Israel, and it may be necessary for Messiah to appear as a warrior chief; but, when the victory is won, the

---

[19] *Israel and the World* (New York, 1948), p. 39.

[20] *Hasidism* (New York, 1948), p. 114. The best known of these pseudo-Messiahs is Sabbathai Zwi 'this wonderful impostor' (as he is called in Hastings: *ERE*, VII p. 605), who drew into his following learned and devout rabbis, and proclaimed the *Annus Mirabilis*, the beginning of the Messianic Age, for the year 1666.

true days of Messiah will come in. There was in the mind of Israel no single picture of Messiah or of the days of Messiah; but in the time of Jesus it is likely that something of this Old Testament vision remained at least in the minds of some.

The figure of Messiah in the mind of Jesus was as different as possible from every form of contemporary expectation. Perhaps that is why he never, till the moment of his trial before the Jewish authorities, claimed explicitly to be Messiah, though he seems not to have rejected the title when addressed by a blind man as Son of David or by an enthusiastic disciple as the anointed one of God. But the supreme picture of the Old Testament is that of the Suffering Servant of the Lord, the one who makes intercession for the transgressors at the cost of his own life.

On the Christian understanding of the terms used, the redeemed are not invited to rest from their labours, to enter now into the joy of their Lord. Precisely the opposite is the case. They are called to take up the Cross of Christ daily, and to suffer with him until the end of the world.

To the question as to how the Jews understand the concept of messiahship today no single answer can be given. The Orthodox probably still cling to the traditional ideas – Messiah is the single mysterious figure, who when the signal is given will bring the age-long process of messiahship out of its hiddenness and proclaim it to all the world. Many liberal Jews have abandoned the concept of an individual Messiah, regarding it as historically conditioned and no more than symbolic in the twentieth century, just as many believing Christians no longer hold to the idea of a literal and visible return of Christ to this earth at the end of the days. Some, thinking in political rather than in religious terms, probably do not go beyond identifying Messiah with the reconstitution of the Jews as a people through the establishment of the state of Israel. To some, perhaps the larger number, it is the people, not the state of Israel, that is itself the messianic figure. What is all important is that the people of God should survive; this survival is itself God's unchanging act of messianic redemption ultimately for the whole world.

In the days of Jesus the Jewish people did not want a Messiah of the kind that Jesus offered them; and so they swept him away. Today Jesus does not fit into any picture of messiahship that the Jews have ever formed. But Jesus does not fit into any of our ideas – about God, or ourselves, or of God's purposes with the world. He has to create his own dimension; we can see him only when we let him shine by his own light, and allow him to create the vocabulary in which we try to express our understanding of what we think him to be. Is it unfair to say that the Jewish people cannot accept Jesus as Messiah today because their minds are not attuned to the revolution in thought that would be involved in such acceptance?

★

Every Christian ought from time to time to attend a synagogue service. The feeling, especially if the service is conducted in Hebrew, is that of being brought into contact with something immensely old and unchanging. What breathes through the service is a sense of tranquil confidence – Israel is the people of God, and this is a reality that nothing can change.

> Blessed art thou, O Lord our God and God of our fathers, God of Abraham, God of Isaac and God of Jacob, the great mighty and revered God, the most high God, who bestowest loving kindnesses, and art master of all things; who rememberest the pious deeds of the patriarchs, and in love wilt bring a redeemer to their children's children for thy name's sake.[21]

The Christian who encounters believing Jews is impressed by the Jewish sense of wholeness, of completeness:

> Judaism *affirms* life, its nobility, its purity, its significance; it is not marked as for Christianity with a minus, it needs no redemption from without. Life is transfigured from within by the constructive effort of men who fulfil the law of God. Community of Law, Judaism entrusts the effort of obedience and edification to the global man. No rent in the nature of man, as Christianity has it; no mistrust of matter, of the flesh, of the letter. All holds together organically, and nothing is to be despised. All contributes to the same objective of sanctification.[22]

---

[21] *The Jewish Prayer Book, Hebrew and English*, p. 44.
[22] André Neher (a French Jew): 'Jews confront Christianity', in *The Student World*, 1959, No. 1, pp. 85-6.

Christians will have some reservations as to the picture of Christianity presented in this passage; but there is no reason to doubt that it faithfully represents some of the highest aspirations of the Jewish faith. There is a tendency among Christians to represent Judaism as a religion of mere arid legalism, and to regard the period of the Law as introduced by Ezra and Nehemiah as one of declension from the purer faith proclaimed by the great writing prophets. This is not the way in which the Jews themselves understood the Law. It was held to be a great gift of God, in the keeping of which man was to find his joy and his delight.

> Thy law is my delight . . . Oh, how I love thy law! It is my meditation all the day . . . I hate double-minded men, but I love thy law . . . I love thy commandments above gold, above fine gold . . . The ordinances of the Lord are true and righteous altogether; more to be desired are they than gold, even much fine gold. (Ps. 119).

'This is the manifesto of a new People of God, which lives in a new obedience. God Himself has made it new, in that He has set His law within its heart.'[23] No doubt seems to enter in as to whether this law can really be kept or not – the world is being saved by 'the constructive effort of men who keep the law'.

It is precisely at this point that danger enters. Privilege can be divorced from responsibility. Favour can be understood in terms of favouritism. It can come to be taken for granted that God will always be unconditionally on the side of his people, and that the Jews who know the law are automatically to be regarded as superior to the Gentiles who do not know it. Amos had laid it down that God would punish his people, precisely because 'you only have I known of all the families of the earth' (Amos 3: 2). The apocryphal book of the Wisdom of Solomon seems to lay down an exactly opposite principle. 'These as a father admonishing them thou didst prove; but those as a stern king condemning them thou didst search out' (11: 9). 'While therefore thou dost chasten us, thou scourgest our enemies a thousand times more' (12: 22). 'Even if we sin we are thine knowing thy power; but we will not sin, because we know that we are accounted thine. For to know

---

[23] H.J. Kraus: *The People of God in the Old Testament* (London, 1958), p. 84.

thee is complete righteousness, and to know thy power is the
root of immortality' (15: 1-3). In Romans, chapter two, Paul takes
up one by one these over-confident assertions of the Jewish
consciousness, and shows that they have no basis in reality.
It is not surprising that Paul is not popular with Jewish readers.
It is not just that he is the renegade Pharisee; Paul never doubts
that Israel is the people of God. But he does attack the Jew's
understanding of himself at its most sensitive point. Paul has not
invented the rent in human nature; he has disclosed it with
remorseless logic and has shown thereby that there is no
essential difference between Jew and Gentile, a conclusion which
has always been a rock of offence to the Jewish reader. The target
of Paul's polemic is not 'work-righteousness', man's attempt to
make himself acceptable in the sight of God, but Jewish pride.

> The way in which for Paul the Jews filled out the sin of Adam was not
> by using the law as a ladder of good works but by using it as a charter
> of national privilege. And this total critique of ... national righteous-
> ness goes back, if we are to believe the Gospels, to John the Baptist
> and to Jesus himself.[24]

So the conclusion is that the way for the Jew is the same as that
for the Gentile – through death and resurrection into peace with
God through the One who died and rose again.
Franz Rosenzweig suggested that the church has need of the
synagogue, if it is to be true to its vocation. The Christian must
ask for liberty to suggest to the Jew that the synagogue has need
of the church, if it is to find its own true fulfilment. The
suggestion must be made with the utmost humility, with a full
sense both of the wrongs for which the church has been
responsible in the past, and of the admiration due to the amazing
faithfulness with which the Jew has clung to the God who has
chosen him. All that he dare ask is that the Jew will look again at
Jesus Christ, without hate and without prejudice, and consider
whether there may not be things in the picture that he has so far
missed. The Jew is not without a sense of sin; in the fifth of the
Eighteen Benedictions regularly recited in synagogue worship,

---

[24] T. Wright: 'The Paul of History and the Apostle of Faith', Tyndale New
Testament Lecture (1978), p. 71

he asks for the forgiveness of his sins. But he has been so much more sinned against than sinning that perhaps forgiveness and acceptance by God are too easily assumed. The rent in human nature is there. But the only thing which fully reveals to man its gravity is the Cross of Jesus Christ, understood both as God's visible judgment on sin, and as the divine act of redemption and mercy on behalf of men who cannot bring in the kingdom of God by their own constructive effort.

We have gone a long way round in the attempt to understand the purposes of God for his ancient people and, when we have done our best, we must admit that much still remains dark to us. But we may rest in the absolute assurance that the faithfulness of Israel is precious in the sight of God, and will in time receive its reward. We can hardly add anything to what was written by Robert Browning a century ago:

God spoke, and gave us the word to keep,
Bade never fold the hands nor sleep
'Mid a faithless world – at watch and ward,
Till Christ at the end relieve our guard.
By his servant Moses the watch was set;
Though near upon cock-crow, we keep it yet.

Thou! if Thou wast He, who at mid-watch came,
By the starlight naming a dubious name!
And if, too heavy with sleep – too rash
With fear – O Thou, if that martyr-gash
Fell on Thee coming to take thine own,
And we gave the Cross, when we owed the Throne,

Thou art the Judge. We are bruised thus.
But, the Judgment over, join sides with us.[25]

---

[25] Robert Browning: *Holy Cross Day*.

CHAPTER III

Islam in Crisis

Among the major religions of the world Islam is unique in that it came into existence later than Christianity, and is in some sense dependent upon it. Like Christianity, from very early times if not from the very beginning, it has laid claim to universality. Because of its assertion that it is the final revelation, the last word of God to man, it stands at certain points in opposition to Christian faith; it must deny that faith's claims and attempt to discredit its credentials.

The Arabic word *Islām* means 'surrender'. The Muslim is the one who is surrendered to the will of God. Christians frequently misinterpret this term, as though it means a quietistic and fatalistic acceptance of whatever happens as the will of God. Its truer and original meaning is 'an acceptance of his pleasure, a dynamic readiness to give oneself to carrying out what ought to happen'.[1] What ought to happen? The Muslim does not make the same kind of distinction as western man between the sacred and the secular, between religion and other concerns of men. He does not think of one community which is the church and another community which is the state. In his view, God through Muhammad revealed a total pattern for the life of man, in which politics, ethics, economics, social order, are bound together in an indissoluble totality by the will of God, which is the transcendental element in the compound. This is the way in which men ought to live. This is human society as it should be. The Muslim is the man who is committed to bringing to realisation, by his devotion and

---

[1] W. Cantwell Smith: *Islam in Modern History* (1957), p. 16 n.10. And see in the Koran, Sūra iii, 78-9.

his efforts, this society as God has willed it to exist to the ends of the earth.[2]

This means that the Muslim, like the Christian and the Marxist, is interested in history. History is the sphere in which the purpose of God is to be carried out. God is omnipotent and sovereign. And since the Muslim identifies his own existence with the will of God, he must expect to see in history, progressively and over ever-widening stretches of the earth, the establishment of the divine society as he has understood it. But the Muslim has been perplexed to find that from his point of view, for a century at least, history seems to have gone wrong.

The Christian can well understand this perplexity since in a measure he shares it. He too believes that the divine community must spread to every part of the earth; he too believes that it is only through the effort and witness of Christians that the community can be extended. But through all the centuries disappointed expectations have been part of the history of the Christian churches.

To put the contrast in straightforward human terms, Jesus was a failure and Muhammad was a success. The Gospel was from the start a story of victory arising out of defeat. For centuries the Christians were a minority of insignificant and persecuted people; they saw the miracle of progress as the direct act of God who uses the weak things of the world to confound the strong.

This being so, it is possible for the Christian, though saddened by Christian reverses, to take them fairly calmly. He may look out on the contemporary world with troubled eyes, seeing the Christian cause so weak and threatened where he had believed it to be strong, but he will not be tempted to identify temporary setbacks with final defeat or extinction. We have not been promised any kind of success story. The church will be to the end of time a persecuted church. The purpose of God will be fulfilled slowly and obscurely, through many disasters and defeats. Accepting weakness and frustration as part of its earthly destiny, the church does not expect to see the glory until the final

---

[2] Sir Muhammad Iqbal (1877–1938) summed up the nature of Islam as a social polity whose purpose is to 'realize the spiritual in a human organization'. Quoted in *Modern Trends in World Religions* (ed. Joseph M. Kitagawa, 1959), p. 24.

manifestation of the Son of man. The Muslim shares with the Christian the conviction that a great purpose of God is working itself out in history. His understanding of history is, however, not the same as that of the Christian. Muhammad was a great leader of men. Finding the Arab tribes of the eighth century weak, divided and purposeless, he, through the force of his personality and through his creed, knit them into a unity, gave them a social organisation, and launched them on an astonishing career of conquest. Some historians take the view that the victories of the Muslims were due rather to the weaknesses of their enemies than to their own skill; all the ancient kingdoms had been eaten away internally by corruption, love of ease or the debility of old age. But this interpretation does less than justice to the facts. The evidence shows that the Muslim campaigns were well organised and well led, and that from early times the soldiers of the Muslim armies manifested themselves as well-disciplined fighters. Within a century of the death of the Prophet, the Muslims had taken over Persia, Mesopotamia, Syria, Egypt, North Africa and the greater part of Spain. They were driven out of France only by the victory of Charles Martel at Tours in AD 732. Later centuries did not quite come up to the surging vigour of the first advance. Yet, in spite of certain set-backs, Islam continued to make progress in many directions for more than a thousand years.

The great thrust of the Crusades, in which the whole weight of resurgent Europe was thrown against Islam and seemed to threaten its very heart, had been thrown back after two centuries of intermittent warfare.[3] From the ninth century on, Muslims penetrated India and established their rule in many areas; in the sixteenth century the greater part of the country fell under the dominion of a Muslim dynasty. In 1453 the greatest Christian city in the world, Constantinople, fell before the invaders; the great church of the Holy Wisdom was turned into a mosque, and the Christian empire of more than a thousand years was brought to an end. Islam continued to press forward into Europe. In 1683 the Turks were at the gates of Vienna – it was the pressure of the Turks on the eastern frontier that more than

---

[3] Jerusalem was captured by the Crusaders in 1099; Acre, their last stronghold, was finally lost in 1291.

anything else saved the Reformation from that threat of extermination which seemed to be always hanging over its head.[4] By the end of the eighteenth century there were many millions of Muslims in China, in Indonesia, in the Philippines and in tropical Africa. There had been set-backs, but the Muslim, looking back on history, might well feel that his faith was justified. Here was a great and solid unity, stretching unbroken across the great land-mass from the Atlantic to the Pacific Ocean.

It was only in the nineteenth century that things began to go seriously wrong from the Muslim point of view. In the Middle Ages Islam had been expelled from Spain, but that loss had quickly been made up by other gains. Now, however, began a steady crumbling of the political power and influence of Islam. The liberation of Greece in 1821 was the portent. This was followed by the gradual detachment of the Balkans from the Turkish Empire. But the withdrawal became a debacle only when Turkey chose the wrong side in the First World War, and suffered all the consequences of the defeat of Germany in that war. The empire of Turkey, ramshackle, incompetent and reactionary, had stretched from Morocco to the borders of Persia, from the Adriatic to the upper waters of the Nile. The Sultan as Caliph (*Khalīfa*) had exercised a shadowy authority as the political, and in a measure also as the spiritual, centre of the whole Islamic world. Now all this was no more.

When the treaty of Versailles was signed in 1919, to an extent unknown even in the days of the Crusades the destinies of the entire Muslim world seemed to be in the hands of alien and Christian powers. The whole of North Africa was under the control of European nations – Spain, Italy and France. Britain effectively ruled the whole of the Nile valley, and was installed in Palestine and Iraq. Even the Arab king who ruled in the Hejaz, and so in the sacred city of Mecca itself, had been installed by the British as their client. The French were in Syria and Lebanon. The British continued to rule serenely over fifty millions of Muslims in India, the Dutch over nearly as large a number in

---

[4] In 1526 the Turkish victory at Mohacs laid Hungary open to invasion. The inveterate tendency of the Christian king of France to ally himself with the Paynim against the Christian emperor did more perhaps than anything else to save Protestantism for Europe. It was the Turkish danger that compelled Charles V to listen to the Protestant princes at the Diet of Augsburg in 1530.

Indonesia. Christian domination had extended itself to the very heart of the Islamic world. Even those countries, such as Iran and Afghanistan, which were technically independent, had, in fact, been deeply penetrated by western influences.

In two generations the situation of the Islamic world has entirely changed. In 1918 it was at its lowest point of humiliation – poor, exhausted, and at almost every point subject to Christian domination. In 1978 it stood before the world free, aggressive, and with a new self-confidence.

After the Second World War the process of decolonisation went forward with extraordinary rapidity. Britain moved out of Egypt and the Sudan. The Italians lost their hold on Northern Africa and Ethiopia which they had occupied for six brief years. The French had to give up their power in Lebanon and Syria. The Dutch lost their eastern empire and Indonesia emerged as the most populous Muslim country in the world. The liberation of Algeria from France was a slow and by no means peaceful process, but by 1962 it was complete. Pakistan and Bangladesh, both overwhelmingly Muslim in character, have successfully asserted their independence from India. At least twenty fully independent Islamic nations have claimed membership in the Assembly of the United Nations.

In the second half of this period great riches have been added to political freedom. Until 1952 the United States produced more than half of the world's supply of oil. Today Saudi Arabia heads the list of the oil-exporting nations, strongly backed by Iran, Iraq, Kuwait and the Arab sheikhdoms.[5] During these years it came home to the nations of the Middle East that it was in their power to threaten the economic life of the great industrial nations of the world, almost all of which were now dependent on supplies of oil, which could come only from these mainly Muslim countries. It is not surprising that these Muslim peoples grasped eagerly at the opportunity to replace their age-long poverty with the inordinate wealth which oil had put within their grasp. The oil-producing countries have used some of their new-found wealth in building up their military power. Perhaps they have seen in economic power an even more effective weapon for paying off old scores,

---

[5] Only the USSR, Nigeria and Venezuela appear, with seven Islamic countries, in the list of the ten top oil-exporting countries.

and for redressing an unfavourable balance which had persisted up to the beginning of their industrial age.[6]

★

Islam is still in the main the religion of the Middle East, but in the course of history it has spread far beyond its original limits. On the map it looks rather like an octopus, with its body in the centre, and its tentacles stretching out in every direction. The body is made up of the ancient Arabic-speaking heartlands, demarcated by lines drawn between Mecca, the religious capital of Islam, and Baghdad, for centuries its political capital; between Baghdad and Damascus, the artistic capital – in the Middle Ages Damascene swords and daggers were highly valued, and the word 'damask' speaks for itself – and from Damascus to Cairo, the intellectual capital – Al-Azhar, with an unbroken history of a thousand years is by far the oldest university in the world, in comparison with which Paris, Oxford and Cambridge look like newcomers. To the west one tentacle stretches right along the coast of North Africa as far as Morocco, then with a southern hook across the Sahara to Timbuktu and the northern regions of Nigeria and the Cameroons; north-westward into Europe as far as Albania, still in spite of communist domination largely a Muslim country, and to wide regions in southern Russia; eastward, through Iran and Afghanistan to Pakistan and India; south-east to Indonesia and the Philippines; due south through the Sudan to the east coast of Africa, strong as far as Tanzania, then gradually dying away at the Cape of Good Hope.

There is a tendency among Muslims to exaggerate the numbers of the faithful but, on the most sober estimate, they cannot be less than 500 million. Thus they considerably surpass in numbers Hindus and Buddhists, and stand second only to Christians among the religions of the world. Muslims claim that, since all Muslims are true believers whereas the vast majority of Christians are only nominal adherents of the faith which they profess, Islam is in fact by far the largest religious community in the world.

---

[6] For a recent survey see E. Mortimer: *Faith and Power. The Politics of Islam* (London, October 1982). Perhaps more helpful is R. Lacey: *The Kingdom* (London, 1981), which gives insight into the Arab world as a whole, and not only into Saudi Arabia.

This Islamic corpus presents itself to the rest of the world as a massive unity.

It finds expression in unity of language. To the devout Muslim the Arabic language is part of the divine revelation as accorded to the Prophet Muhammad. This cannot be changed; therefore every good Muslim must learn the obligatory prayers in Arabic – this is the only language used in public worship. Many Muslims know the entire Koran by heart, and can be seen endlessly repeating it to themselves. The words seem to exercise an almost hypnotic power on the minds of even those who only imperfectly understand the meaning. Whereas Christians maintain that the miracle of the Bible is that parts of it have been translated into more than 1,700 languages, and that it conveys essentially the same message to the speakers of all these myriad tongues, the Muslim asserts the exact opposite – the excellence of the Koran is such that it can never be the same in any language other than that in which it was given by God himself. The Koran has indeed been translated into many languages, but almost all these translations have been made by those who were not Muslims. Some Muslims are prepared to commend the accuracy of the best of these translations, and to admit their value as interpretation, though not official interpretation, of the meaning of the sacred text.[7]

Muslims claim that, though Christians maintain that Christ has made the whole world one in him, the brotherhood which Islam has established is far deeper and more real than anything which Christians have achieved. This unity finds visible expression in the pilgrimage to Mecca, which each adult male Muslim ought to accomplish once at least in his life. At the appointed time Muslims, yellow, white, brown, black, stream together to the sacred city. Some of the ceremonies to be carried out in the neighbourhood of Mecca seem to the western mind to be trivial or primitive. But those who have made the pilgrimage speak of a profound spiritual experience, in which all the differences of race, language and background sink into insignificance.

So the Islamic world has entered on a new phase of prosperity. And yet, for all its power, that world seems to be pervaded by a sense of anxiety.

---

[7] For divergent views, see H.A.R. Gibb: *Modern Trends in Islam*, p. 131, n. 1.

For this anxiety there are several reasons. The immense increases in the price of oil have had less effect on the world's economy than might perhaps have been expected. The oil-producing countries seem to have underestimated the resilience and adaptability of the industrial west. The increases have been absorbed, not without inconvenience but without disruption of the economy. Attention has been directed towards possible new sources of energy; the ingenuity of western technicians may yet succeed in harnessing the sun and the tides to the production of the power that is needed.

All attempts to bring about a united voice of Islam have been unsuccessful. The unity of Islam is impressive, yet it is less commanding than at first it might appear. Islam actually exists in three overlapping, but in many respects independent, zones.

First there is that area, already mentioned, of the heartlands, where Arabic is the national language, where culture has exclusively Islamic roots and where Islam is for the most part fully orthodox.

There are the lands which have been Islamic for centuries, yet have retained their own language – Turkish in Turkey, Persian in Iran, Urdu in Pakistan. In Iran the vast majority of the population adhere to the Shi'ah form of Islam, and are thus divided from the Sunnis, who in their own judgment are alone in maintaining the fully orthodox form of the Islamic faith. During the period of Turkish revolution under Kemal Atatürk after the First World War, Turkey went far to identifying itself with the west, so far that many Muslims questioned whether Turkey could in any sense be considered a Muslim country. For forty years, however, the tendency has been all in the direction of the re-establishment of Islam; this suggests that the revolution had touched the surface of life at many points, but that essentially Islamic convictions were only waiting the opportunity to reassert themselves.[8]

The third zone is that of the areas such as Indonesia and Africa,

---

[8] G.H. Jansen writes in *Militant Islam* (1979), p. 114: 'The sad fact about Kemal Atatürk is not merely that he was a very shallow reformer, but that he has been proven an unsuccessful reformer. The main reason for his failure is that he did not know his people. He refused to acknowledge that the Turks have always been and for the foreseeable future will remain very devout Muslims.' This perhaps overstates the case; secular influences are still strong among the Turkish peoples.

which have somewhat recently become part of the Islamic world. Here the process of Islamisation, like the parallel process of Christianisation, has been rather superficial and much of the old tribal religion survives not far below the surface. It is perhaps for this reason that in Indonesia alone there is a significant movement of the population from Islam to Christianity.[9]

When such diverse elements are included in one religious system, it can hardly occasion surprise that it is not easy for the system to speak with a single voice. What is perhaps most disturbing from the Islamic point of view is that grave tensions exist within the Islamic quadrilateral itself. Saudi Arabia and Egypt are competitors for leadership in the Islamic world. President Sadat of Egypt was widely regarded in the world outside as the most notable of the statesmen whom the Islamic world has produced in recent times. In other circles his willingness to make a friendly approach to Israel caused him to be regarded as a traitor to the Islamic cause. His assassination, though widely regarded as a major disaster, was not wholly unexpected.

If we look beyond the Arabic quadrilateral there are several other causes for anxiety, if not for dismay.

The year 1981 saw Iraq and Iran engaged in a war, the causes of which seemed to the outside world to be trivial, and which has not at the time of writing come to an end. Religious tensions seem to have contributed to the outbreak of hostilities, since the vast majority of Iranians are Shi'ahs, whereas in Iraq the Sunnis have a prevailing voice.

Pakistan was founded as an Islamic state, to give to Muslims a home in which they could practise their religion in its fullness. Friendly observers wondered whether a country which existed in two entirely distinct divisions, separated not merely by a thousand miles of the land-mass of India but by diversity of language and tradition – West Pakistan speaking Urdu, East Pakistan Bengali – could ever hold together. Tensions were many from the start; these gradually grew in intensity and finally resulted in a civil war, fought with extreme ferocity on both sides until, with the help of India, Bangladesh attained its independence. Two populous Islamic states have taken the place of one; the

---

[9] See Jansen, p. 54, and for earlier years, K.S. Latourette, *History of the Expansion of Christianity*, vol. V, pp. 291-2.

bitterness surviving from the days of war has gone very deep and will not easily be assuaged.

The fifty million Muslims in India present a continuing question-mark to the Islamic world. The rights of Muslims are safeguarded by the generous provision for religious liberty in the Indian constitution. A number of Muslims have attained to positions of eminence in independent India. Many, perhaps the majority, have settled to acceptance, not necessarily willing, of the status of a minority in a country in which they can never hope to exercise a prevailing influence, and not without some anxiety as to the activity of those extreme Hindu sects which desire to ensure that India becomes Hindustan, the country of the Hindus.

The politics of Libya, now one of the rich oil-producing countries, especially the intervention of its ruler in the unhappy civil war which for long years has devastated the republic of Chad, have not won universal approval in other Islamic countries.

It is right to take note of such tensions within the Islamic world. But it is important not to exaggerate their significance. For all the differences there is a deep underlying sense of Islamic unity. This does not at present find any political expression; that it exists as a religious reality is a fact of immense significance in the life of the entire world of nations.

In the religious sphere also, however, observers of the Islamic scene are aware of elements of anxiety.

Islam is a missionary religion. Through the centuries it has been aware of numerical success and steadily increasing strength. It has lived through the years in the expectation that this experience will be continued. But in recent years this high expectation has been disappointed. Vigorous Islamic propaganda has been carried on in the west, especially by the Ahmadiyya movement – albeit this active group is not recognised by the Islamic world as a whole as genuinely Islamic. But the results have been less than had been hoped for. Converts to Islam in the west have been few. Muslims now in Great Britain make up a sizeable proportion of the population, but almost all of these are immigrants from Pakistan or other Muslim countries – converts from other sections of the population are very few indeed.

Until recently Muslims pointed to Africa as the scene of their most triumphant progress. In the early years of this century Islamic advance in tropical Africa seemed to be so rapid that there was much talk in Christian circles of 'the Muslim menace'. G. H. Jansen states confidently that 'Islam's strength in Africa is rapidly growing ... by the early 1980s over half of the population of Africa should be Muslim.'[10] The cry has been taken up by Christian pessimists, who have stated so often that in Africa five times as many people are becoming Muslims as are becoming Christians that this has come to be believed by a number of Christians. In point of fact none of this is true; a careful study of the statistics yields a very different picture of the situation.

In 1958 the then governor of Tanzania asserted that 65 per cent of the population was Muslim. This may be true of certain areas near the coast, but more careful enumeration has shown that for the country as a whole the correct figure is 20 per cent or a little over. In Kenya Muslims are a highly respected minority, but they do not amount to more than 10 per cent of the population, and there is no sign of any rapid increase in numbers to compare with the startlingly rapid growth of the Christian churches. In such countries as Zaïre, Zambia and Zimbabwe, Islam is almost unknown and there is no sign of any rapid penetration. In northern Nigeria and the northern Cameroons, where it is generally believed that the greater part of the population is Muslim, research has shown that, with rare exceptions, Muslims are to be found mainly among the ruling class, and that the majority of the population still adheres to the ancient African traditions in religion.

It might be thought that these figures represent Christian triumphalism based on rather limited successes. The best evidence that this is not so is to be found in figures supplied by the World League of Muslims. Here it is stated that, according to the latest available figures, there are in Africa 190 million Muslims as against 141 million Christians. This includes 80 million Muslims who live in countries north of the Sahara, and who therefore belong to the Mediterranean area rather than to tropical Africa. If these Muslims are omitted, and the Coptic Christians in Egypt, reckoned at 6 million, are also omitted, Christians already exceed Muslims in tropical Africa by about 20 million. If the same source is correct in stating that the annual rate of increase among Christians is 6 per cent and among

---

[10] *Militant Islam*, p. 16.

Muslims 2 per cent, this would give for the year AD 2000 an estimated total of 210 million Muslims to more than 300 million Christians.[11] In all such demographic projections there is a large measure of uncertainty, and in any case mere numbers can never give a true picture of the vitality of a religion. What is significant is that these figures come from a Muslim source, and give a picture of the situation different from that presented by the Ahmadiyya and other groups whose aim is to glorify the Muslim cause.

The Muslim world, then, finds itself in 1982 in a state of considerable perplexity. The most recent survey of a considerable part of the Islamic world – from Iran to Indonesia – has been made by the novelist V.S. Naipaul, in *Among the Believers: An Islamic Journey*.[12] Naipaul, a non-practising Hindu from the Indian community in Trinidad, is a good observer and sympathetic to the many Muslims of varying traditions with whom he entered into conversation. The word that recurs in his book with almost monotonous regularity is 'perplexity'. Almost all those whom he encountered were fervent believers in Islam.[13] They had believed that the restoration of Islamic faith in its purity would solve all problems, would bring about the *jamā tauhid*, the society of true believers. The revolution had come, Islam was again triumphant – and yet the problems had not been solved. The *Tehran Times* proclaimed that 'the Iranian nation launched the unique and most courageous revolutionary movement in the history of mankind to establish the rule of Islam'. Yet 'out of that society had not come law and institutions; these things were as far away as ever. That society had brought anomaly, hysteria, and this empty office'.[14]

So, as a result of these perplexities, the Islamic world finds itself engaged in an immense task of re-assessment, of re-thinking of what it means to be a Muslim in the late twentieth century.

[11] See P.J. Meiring in *Missionalia* (April 1980), p. 18.
[12] London, Andre Deutsch, 1981.
[13] Not all; naturally Mr Naipaul also met sceptics, and a not inconsiderable number of communists.
[14] Naipaul, pp. 398, 397.

Three distinct tendencies can be identified in Muslim thinking at the present time.

1. The conservatives, the fully orthodox, hold that the answer to the problems is perfectly simple; the four words 'back to the Koran' hold within them the solution to every problem and the supply of every need. Every pious Muslim holds that the Koran is in the simplest and fullest possible sense the word of God. There is no human element in it at all. It has existed from the beginning with God in the Arabic language, to be revealed at the appropriate moment to the chosen apostle of God. Muhammad made no contribution to it whatever. He simply listened, and then recited exactly what he had heard. Every word is a word of God. This is a claim different from that which even the most conservative Christians make for the Bible. They recognise that God has been pleased to make himself known through human instruments, and that the style of Paul is not the same as the style of John. Part of the charm of the Bible is precisely its variety. But this is what makes it hard for Muslims to understand how it is possible for Christians to claim that the Bible is the word of God. No Muslim could put such a book on a level higher than that of tradition, and this gives it only a minimal share in the glory which the Koran has in its fullness.

Muslims claim that the Koran is the culminating point of divine revelation, the source of truth by which they live, and that, if the Koran is rightly understood, it will supply the right answer to every question that man can seriously ask. But the Koran is by no means an easy book, either to understand or to apply. Therefore the learned through the ages have applied their brains to it, have worked out rules of exegesis, and have not always been unanimous in the interpretation that they have given. What they have done to some extent resembles what Christian scholars have done through the ages in the interpretation of the Bible.

The Koran stands alone for the Muslim, and may not be subjected to any form of criticism. But beside it stands a vast collection of texts which are to be treated with respect, though not with the veneration accorded to the Koran. These are the *ḥadīth* and the *sunna*, the traditions of what the prophet said and did on a great variety of occasions. Thoughtful Muslims are willing to admit that some of these traditions are not authentic, in the sense of going back to the prophet Muhammad himself or to the days in which he lived; they represent rather the development of Muslim thought, as controversies arose and teachers strove to find justification for their views in a past which had never had any very real existence.

The third great factor is the sharī'ah, the traditional Islamic code of law. This, based on the Koran, shares at least to some extent in the infallibility of the sacred book. That there are for the Sunnis four schools of legal interpretation is only to be expected, but is not regarded as contravening the essential unity of the codes. Muhammad was undoubtedly a reformer, who revised at many points and gave shape to the chaotic legal traditions of the pre-Islamic period in Arabia. But only a rigidly orthodox Islamic faith can regard what was appropriate in the seventh century as being wholly suited to the conditions of the twentieth. The Islamic code undoubtedly permits slavery to exist in the world of faith; memories of Arab participation in the slave-trade are still so vivid in parts of Africa, where many people now living have been acquainted with those who have been slaves, that Islam has difficulty in finding acceptance among those to whom liberation and freedom are sacred words.

2. Such difficulties arising from Muslim tradition lead on to the second tendency that is noticeable today in many parts of the Islamic world – the belief that it is possible to maintain unimpaired the great tradition of Islam without being tied to every letter of that tradition. The Islamic reformers desire to make their voices heard.

The reformers make their appeal to the principle of ijtihād, exercise of judgment, in addition to other principles of interpretation, of which ijmā', consensus, is the most widely accepted.

One of the ḥadīth, traditions, affirms that, on one occasion the prophet said: 'My community will never agree in error.' This clearly implies the possibility of disagreement and discussion as to the meaning of the faith. Out of such discussions arises consensus, ijmā', as demonstrated by the slowly accumulating pressure of opinion over a long period of time.[15] Is such debate

---

[15] H.A.R. Gibb: *Modern Trends in Islam*, p. 11.

and discussion legitimate today? To the orthodox this admission would seem to be dangerous. Such discussion may have been possible in the early days, when the first Muslims were nearer to the great events of the days of the Prophet, and were in a position to elucidate what was not clear in the words of the Koran; but this process has long since come to an end, the gaps in revelation have all been filled in, the structure of Islam is stable, and any questioning of it is heresy.

If this is accepted, would-be reformers are driven back on the other principle of *ijtihād*, exercise of judgment. This sounds a little like the principle of private judgment introduced in the Christian world at the time of the Reformation; undoubtedly some of the extreme liberals among the Muslims would interpret it in this way. In reality the scope of *ijtihād* is rather narrower than this. Its meaning, taken strictly, is exerting oneself, striving to discover the way in which the Koran and its teachings may be applied to a particular situation; but in no circumstances may it go against the plain teachings of revelation.[16] Nevertheless it is to this principle that Islamic reformers have appealed in their efforts to make the ancient system more acceptable in a greatly changed situation.

Reform movements began in the nineteenth century in India, where Muslims were confronted with special intensity by the teachings and practice of the west. One of the first of the reformers was Sayyid Amir Ali, whose work *The Spirit of Islam* was first published in 1891, but has been reprinted as recently as 1965. In one context Amir Ali goes so far as to say: 'It is earnestly to be hoped that before long a general synod of Muslim doctors will authoritatively declare that polygamy, like slavery, is abhorrent to the laws of Islam.'[17] The distinguished poet Sir Muhammad Iqbal, who was perhaps the first to put forward the idea of Pakistan as a separate Islamic nation within the limits of India, in his work on *The Reconstruction of Religious Thought in Islam* (1934[2]) also challenges the immobility of the Islamic system of law: 'Did the founders of our schools ever claim finality for their reasonings and interpretations? Never. The claim of the present generation of Muslim liberals to reinterpret the foundational legal principles, in the light of their own experience and the

---

16 Gibb, pp. 12–13.
17 Quoted by Gibb, p. 97.

altered conditions of modern life, is in my opinion perfectly justified.'[18]
The movement of liberal questioning passed in this century from India to Egypt.[19] Later times have directed against the Egyptian thinkers the criticism that, though engaged in controversy with the west, they were unconsciously far too much influenced by western ideas and standards to be able to work out an acceptably Islamic understanding of the world and of human life.

The same objection may be raised against interesting discussions being carried on in a country such as Tunis, where a great tradition of Islamic scholarship is combined with a frank acceptance of much that is valuable in French culture. What is to be thought, ask some of these reformers, of the regulations governing the fast of Ramaḍān? These rules may not have been unduly burdensome in days when society was mainly pastoral, and in countries not too far from the equator. But, as Muslims observe the lunar calendar of twelve months of thirty days each, Ramaḍān moves round through the seasons of the year. If it comes in June or July, will it not prove unbearably demanding for Muslims living north of the 40th or 50th parallel of latitude? And is it reasonable to expect a man to be able to carry out a full day's work in the exacting atmosphere of a factory, if he has had nothing to eat since the first light of day? Cannot the spirit of the fast as self-discipline be maintained, even though details of its observance are changed under conditions which the founders of Islam could in no way have foreseen?[20]

The camera turns back to India, where an even more radical stance is that of a distinguished Islamic scholar, A.A. Fyzee, who has been Indian ambassador in Egypt and vice-chancellor of the University of Kashmir. Fyzee draws a radical distinction between universal moral principles, such as kindness, honesty and loyalty, and detailed prescriptions relating to food and drink and matters of personal hygiene. The former are of unchanging obligation; the latter may be less appropriate under some social

---

18 *Reconstruction*, pp. 159-60.
19 Three names may be specially mentioned – Jamal ad Din al-Afghani (1839-97), Muhammad Abduh (1849-1905), and Muhammad Farid Wajdi (1875-1954).
20 Tunis is the only Islamic country in which polygamy has been abolished.

conditions than others. The *Shari'ah* was undoubtedly suitable to the Bedouin of Arabia in the seventh century; it can hardly be regarded as applicable in every respect to the life of the Eskimo or Bushman in the twentieth.[21]

3. A third tendency is much alive in the Islamic world today – the mystical tradition. It may seem strange that mysticism can exist in what seems to be the least mystical of all the great religions. But perhaps it was just in reaction against what appears to the Christian, and seems to have appeared to some Muslims, to be the rigidity of over-formalised worship, the sterility of Islam in piety, that this other concept of the approach of man to God came into being in the Islamic world. In the early days of Muslim domination Christians and Muslims lived in close contact with one another in the country now called Iraq. Christians helped Muslims in the administration of their new dominion. They enlarged their horizons by the translation into Arabic of many Greek masterpieces in philosophy, thus making possible new developments in Muslim philosophy and theology. Among the works translated were those of Plotinus, the greatest of the neo-Platonists, the influence of whose writings is clearly to be traced in the Jewish mysticism of the Qabbalah, and in that long tradition of Christian mysticism which, through the sixth-century writer who called himself Dionysius the Areopagite, goes directly back to Plotinus.

The aim of the *Sūfī*, as of all mystics, is union with God. This is vividly expressed by the great poet Jalal al-Din Rumi (1207–73) in his book the *Masnawī*:

One knocked at the door of the Beloved, and a voice from within enquired, 'Who is there?' Then he answered '*It is I.*' And the voice said 'This house will not hold me and thee.' So the door remained shut. Then the lover sped away into the wilderness, and fasted and prayed in solitude. And after a year he returned, and knocked against the door, and the voice again demanded, 'Who is there?' And the lover

---

[21] A.A. Fyzee: *A Modern Approach to Islam* (Bombay, 1978²), Fyzee has defined his position in the words 'If we cannot go "back" to the Koran, we have to go "forward" with it.' For a notably 'ecumenical' statement of the Islamic position, see Mushir-ul-Haq: 'The Universal Aspects of Islam' in *Towards World Community*, ed. S.J. Samartha (WCC, Geneva, 1975).

said 'It is thou.' Then the door was opened.[22]

The Sūfī believes that he can find support from the Koran for his interpretation of the faith. He can also cite from the ḥadīth the venerable tradition which says: 'My servant draws near to me by works of supererogation, and I love him; and when I love him, I am his ear, so that he hears by me, and his tongue so that he speaks by me, and his hands so that he takes by me.'[23] Many utterances of the Sūfīs have in Christian ears, a startlingly Christian sound. A notable Sūfī Hallāj was put to death in AD 922, among the accusations laid against him being the charge that he said of God 'I am he'. The prayer that he uttered at the time of his execution has become famous:

And those thy servants who are gathered to slay me, in zeal for Thy religion and in desire to win Thy favour, forgive them, O Lord, and have mercy upon them; for verily if Thou hadst revealed to them that which Thou hast revealed to me, they would not have done that which they have done; and if Thou hadst hidden from me that which Thou hast hidden from them, I should not have suffered this tribulation. Glory unto Thee in whatsoever Thou doest, and glory unto Thee in whatsoever Thou willest.[24]

Many Muslims, who would not go all the way with the Sūfī hope of unity with God, might find themselves much in sympathy with the inwardness of this understanding of their religious tradition. These are the

Muslims whose concern for the forms and institutions evolved in Islamic history is subordinate to their lively sense of the living active God who stands behind the religion... The Islam that was given by God is not the elaboration of practices and doctrines and forms that outsiders call Islam, but rather the vivid and personal summons to individuals to live their lives always in His presence and to treat their

---

[22] Quoted in Idries Shah: The Way of the Sufi (1979⁵) pp. 207-8.

[23] 'O God, grant me to love thee, and to love those who love thee, and whatsoever brings me nearer to thy love, and makes thy love dearer to me than cold water to the thirsty traveller in the desert.' I have not been able to trace the source of this beautiful Sūfī prayer.

[24] Quoted by R.A. Nicholson in The Legacy of Islam (1931), p. 217.

fellow men always under His judgement.[25]

It is hard to say how far this spirit has penetrated the Islamic world, though it is likely that this is the inner conviction of many who maintain a perfectly orthodox outward appearance. Clearly, if this became the dominant outlook of convinced and believing Muslims, Islam would undergo a re-creation of itself comparable to that occasioned in Christianity by the Reformation.

★

Islam throughout the world is subject to grave inner tensions. This situation should be viewed by Christians with understanding and sympathy, since we also have experienced similar tensions, and have lived with them through centuries.

The central problem for Islam has been succinctly expressed by Professor H.A.R. Gibb:

> The question for the future is whether Islam will remain what it has been in the past, a comprehensive culture based on a religion, or become a 'church', a religious institution accepted by larger or smaller bodies of adherents within the framework of secular civilisation.[26]

The Christian attitude must be marked not merely by sympathy; it must be marked by penitence. We have already spoken of the tension between the dār-ul-Islām, the world of Islam, and the Christian west, which has been one of the dominant factors in world history for a thousand years. There have been faults on both sides, and these we can leave to the judgment of God. What is essential is that we should understand the dark shadow which has been cast everywhere on the Muslim mind by the wanton aggressiveness of the west. Like the Jew, the Muslim may forget his own faults in the contemplation of ours; we may leave him to this occupation, and welcome only the service that he has rendered in calling our attention to our own. Memories are long in the east. To us the Crusades are very ancient history; to the Muslim they are as though they had

---

25 W. Cantwell Smith: *Islam in Modern History*, p. 308.
26 In the *Concise Encyclopaedia of Living Faiths* (ed. R.C. Zaehner, 1959), p. 208.

happened yesterday.

It may be profitable at this point to cite a judicious estimate of the Crusades by an outstanding western historian. Sir Steven Runciman, who has an incomparable knowledge of the Byzantine and eastern authorities of the period, ends the third volume of his great *History of the Crusades* with a melancholy chapter, entitled 'The Summing Up', of the force of which the following brief quotation can give only a very imperfect impression:

> The Crusades were launched to save Eastern Christendom from the Moslems. When they ended the whole of Eastern Christendom was under Moslem rule ... Seen in the perspective of history the whole Crusading movement was a vast fiasco ... The triumphs of the Crusade were the triumphs of faith. But faith without wisdom is a dangerous thing ... In the long sequence of interaction and fusion between Orient and Occident out of which our civilization has grown, the Crusades were a tragic and destructive episode. The historian as he gazes back across the centuries at their gallant story must find his admiration overcast by sorrow at the witness that it bears to the limitations of human nature. There was so much courage and so little honour, so much devotion and so little understanding. High ideals were besmirched by cruelty and greed, enterprise and endurance by a blind and narrow self-righteousness; and the Holy War itself was nothing more than a long act of intolerance in the name of God, which is the sin against the Holy Ghost.[27]

These are hard words. But they may well be pondered by those who would enter the mind and the heart of the Muslim today.

Christian approach to the Muslim, Muslim approach to the Christian – these have been carried on in many ways and through many centuries, sometimes with acrimony and bitterness and unwillingness to understand, at other times with learning and sobriety and with that respect for the opponent without which no meeting of mind with mind can take place. On the Christian side, the most notable name in the early days of controversy is that of John of Damascus (*c*.675–*c*.749), who in 1890 was declared by Pope Leo XIII to be a doctor of the church; his *Disputation between*

---

[27] Steven Runciman: *A History of the Crusades*, vol. iii, *The Kingdom of Acre* (1954), pp. 469, 480.

a Christian and a Saracen, based on long contact with Muslims in Damascus, was an armoury for many later defenders of the Christain faith. Al Ghazzālī (1058-1111), perhaps the greatest among Islamic philosophers, shows a more than superficial knowledge of Christianity. Best known of those who pleaded for a Christian understanding of Islam on the part of those who would enter into theological discussion with Muslims was Raymond Lull (*c*.1233-*c*.1315), who wrote:

> It seems to me therefore, O Lord, that the Holy Land will never be conquered except by love and prayer and the shedding of tears as well as blood. Let the knights go forth adorned with the sign of the Cross and filled with the grace of the Holy Spirit, and preach the truth concerning Thy passion.[28]

Unhappily controversialists on either side of the argument did not always maintain this even temper, or this level of awareness each of the treasured beliefs of the other. All too often controversy has become shrill and acrid, aiming rather at the destruction of the other than at mutual understanding, let alone reconciliation.[29] It is good to be able to cite from more modern times examples from both sides of those who have entered the field of discussion with the same charitable and temperate spirit as was manifest in their great predecessors.

Many of us learned something of it more than a generation ago from a great scholar in this field, Duncan Black Macdonald. Macdonald describes for us his perplexity, when he first travelled in the east, as to the way in which he should approach the tombs of Muslim saints, access to which had been opened for him by the authorities, and the decision that he made:

> The course that I followed . . . was to visit them frankly in reverence, and I found that the fact that I did so - that I behaved, as my Eastern friends would say, like a religious-minded man and a gentleman - helped me indefinitely in my intercourse with Muslims. There is one usage, for example, that is of rule when visiting the tombs of Muslim

---

[28] From his work written in 1312, *Liber de participatione christianorum et sarracenorum*.
[29] Perhaps the fullest account of the long process of argument and discussion is the massive work of J. W. Sweetman: *Islam and Christian Theology* (2 vols, London 1955 ff).

saints. You advance to the railing that surrounds the tomb, you hold it in your right hand ... and you recite the *Fatiha*, the first chapter of the Koran, which holds pretty much the place with the Muslim that the Lord's Prayer does with us.

I do not know whether any one of those standing there were especially spiritually benefited by it. I do know, however, that I was benefited by feeling the nearness of the spiritual kindred of all that call upon the Lord, and I know too that those Muslims who saw me do this or who knew that I did it, felt that here was a spiritual unity, that this man, Christian though he might be, reverenced their saint and knew what it meant to recognize holiness and the life hid in God.[30]

I have always liked this picture of the reverence of a Christian man in a place which to the believers of another faith was holy ground. We shall understand at once why a much more recent expositor of Islam, Bishop Kenneth Cragg, has called one of his books *Sandals at the Mosque*.[31] In the east you enter a temple, a mosque, or a church barefoot. Bishop Cragg is teaching us that, unless we approach that which to others is holy, even though it may not in the same sense be holy to us, in that spirit of humility and reverence, we shall find all the doors barred and bolted against us. We may attain to intellectual knowledge; but that is far removed from the inner understanding which it ought to be our desire as Christians to attain.

In all his writing Bishop Cragg stresses the truth that, if we wish to understand the Muslim, we must approach him by way of his worship. Five times a day the Muslim is supposed to say his prayers. It cannot be doubted that this prayer, by the very fact that it is endlessly repeated from day to day, impresses on the Muslim soul a certain pattern, a certain temper. And what is it that the Muslim says?

God is most great. God is most great. I bear witness that Muhammad is the apostle of God. God is most great. In the name of God, the merciful Lord of mercy. Praise be to God the Lord of the worlds, the merciful Lord of mercy, Sovereign of the day of judgment. Thee alone it is we worship; Thee alone we implore to help. Guide us in the

---

[30] D. B. Macdonald: *Aspects of Islam* (1911), pp. 24–6.
[31] London, 1959.

straight path, the path of those to whom thou art gracious, who are not the incurrers of thine anger, nor wanderers in error. God is most great, God is most great... I bear witness that Muhammad is the apostle of God... May God send down blessing upon him and preserve him in peace. Peace rest upon you and the mercy of God.

Even a cursory reading of this prayer must suggest to the Christian that Islam and the Gospel are concerned about the same things. They are concerned about the reality, the oneness and the sovereignty of God, about revelation and mercy, about the responsibility of man, about eternal life and destiny, about God's call to submission and obedience, about the need for decision on the part of man.

Both the Roman Catholic church and the World Council of Churches have taken the initiative in developing dialogue between Christians and Muslims. It has been found possible for the adherents of two different faiths to spend time together, to some extent to share in each other's worship, and to exchange ideas with a considerable measure of frankness. One statement of the spirit expected of participants, and to a large extent enjoyed by those of both persuasions, may serve as a specimen of many:

> Dialogue was not a sentimental process of easy agreement but could mean a rigorous facing of differences and a stripping away of pretence. Dialogue was not coldly objective analysis of the other man's religious tradition although there was a real place for some to use their gifts for disciplined descriptive statements. Dialogue was essentially to be understood in a spirit of repentance wherein we turned our backs on past and present prejudice, wherein we turned to our neighbours in the spirit of love, and wherein we turned to God, as he offered Himself to us. Our Muslim observers shared this point of departure, in self-criticism and openness.[32]

This emphasis on gentleness, and a more sympathetic approach is highly to be commended. But it takes two to make

---

[32] *Dialogue between Men of Living Faiths*, ed. S. J. Samartha (WCC, Geneva, 1971), p. 60. The Christian writer was John B. Taylor. Reference to the Muslim reply by Muzammil H. Siddiqi (pp. 73-4) shows that the Christian was generous in his estimate of the Muslim attitude.

dialogue possible. The most disappointing factor in the history of the past twenty years is the failure, which is still almost universal in the Islamic world, of the Muslim scholar to approach Christianity with that reverence and open-mindedness which he rightly demands of the Christian scholar in his approach to Islam. Dr Cantwell Smith, a scholar who cannot be accused of lack of sympathy for Islam, wrote sadly in 1957:

> The present writer knows no book by a Muslim showing any 'feel' for the Christian position; nor indeed any clear endeavour to deal with, let alone understand, the central doctrines. The usual Muslim attitude is not to take the central doctrines seriously at all. That is, they do not recognise that Christians take them seriously; and that however absurd they might seem to outsiders (to Muslims they appear both stupid and blasphemous) the Trinity, the Deity and Sonship and Crucifixion of Christ, and the like are affirmations deeply meaningful and precious and utterly integral to the Christian's faith.[33]

This is echoed from the Muslim side by Muhammad Talbu in Tunis: 'In particular, as far as I am aware, it is not possible to name a single real Muslim Christologist.'[34]

It would be a mistake, however, to disregard the possibilities of a more sympathetic understanding of Christianity from the Muslim side. One of the most remarkable of these has been made accessible to the English reader in an excellent translation by Bishop Kenneth Cragg, *City of Wrong* by Kamel Hussain.[35] What actually happened in Jerusalem on Good Friday? The writer, a devout Muslim, leaves an atmosphere of mystery surrounding the events of that fateful day. He cannot go so far as to affirm that Jesus Christ was actually crucified; yet his vivid depiction of the various forces at work in the city, of the personalities involved and of the concentration of them all on one central and mysterious figure, draws us very near to an understanding of that mystery which in another way has been presented to us in the Gospels.

---

[33] W. Cantwell Smith: *Islam in Modern History*, p. 104, n. 1.
[34] *Islam in Dialogue* (Tunis, 1972), p. 14.
[35] Amsterdam, 1959.

★

Did Jesus die on the cross? In any honest dialogue between
Muslims and Christians this issue cannot be avoided. If
discussion is to be fruitful, it is necessary to look carefully at what
is actually said on the subject in the Koran:

> They [the Jews] said
> See, we have killed the Messiah Jesus the Son of
> Mary
> the sent one of God –
> they killed him not,
> they did not crucify him
> but it was made to appear that way to them...
> they did not kill him in reality,
> but God exalted him to himself,
> and God is mighty and wise.

It might seem that the words can have no meaning other than
that which is most obvious – that the Jews did not kill Jesus and
therefore that Jesus did not die on the cross. But in recent times a
number of scholars have argued persuasively that the meaning is
less clear than at first appears.

For instance R. C. Zaehner has written: 'It is really asserted
that the *Jews* neither slew nor crucified the Messiah Jesus, Son of
Mary, but that God raised him up to Himself, the implication
being that it was God himself who slew and crucified Jesus. The
Jews took the credit for what was really God's own initiative.'[36]

E. G. Parrinder follows somewhat the same line of thinking:'We
must try to understand what the Qur'ān really teaches and
Muslims believe. The great Quranic and Islamic emphasis upon
the will of God, apart from which no man could kill the Messiah,
needs to be understood.'[37]

Scholars, both Muslim and Christian, will continue to debate
the exact meaning of the words of the Koran. It is, however, clear

---

[36] *At Sundry Times* (1958), p. 212; and see the whole Appendix, pp. 195-217. The
same view is taken by the editor of *Operation Reach*, the valuable series of booklets
put out by the Near East Christian Council (now the Middle East Christian
Council).

[37] *Truth and Dialogue*, ed. J. Hick (1974), p. 123.

that the vast majority of Muslims believe, and have been taught, that Jesus was not crucified but that God rescued him and carried him away to a safe place in the heavens. Traditions tell that some other was substituted for Jesus, and was crucified in his place.[38] If there was no death, there was no redemption through the death of the Messiah; thus one central article of the Christian creed is found to be baseless, and to rest on nothing other than a misunderstanding propagated by the Christian.

It is hard to see how on this point a meeting of minds between the Christian and the Muslim can be brought about. The Christian student, trained in historical methods, is not likely to wish to diverge from the almost unanimous agreement of historians, Christian and secular alike, that the crucifixion of Jesus is one of the most assured events of ancient history, at least as assured as the departure of Muhammad from Mecca to Medina in the year 622 of the Christian era. He is no more likely to doubt the historicity of the crucifixion than the Muslim is likely to doubt the historicity of the *Hijra*, the event which for him marks the dividing point of history.

On this point, as on others, there are considerable differences between the New Testament and the Koran. If this is the case, the Muslim controversialist is ready with an explanation. To him the Koran is the very word of God, and it is therefore impossible that it should contain any error. The picture of Jesus given in the many passages of the Koran which refer to him is the only authentic picture. The New Testament as Christians read it today cannot be the original message of Jesus, the *Injil* commended by the Prophet Muhammad in twelve passages of the Koran. It must have become corrupted in the process of the handing down of the New Testament by Christians.

Here again is a point at which it is difficult to see how there can be a meeting between the Christian and the Muslim mind. The

---

[38] There is no support in the Koran itself for this view. Muslim controversialists sometimes quote as an authority the *Gospel of Barnabas*, a strange work which cannot be earlier than the sixteenth century, and which puts forward the view that it was Judas Iscariot who was crucified. This Gospel, apparently by a Christian who had turned Muslim, exists only in Italian; it was translated into English by Laura and Lonsdale Ragg (1907). It has been translated into Arabic for use in argument with Christians. Some of the Gnostics (Basilidians) seem to have believed that it was Simon of Cyrene who was actually crucified.

Christian student is familiar with the fascinating process through which scholars have recovered and established the original Greek text of the New Testament. He has followed the process, through the discovery of the great fourth century manuscripts, back to the papyri of the third century discovered in Egypt, behind them to even older fragments which give evidence that, allowing for some minor variations, the text of the New Testament in the second century was very near to that which we have today. When to this is added the immense weight of the early translations of the New Testament into Latin, Syriac and Armenian, and the massive testimony of the Christian fathers of the second and third centuries, he feels justified in the affirmation that, for about 98 per cent of the text of the New Testament, we have before us exactly the words which the original authors wrote; it is impossible that any extensive corruption can have taken place between their time and ours. In the days of the Prophet Muhammad the New Testament was available in both Syriac and Arabic; this was the *Injil* which was conveyed to the Prophet, probably by word of mouth; in the Koran itself there is no suggestion that the New Testament as put forward by the Christians was different from that revelation communicated by God Himself to Jesus the Son of Mary.[39]

The Muslim missionary is sincerely convinced that it is he, and not the Christian, who has the true picture of Jesus of Nazareth. His task, therefore, is to help Christians to discover what it really means to be a Christian. If they will only use their reason, cast away the later absurdities of Christian doctrine, and come back to the simple prophetic faith of Jesus in God, they will find that this is the same as the faith proclaimed by Muhammad, who himself claimed that he was doing no more than to set forth the original prophetic faith as it had been proclaimed by all the prophets from the time of Abraham to the time of Jesus, the last in the succession before Muhammad himself. In this proclamation faith is entirely set free from idealistic fancies, and

---

[39] This historical and critical question must not be confused with another different, though related, question. Is it possible that the very earliest Christians misunderstood, and therefore distorted, the message that their Master had delivered to them and the claims that he made for himself? This is arguable. If this is affirmed by Muslims, there is a place for patient and rational Christian apologetic.

brought within the compass of the ordinary practical man who has to live and earn his daily bread in the world. Let us start with those principles on which all the prophets agree.

Dr Guillaume has conveniently set out for us the extent of agreement and disagreement between Christian and Muslim in terms of the Apostles Creed.[40] The words in italics are rejected by Islam:

> I believe in God
> *the Father*
> Almighty, Maker of heaven and earth:
> And in Jesus Christ
> *His only Son our Lord*
> Who was conceived of the Holy Ghost
> Born of the Virgin Mary
> *Suffered under Pontius Pilate*
> *Was crucified*
> *Dead and buried*
> *He descended into Hell*
> *The third day he rose again from the dead*
> He ascended into heaven
> *And sitteth on the right hand of God the Father Almighty*
> From thence he shall come
> *To judge the quick and the dead*
> I believe in the Holy Ghost
> *The Holy Catholic Church*
> *The Communion of Saints*
> The Forgiveness of sins
> The Resurrection of the body
> And the life everlasting.

The agreements are impressive. Yet the Christian must ask himself whether the nature of the massive denials is not such that by their existence they change even the agreements into disagreements. Even when we use the same words, do we not use them in totally different senses?

We have a common starting point in that Christians and

---

40 A. Guillaume: *Islam* (Pelican Books, Second Edition (revised) 1956) p. 194 copyright © the Estate of Alfred Guillaume, 1954, 1956. Reprinted by permission of Penguin Books Ltd. Dr Guillaume follows this paradigmatic statement with a useful comment on each clause of the Creed.

Muslims alike passionately proclaim belief in one God. But
everything depends on the meaning we put into the word 'God'.
Islam conceives the possible relationship of man to God in one
way and the Christian Gospel in another:

> While God was the exclusive source of the revelation to Muhammad,
> God himself is not the content of the revelation. Revelation in Islamic
> theology does not mean God disclosing himself. It is revelation *from*
> God, not revelation of God. God is remote. He is inscrutable and
> utterly inaccessible to human knowledge ... Even though we are his
> creatures whose every breath is dependent upon him, it is not in
> inter-personal relationship with him that we receive guidance from
> him.[41]

At this central point the teaching of Jesus diverges from what
the Muslim believes to be the essential prophetic witness. The
God of Jesus is a God who cares for his creatures, who is prepared
to enter into fellowship with them, and is concerned that they
should love him in response to his love. The Koran never uses the
word 'Father' of God. Jesus taught his disciples to address God as
'Our Father'. The essence of the Gospel is summed up in these
two words.

This is a point of special difficulty. Muhammad seems to sweep
away completely the idea of fatherhood in God, and to reject
unconditionally the Christian idea of incarnation; 'God resist
them: how they are perverse' (Sūra 9: 30) sums up his attitude to
the Christians of his day. But is it certain that what the Prophet
was rejecting was the doctrine of incarnation as Christians
understood it? Had this doctrine ever been explained to him?
There can be no doubt that there were Christians in Arabia in the
seventh century, and that Muhammad had some contacts with
them, apparently in the later rather than in the earlier periods of
his ministry. But there were various Christian sects at the time.
There is reason to think that what the Prophet was condemning
was not the doctrine as the church has understood it through the
centuries but the heresy known as adoptianism – the idea that a
man somehow climbed up to be God, or that God in some way
acquired a son. Bishop Cragg draws attention to the fact that in

---

[41] Edmund Perry: *The Gospel in Dispute* (1958), pp. 155, 157.

Arabic the recurrent term is *ittakhadha*, to take to oneself – 'Far be it from the eternal to take to himself a son' (19: 35, and 19: 92, 25: 2). 'Adoptianism is broadly what it has in mind. It is possible in this way to relieve the orthodox Christian faith of much of the burden of explicit Quranic repudiation.'[42]

It can hardly be doubted that Muhammad understood the terms 'father' and 'son' in a purely physical sense, and was unaware, or perhaps refused to recognise, that they could be used in any other sense. If this were, indeed, the only sense in which the words could be used, Christians would be the first to repudiate them. But, in the New Testament, the word 'Father' as used by Jesus stood for trustful affection, confidence in a higher wisdom, understanding, rational obedience, intelligent co-operation. Such an attitude is reasonable only if there is a God in relation to whom such words have meaning. It is the affirmation of the Prophet Jesus that there is such a God, and that he can be known and loved.

To the Christian the incarnation means that that which is inherent in the very being of God from the beginning has now been made manifest in the three-dimensional world of space and time, and under the conditions of human existence. The Koran speaks of Jesus both as a spirit from God, and as a word from God. If these terms, which to the Muslim are inspired truth, are taken in the full range of their being, it might seem that the incarnation, so far from being a blasphemous absurdity, could appear as inevitable in the light of what the fatherhood of God is now revealed to be.

Muslim tradition, as we have seen, rejects the very idea of the crucifixion, though it is less than clear that in doing so Muslims are interpreting the Koran correctly. The origin of this idea may have been a generous desire to safeguard the honour of God from the charge that he could be either unable or unwilling to deliver so eminent a prophet from so shameful a death, and perhaps also to pay honour to the prophet concerned. If so, credit must be given to those who held and hold this view, though the Christian must maintain that it is based not only on disregard of historical evidence, but also on unacceptable presuppositions as

---

[42] 'Islam and Incarnation' in *Truth and Dialogue* (ed. J. Hick, 1974), pp. 138–9. See also R.C. Zaehner: *At Sundry Times* (1958), pp. 195–218; and the full discussion in E.G. Parrinder: *Jesus in the Qur'an* (1965).

to the nature and activity of God. If we know exactly what God is like, we can predict exactly what God will do in any circumstances and there can be no exceptions. The Christian cannot feel himself tied down by any such certainty. The biblical emphasis is on the freedom of God, a God 'afar off', who cannot be limited by any human understanding or expectation. His action is unpredictable and may go far beyond the limits of the highest and best imaginations of men. The Muslim starts from the assumption that God will not leave so great a prophet helpless in the hands of his enemies. The more flexible Christian approach leaves open the possibility that, for good reason, God might do just that. The Muslim feels that the Christian is denying or calling in question the omnipotence of God; the Christian might answer that, in his doctrine of the death and suffering of Jesus Christ, the omnipotence of God is the very thing that he is defending.

Muslims are resentful when Christians call them Muhammadans, and object strongly to the title of Professor Gibb's excellent little book *Mohammedanism* (1953). This suggests to them that Christians regard Muslims as standing in the same relationship to the Prophet as Christians believe themselves to stand to Jesus Christ. No Muslim imagines himself to have a personal relationship with the Prophet here and now. It is true that in popular Islamic faith the Prophet is almost divinised; glory is ascribed to him such as is ascribed to none other but God himself. But this is not part of orthodox Islamic theology.The glory of the risen Jesus is part of orthodox Christian theology.

Moreover, that which we ask the Muslim to look for in Jesus is in itself a cause of grave offence to Muslim pride. We suggest – we cannot do otherwise – that he find a Saviour. The Muslim affirms that he has no need of any such thing. In modern Muslim propaganda in the west nothing is more strongly emphasised than the feasibility, the viability, of Islam. Men can turn and obey, if they will. Islam makes only reasonable demands upon men. This is part of the mercy of God – he knows what men can do, and does not lay upon them burdens too heavy to be borne. A contrast is drawn between the unpracticable idealism of Jesus, suitable perhaps for ascetics and those who can flee entirely from the world, and the practical down-to-earth regulations of Islam. And the Muslim objects strongly to Christian stress upon the sinfulness of man. This seems to him to be mere evasion. By pleading his weakness man tries to excuse his failure to obey, and so to withdraw himself from the just judgment of God on disobedience. Instead, he should gird himself to the not overwhelmingly difficult effort of obedience.

At the heart of the Muslim-Christian disagreement, we shall find a deep difference in the understanding of the nature of sin. It is not true to say that the Muslim has no sense of sin or of the need for forgiveness. He has both. But an understanding of sin is directly related to an understanding of the nature of God. The New Testament doctrine of God as love involves a deepened understanding of the nature of sin, such as seems not to be involved in the Islamic concept of the relation between the believer and the God in whom he believes. The believer may sin against the law and the majesty of God, and if he does so he deserves to be punished. The idea that man by his sin might break the heart of God makes sense only on the basis of the Christian understanding of the nature of God as love.

It is at this point that Bishop Cragg, who has gone perhaps farther than any other Christian student of Islam in the attempt to understand and sympathise, changes from expositor to evangelist; and, coming after 120 pages of profoundly sympathetic exposition, the change is all the more impressive:

> Law informs our ignorance, and when the problem is no longer ignorance but obduracy, this it will rebuke and condemn. Then the gulf widens and the righteousness of the law goes, by the way of the law, ever further from our reach. If we acquiesce in this situation we are complacent sinners; if we deplore it we are despairing ones. The Gospel of grace is beyond this dilemma of the law. It assures us in the Cross that it reaches beyond our despair, while leaving us no ground for refuge in complacency...
>
> Even where it is despised and rejected by the soul of man, the Cross stands majestically. It has a patience and a promise, beyond the competence of law. Its grace will never let us go, as at some point law necessarily must. If we are burdened by the length of human waywardness, as in our questions we confessed to being, we shall find in the Cross alone a commensurate enterprise of God for its redemption.[43]

---

[43] Kenneth Cragg: *Sandals at the Mosque* (1959), pp. 138-9.

So, if the Christian desires to approach the Muslim with the message of the Gospel, he will find that there are immense obstacles in the way, and that these have to be removed if reasonable discussion is to become possible. But he must never give way to despair, and may not suppose that there will never be response from the Muslim side to a friendly and modest approach on the part of Christians.

Just in time to be included in the final revision of this chapter has come news of a conference, held in Colombo and attended by Christians and Muslims from nearly forty countries, an outcome of which was a recommendation for the formation of a joint committee to 'promote further dialogue and co-operation'. The sponsoring bodies would be the World Council of Churches and the World Muslim Congress based on Karachi. One of the special tasks of such a committee would be precisely to identify and try to redress obstacles and difficulties which stand in the way of understanding and co-operation.[44]

So, if undeterred by hindrances and obstacles, the Christian girds himself to the finding of his Muslim friend and to the effort to introduce him to the things that Christians really believe, what is the principle on which his efforts must be based?

The Christian has no other message for the Muslim than Jesus Christ himself. He asks no more of the Muslim than that he will look at Jesus Christ, as he is presented in the Gospels, patiently, sincerely and without prejudice. But this is the very thing that it is most difficult to persuade him to do. The Muslim thinks that he already knows about Jesus all that it is possible to know; why should he suppose that he still has anything to learn? But it is not the case that the Muslim has seen Jesus of Nazareth and has rejected him; he has never seen him,[45] and the veil of misunderstanding and prejudice is still over his face. But, if he can be persuaded to look at Jesus, strange things may happen.

The Muslim is convinced that no Muslim has ever sincerely become a Christian, though some have been persuaded to profess conversion for base and unworthy reasons. They are

---

44 *Greetings* (1982), No. 2.

45 'There is no evidence that Muslims saw either . . . Jewish or Christian faith at all. What they saw in fact were images developed within their own religious and cultural orbit.' J. Waardenburg: *Islam: Past Influence and Present Challenge* (Edinburgh, 1979), p. 268.

mistaken. Genuine conversions may be rare; but sufficient cases are on record of Muslims who after long and painful seeking have reached the conclusion that in Jesus Christ alone the answers to their perplexing questions are to be found. No question should be raised as to the sincerity of such earnest seekers. An experienced missionary, who had spent many years in Christian work among Muslims, when asked what it was in the Christian faith that drew Muslims towards it, answered without hesitation, 'the person of Jesus Christ'. In the story of the transfiguration, it is recorded that the disciples saw Jesus speaking with Moses and Elijah; when they looked up again, they saw Jesus only and no man with him. This is a kind of parable of what happens when Jesus is set alongside any other religious teacher. The other gradually recedes into the background and Jesus alone is seen in the simplicity and grandeur of what he is.

A strange tribute has been paid in this century by Muslims to this reality. Many lives of the Prophet Muhammad have been written by Muslims for western and Christian consumption. In all of these the less agreeable features in the character of Muhammad have been softened down and subtly christianised, so that the rugged Prophet of Arabia has been transformed into a kindly and beneficent reformer. If the enquiring Muslim student is prepared to turn from this composite picture to Muhammad as he is actually portrayed in the Koran and the traditions, and to Jesus of Nazareth as he is actually portrayed in the Gospels, he may discover, perhaps with dismay, that his understanding of religion is undergoing a subtle change, and that the attractive power of Jesus is a force which he is finding it increasingly difficult to resist.

CHAPTER IV

Renascent Hinduism

Hinduism is not so much a religious system as a vast complex of systems, not all of which are consistent with one another. It has incorporated into itself many and various forms of thought and worship, from the lofty thinking of the philosophers to the adoration of evil spirits practised by simple villagers and what to the Westerner must seem to be the excesses of Tantric rites.

When Europeans, missionaries among them, began to concern themselves with the religion of their neighbours, their first encounters were almost invariably with what from the western point of view was repellent and degrading – animal sacrifice at the Kālighāt in Calcutta, the burning of sometimes unwilling widows on the funerals pyres of their husbands, and the presence of the harlots' houses around the temples as in the Ephesus of the days of St Paul. Indian scholars had, of course, guarded the ancient tradition of learning; there was never a complete breach in the continuity of philosophic thought and contemplation. But little of this was apparent in Hinduism as it was seen in the practice of the ordinary worshipper; the content of religious understanding seemed to be conditioned by late and not very edifying Purānic tales of the doings of the gods.

The same problem today confronts the enquiring student of religion, who moves from the calm atmosphere of academe to direct confrontation with the Indian peoples as they are today. In the course of his studies he will have been introduced to the classical traditions of Hinduism. He will have started with the Rg Veda, one of the very oldest monuments of human literary skill. He will have ploughed his way through the Taittiriya and Chandogya Upaniṣads and made himself familiar with the lively beginnings of Indian speculation. He may have gained some acquaintance with the six systems of Indian philosophy, and become aware that that capacious religion can make room within itself both for theistic and for atheistic understandings of the universe. But he will find in India that many of these things are outside the imaginative world of people, other than scholars, with whom he has to do. The vocabulary of the classics, even when adapted to the modern forms of Indian speech, is unfamiliar to them. The ideas of the ancient religion are not theirs. He begins to wonder whether those whom he encounters are Hindus at all and, if so, in what sense.

This perplexity arises in part from the simple fact that, though urbanisation is advancing, in India as elsewhere, more than two-thirds of the population is still made up of village dwellers. The villager is not unaware of the existence of one supreme deity. But for the most part he has to do with spirits rather than with gods. In all probability the very names of the Vedic gods are unknown to him. Every village has at least one shrine, more probably several. But the spirits, male or female, which are worshipped at these shrines, are not those of the Hindu pantheon. Much that is primitive has survived. Even on a higher level of sophistication, popular Hinduism bears little relation to the classical tradition as this is set forth in most of the western books on Hindu religion.[1]

Yet those who treat Hinduism as essentially a unity, and as the bond which has created a measure of cultural and religious unity among many of the races which inhabit the Indian sub-continent, have a good deal to be said on their side. There are perhaps three elements of the Hindu system that have penetrated to the remotest Hindu village and condition the minds of those who stand in any kind of relation to the Hindu tradition:

1. Every individual who has any claim to the Hindu name is a member of one of the innumerable castes into which society is divided, and by his membership is pledged to keep its rules. Each caste has its own traditions, its own way of living, and these lay

---

[1] There is now a considerable literature on this more popular Hinduism. Two striking works of recent years are Carl Gustav Diehl: *Instrument and Purpose* (Lund 1956), in which a good bibliography is provided, and by the same author, *Church and Shrine* (Uppsala, 1965). An exceptionally valuable study of village Hinduism is M. L. Reiniche's *Les Dieux et les Hommes. Étude des Cultes d'un village du Tirunelveli Inde du Sud* (Paris, 1979); on which see a penetrating but on the whole favourable review by Richard Bunghart in *Bulletin of the School of Oriental and African Studies*, XLV, 1982, pp. 379-81

their iron hand on every part of the life of man and woman – on what they wear and what they eat, on the words they use, the gods they worship, and the manner in which they order their social relationships. In the cities the old ways are rapidly changing; in the village their sway has hardly been affected by the transformations of the times.

Western observers have in the main been impressed by the divisiveness and wastefulness of caste. Individual initiative is at a discount. A man's occupation is determined for him by his birth and not by his choice; and the exclusion of nearly a sixth of the population from social privilege and participation in the cultural heritage of the nation must involve not only the sufferers but the whole people in grave national impoverishment. The Indian sees the other side of the picture.[2] This marvellously ingenious fabric has secured to Indian society a stability unknown for centuries in the west. Individuals understand exactly what their place is in society, and unless they flagrantly break the rules are assured throughout their life of the support and help of a close-knit community. All have some kind of rights. All render some kind of service to the community, and for this there is reward. The rights of the scheduled communities, formerly known as outcastes, may be so limited as to be almost invisible; but they are not non-existent and are maintained both by the general good sense of the community, and by legal enactment carried through, greatly to its credit, by the government of independent India. The process by which the casteless aboriginal peoples of the mountains and jungles are being absorbed into the caste system continues to the present day.

2. Almost everyone who belongs to any Hindu community is likely to have some idea of the law of retribution, by which life and fate in this world are determined. Every human being must eat the fruit of ancient deeds until they are wholly consumed. If there has not been time in one life for the debt to be fully paid, then the one who has incurred the debt must be born again upon earth, and so on endlessly until the uttermost farthing has been paid. Here the Hindu finds the explanation of all inequality and

---

[2] A good and balanced statement in Duncan B. Forrester: *Caste and Christianity* (London, 1979), pp. 2–6.

misfortune in this earthly life, and to him the explanation is complete and logically irrefragable. 'One man is borne aloft in a litter', says the ancient Tamil classic; 'four men sweat at the pole. What can this be, other than the fruit of ancient deeds?' This is a fatalistic creed as far as present existence is concerned, yet not merely fatalistic, since there is always the hope that by acquiring merit in this life the Hindu may attain to a higher stage in the next existence, and ultimately to release from the *samsāra*, the endless wheel of existence and change.

3. Everywhere in the Hindu world there is an all-pervading sense of the reality of the unseen and the spiritual. The great prayer of the Bṛhadāranyaka Upaniṣad splendidly sums it up: 'From the unreal lead me to the real; from darkness lead me to light; from death lead me to immortality.' To the Hindu the visible is the unreal, the illusory; the real is the invisible. In contact with Christians this is what the Hindu finds lacking; the Christian seems absorbed in the visible world and its concerns; he lacks what to the Hindu is the essential quality of spirituality. It is true that for the simple villager the unseen is often a menacing reality; yet even to him the real is always present on the fringe of consciousness. For many this is a distant reality hardly ever invoked in worship. Yet for almost all there is this awareness of the Other, the ultimately real, and it is precisely of this that western man, as the Hindu sees him, has been deprived by the progress of secularisation.

*

The visitor to an Indian village becomes aware of a culture that to a large extent has resisted the threats of time. Even today the most characteristic sound in the village in the early morning is the creak of the well-wheel, as the bulls go up and down the ramp, drawing the water from the well for the thirsty fields. But for nearly five centuries India has, for good and ill, been in close contact with the west, and particularly with the English-speaking west. English is the most widely spoken language in India, though it is readily spoken by less than five per cent of the population. But the western influence goes far beyond this highly educated élite. And, wherever it has penetrated, it has brought about tensions and frustrations; resistance to change has been at times almost frenetic; yet change has taken place, at times against the will, at times almost without the consciousness, of those who have been subject to it. The assault from the west took on a variety of different forms. The religious aspect of this assault could not fail to produce a variety of reactions. The first was, naturally, the reaction of refusal. Those who by temperament or status were inclined to conservatism refused to have anything to do with the new ways. The old is better, sanctioned by immemorial custom. Any hand which is laid on any part of the structure must of necessity be a sacrilegious hand. Dr Percival Spear has strikingly interpreted the great uprising of 1857 in terms of emotional self-defence against a threat to the familiar world order:

> The supreme expression of the reactionary spirit was the Mutiny of 1857. In one tense and tragic moment all the country's love of its old way of life, regret for past glories, and distrust of and disgust at foreign innovations flared up in a violent explosion of emotional resentment... So far from being the first war of independence or a national revolt in the modern sense, the Mutiny was the final convulsion of the old order goaded to desperation by the incessant pricks of modernity.[3]

A great deal of this sheer, emotional rather than intellectual, conservatism survives, especially perhaps among the Brahmans, the traditional guardians of the law and practice of Hinduism. It underlies one of the modern movements by which the Hindu scene is diversified.

Dayānand Sarasvati (1824–83), a Gujarati, became convinced that the only way by which Hinduism could recover vitality and power was a return to its first sources in the Veda. To the Veda he was prepared to attribute almost verbal inspiration, and in the light of his understanding of it to abandon such venerable Hindu customs as idolatry and the caste system.

In 1875 Dayānand founded the Ārya Samāj to propagate his ideals and to put into effect his ideas. From the start this was a polemical movement: 'For the first time for centuries Hinduism

---

[3] Percival Spear: *India, Pakistan, and the West* (1967⁴), p. 115.

took the offensive.'[4] Corrupt Hinduism, no less than Christianity and Islam, was the object of the attacks launched by Dayānand. Unlike the majority of Indian reformers, who have shown marked regard for Jesus Christ, Dayānand treated him with bitter ridicule and contempt, as one hardly deserving the title of teacher. His knowlege of the Bible was limited, and his polemic at many points was naive; but his book *Satyārtha Prakāsa (The Light of Truth)* has left a deep mark on subsequent Hindu-Christian controversy, having served as an armoury of arguments for those who have desired to confute Christianity rather than to understand it. Membership of the Samāj has never been large; but it still exists and carries on vigorous anti-Christian propaganda in a number of countries. One of its activities has been to open a way back to the Hindu fold for members of the scheduled classes who have been so imprudent as to forsake the faith of their fathers and to embrace the Christian way.[5]

Dayānand has his heirs in the political as well as in the religious sphere. India has chosen to be a *secular* democratic republic. Certain political groups, notably the Hindu Mahāsabha and the Rāshtriya Sevak Sangh, regard this as basic error and betrayal. In sharp contrast to the international understanding of Hinduism to which we shall come later, such groups maintain that Hindustan must be the land of the Hindus and its whole life an expression of a certain spiritual ideal. This point of view can be carried to extremes, as will be evident from the following utterance of Shri Golwalkar, one of the leaders of the Rāshtriya Sevak Sangh:

> The non-Hindu peoples in Hindustan must either adopt Hindu culture and language, must learn to respect and hold in reverence the Hindu religion, must entertain no ideas but those of glorification of the Hindu race and culture, or may stay in the country wholly subordinate to the Hindu nation, claiming nothing, deserving no privileges, far less preferential treatment – not even citizenship rights. There is, at least there should be, no other course for them to

---

[4] A. L. Basham in *Concise Encyclopaedia of Living Faiths*, p. 256.
[5] News of the reconversion of nine Christians to Hinduism was published in the Indian press while this chapter was in process of revision.

adopt. We in Hindustan cannot give up religion in our national life as it would mean that we have turned faithless to our Race Spirit, to the ideal and mission for which we have lived for ages.[6]

The second reaction was a warm welcome to the new ideas. In the case of some high-caste Hindus, this led to the acceptance of the Christian faith. Of the converts in the early days the majority came from the notable educational institution founded in Calcutta by the Scot, Alexander Duff; these became the ancestors of many of the most outstanding Christian families in India. The majority of those affected would not go so far; they were prepared to accord great regard to Jesus Christ and to his teaching, and tried to work out a syncretistic religion, in which Christian truth would be used as a leaven to vivify the somewhat moribund traditions of the ancient Indian faith.

Most notable of all these early Indian reformers was Rāmmohun Roy (1770–1834), who is generally regarded as being, more than any other single man, the creator of modern Hinduism, indeed of modern India. In 1820 he published a remarkable book with the title *The Precepts of Jesus the Guide to Peace and Happiness, extracted from the books of the New Testament ascribed to the four evangelists.* Rāmmohun Roy never intended to become a Christian; what he did was to restore to the thoughtful Hindu his confidence and his self-respect, in the belief that, profiting by the new knowledge brought by Christ, he could stand firm in his own traditions and meet the west without shame and without fear.

Rāmmohun Roy and his followers brought into being the syncretistic body known as the Brahmo Samāj. Of special interest was the connection of the Tagore family with this body through three generations. Dwarkanāth Tagore was an immensely wealthy merchant, who embraced western ideas so eagerly that he believed that India could be benefited by an increase of British immigration into Bengal. His son Debendranāth renounced such commercial interests, and became head of the Brahmo Samāj. His autobiography, a fascinating work, more than any other book of the period carries the reader into

---

[6] Quoted in J. R. Chandran and M. M. Thomas: *Political Outlook in India* (Bangalore, 1956), pp. 112, 113.

the life of a high-minded, thoughtful Indian family. But Debendranāth was deeply grieved when some members of the family deserted the Hindu for the Christian way. His son Rabindranāth (1861–1941) was the distinguished poet, whose writings won great acclaim in England, and made English readers aware of the strength and richness of the Indian renaissance.[7]

A generation later than Rāmmohun Roy, another Bengali, Keshub Chander Sen, less intellectual and more emotional than his predecessor, could speak of Jesus Christ in terms of passionate devotion, so much so that many of his hearers found it hard to understand why he never became a Christian. The Unitarian scholar Dr James Martineau has recorded this impression of his meeting with Sen in London:

> The impression was so powerful upon most of us, at least in London, when we heard him preach, that I venture to say that few of us had ever been under a Christian preacher and been moved to so deep a sense of Christian conviction and of Christian humility ... It appears to me that the visit of Keshub Chander Sen was a demonstration that our churches are wrong in their definition of Christianity, and that the very essence of it lies, not in the doctrinal and historical machinery, but in the spirituality of which this machinery is the mere vehicle to our souls. If this be so, I think it a lesson of the deepest moment to our Christian churches.[8]

The fact was, however, that Sen was worshipping a Christ of his own imagination, an Asian Christ, and not the historical figure depicted in the Gospels. Towards the end of his life, imprudent actions on his part brought discredit to him, and division to the movement of which he was the head.

The membership of these movements has always been limited. The Brahmo Samāj still exists, though it attracts few outside the intellectual élite. But India owes a great debt to these pioneers;

---

[7] See the essay by Amiya Chakravarty: 'Rabindranāth Tagore and the Renaissance of India's Spiritual Religion' in *Modern Trends in World Religion*, ed. J. M. Kitagawa (1951), pp. 157–192.

[8] Quoted by P. D. Devanandan: 'Hindu Missions to the West', in *International Review of Missions*, October 1959, p. 402, from P. K. Sen: *Biography of a New Faith*, vol. II, p. 49. Dr Martineau must have heard Keshub Chander Sen preach during 1870.

without their achievements India would not be what it is today, and the third of the Indian reactions to the challenge of the west could hardly have come about. This third reaction is more difficult to define in a single phrase. Hinduism has always been polymorphous. It has manifested through the centuries an astonishing capacity for taking into itself the most disparate elements and yet itself remaining essentially unchanged. Those who stand in this third tradition would perhaps maintain that Hinduism has within itself all needed truth, indeed the highest truth yet manifested to mankind, but that it needs to purify itself from the confusions and accumulations of the centuries by going back to its own earlier sources, and that it can be stimulated and even helped in this task by insights that have come to it through contact with other religions. To put the matter briefly, Swāmi Vivekānanda lighted the spiritual flame of this ideal; Mahātma Gāndhi interpreted it in terms of practical activity; and Dr S. Rādhākrishnan restated it in terms of intellectual validity.

Behind Swāmi Vivekānanda (Narendranāth Datta, 1863–1902) lies the greater figure of Rāmakrishna Paramahamsa (1834–86), the devotee whom modern Hindus constantly cite as the most notable example of a human being who attained in this life to perfect union with the divine. About 1871 Rāmakrishna began to study other religions, in a spirit which many Hindus would point to as an ideal example of the tolerance with which all believers should approach a religious system other than their own. For a certain period he would read only the scriptures of the faith that he was studying, as far as was possible carrying out all the appointed prayers and rituals.[9] At the end of several years of such study and experiment he reached the conclusion that all religions in their inmost content are one – they all lead back to the truth apprehended by the mystic of the unity of all things in the supreme and universal Spirit.

To carry this message of the unity of all faiths to the west was the self-chosen task of Swāmi Vivekānanda. His opportunity came with the Parliament of Religions held at Chicago in 1893, one of the most striking events in the religious history of the late

---

[9] This is the generally accepted story. Some doubt has been cast upon the details by recent and more critical study.

nineteenth century. The young Bengali, eloquent in English as are so many of his race, carried all before him, and made himself the most conspicuous figure of the entire assembly. Widely heard were comments to the effect that, if India could produce religious thinkers and speakers of this calibre, it was a monstrosity to think of sending missionaries to India.

In the earlier stages of his journey Vivekānanda had been overwhelmed by the wealth and power of the west. What reply could the east make to the crushing weight of this power? Vivekānanda's solution of the problem was brilliant and lasting in its effects; he invented the myth of the spiritual east and the material west. The myth disregards both the glorious spiritual history of the west and the materialism that is to be found on certain levels in the east as much as in any other part of the world. But, sedulously propagated by eastern emissaries in all the countries of the west, the message has proved attractive in a period when the west has begun to be weary of its own material triumphs.

Vivekānanda was prepared to accord a high place to Jesus Christ as one of the great incarnations of God – Krishna, Buddha, Jesus, and Rāmakrishna. 'Christ, the special manifestation of the Absolute, is known and knowable.' But he would not grant to him such a splendour of uniqueness as the Christian gives him. He was prepared to admit that man needed to be delivered from the darkness of ignorance; but to speak of men as miserable sinners was in his judgment a crime:

> The greatest error is to call a man a weak and miserable sinner. Every time a person thinks in this mistaken manner, he rivets one more link in the chain of *avidya* that binds him, adds one more layer to the 'self-hypnotism that lies heavy over his mind'.[10]

Following the conviction of his master Rāmakrishna that all religions are in essence one, Vivekānanda proclaimed a doctrine of enlightenment and goodwill free from any sectarian bias. Thus he disclaimed any intention of making converts: 'Do I wish that the Christian would become Hindu? God forbid! Do I wish that the Hindu or Buddhist would become Christian? God

---

10 See M. M. Thomas: *The Acknowledged Christ*, p. 123.

forbid ... Each religion must assimilate the spirit of the others and yet preserve its individuality and grow according to its own laws of growth.' There is no reason to doubt the sincerity of these words uttered at the final session of the Parliament of Religions. It did not seem to Vivekānanda paradoxical that Christians should accept the principles of Hindu Vedānta and at the same time continue to be Christians.

★

When Vivekānanda made his famous appearance at Chicago, Mohandas Karamchand Gāndhi (1869-1948) was a young man of twenty-four, then recently settled in South Africa and engaged in the practice of law in the courts of that country.

During his years in South Africa Gāndhi was in close touch with Christian friends, and under their influence made a careful study of the Gospel. There can be little doubt that at one time he was near to accepting the Christian faith. But the decision was never made; as the years passed Gāndhi moved farther away from the Christian position, though he always retained his deep regard for Jesus Christ. Many of his views, though akin to Christian ideas, seem to have been derived from sources other than the New Testament. His view of social equality is akin to that put forward by John Stuart Mill. His dislike of industrial development, and his preference for the old simple ways of India, show the influence of Ruskin and William Morris. His characteristic doctrine of non-violence seems to be related to the views put forward by Tolstoy in his later years.

Gāndhi was first and foremost and at all times an active and extremely astute politician. His one overmastering concern was that within his lifetime India should become a completely independent nation. 'His plea for religious tolerance was motivated primarily by the desire to achieve the goal of Indian independence... The dominant motive was nation-building.'[11]

This is not to call in question the sincerity of Gāndhi's religious convictions; but in him it is hard to draw a clear distinction between the political and the religious.

Religious conviction has in the past led to bitter strife and division, as in the religious wars in Europe. Therefore, as Gāndhi

---

[11] P. D. Devanandan: *The Gospel and Renascent Hinduism* (1959), pp. 16-17.

taught his followers, India must learn that all religions are essentially the same; none must make such an exclusive claim as would justify it in setting up barriers in the way of national unity. So, in the regular meetings for prayer in his *āshram*, he would read selections from the scriptures of many faiths, and the adherents of all religions were encouraged to feel entirely at home in this atmosphere of tolerance and mutual respect.

The degradation of the depressed classes presented another grave problem.[12] National unity cannot be achieved when a sixth of the population is excluded from social privilege and economic equality. Gāndhi was also well aware of the success of Christian propaganda among these impoverished communities, and of the grave danger that the whole fifty millions of them, or at least a very large section, might be seduced into separation and the formation of yet another large non-Hindu community. So at all costs the oppressed must be taught to regard themselves as Hindus, and to believe that their future and their destiny were to be found in adherence to Hindu society. They must be called the Harijans, the people of God, and welcomed with open arms into the fellowship of the movement for national independence.

When the British government, in its desire to secure political representation for these suppressed communities, put forth a plan to give them status as a separate community, Gāndhi declared that he would fast to death, unless this proposal was withdrawn. Hindus the depressed people are, Hindus they must remain.

This action on his part did not meet with universal approval. The outstanding leader of those communities, Dr B. L. Ambedkar, did not believe that there was any prospect of liberation for them within the Hindu fold. Looking with disapproval on the many divisions among Christians, he felt unable to encourage a movement towards Christian conversion. He believed that the ancient Indian religion of Buddhism, which had entirely died out in India, would offer them the best chance of a religious sanction for their desire for social equality with

---

[12] For Gāndhi's views on 'untouchability' see his striking declaration in 1915: 'If it was proved to me that this is an essential part of Hinduism I for one would declare myself an open rebel against Hinduism itself.' *Collected Works*, XIII (1964), p. 69.

others. As many as three million from among these people professed adherence to the Buddhist faith.[13]

Gāndhi's noble plea for respect for these communities has not led to the emancipation for which he hoped. The government of independent India has abolished untouchability. But every day the Indian papers carry accounts of violent assaults carried out by those of higher social status on those who try to assert claims to equality which those who cling to the religious sanctions for the inequality of castes are not prepared to recognise. Discrimination against those regarded as ritually impure is still one of the unsolved problems of independent India.[14]

Gāndhi never wavered in his resolve that India must become independent of the west. But how was this to be brought about? India was weak when face to face with the strength of one of the greatest of western powers. A virtue must be made of weakness, and a demonstration given of the superior efficacy of 'soul-force' as against the mere brute force available to the militarised power of the west. The idea of soul-force lies deep in the Indian consciousness; this was the kind of force that the sages and wise men of old acquired by the tremendous penances that they imposed upon themselves. But the idea that all alike are required to practise complete non-violence is not to be derived from the Hindu Scriptures, and least of all from the *Bhagavadgītā*, that ancient classic in which Gāndhi declared himself to find deeper truth than in the Sermon on the Mount.

The idea of non-violence, *ahimsā*, is complex, and in part of non-Indian origin. But it is this that has made a deeper impression on India and on the world than any other part of Gāndhian doctrine. Where Europeans and Christians have blundered over centuries, so the Gāndhian doctrine runs, Asia has at last come to the rescue with a new principle of political action through which all the

---

[13] The original momentum has not been maintained. The high point seems to have been reached in 1951. The census of 1971 shows that the proportion of Buddhists to the total population had declined, and is far less than that of Christians.

[14] On 22 December 1981 *The Times* of London carried an article on the question 'Why are the Harijans persecuted?' An open letter, signed by a number of Christian leaders, and drawing attention to the grave disabilities under which the now ninety million of Harijans suffer, was published in the periodical *Missiology* for July 1982, p. 346.

problems of men can be worked out to a peaceful solution.
Gāndhi never pretended to be anything but a Hindu. His kindly
remarks about other religions, and the evident parallels between
some of his teachings and those of the Gospel, sometimes led his
friends and admirers to think otherwise. But they were
mistaken. He was and remained a Hindu, and was in fact 'the real
architect of the new Hinduism'.[15] Everything in existing
Hinduism of which he disapproved, such as caste distinction, the
idea of ritual pollution, animal sacrifice and so forth, he regarded
as corruptions which had somehow slipped into the pure waters
of Hinduism; all these he was prepared ruthlessly to expel.
Conservatives could not but be aware of what would happen to
Hinduism if this teaching were widely accepted. The assassination of the Mahātma in January 1948 by a young fanatic of the
Hindu right wing came as a terrible shock to the world. Yet those
who had closely watched the course of events were hardly
surprised; the challenge presented by Gāndhi to the whole of
Hinduism as traditionally understood was so intense that the
surprising thing, in that land of continual violence, was not that
he died but that he lived so long.

The history of India since independence has not been as the
Mahātma would have wished it to be. Non-violence has remained
officially enshrined in the national creed, but the rule has not
been consistently observed. Police fired on Indian crowds more
often in the days of Nehru rule than in the period of British
domination. India spends on defence, primarily against Pakistan,
a higher proportion of the national income than was so expended
in British days. Some years after independence, India invaded the
Portuguese territory of Goa and brought to an end more than
four centuries of European rule. When Mr Nehru was asked how
he justified the invasion in the light of Gāndhi's teaching, he
replied simply that non-violence is not a creed by which it is
possible to live in the modern world.

But it would be a grave mistake to suppose that nothing has
survived from the period when Gāndhi's influence was at its

---

[15] A. L. Basham in the *Concise Encyclopaedia of Living Faiths*, p. 259.

height. The leader can be killed but his ideas live on. In 1907 Gāndhi read Ruskin's *Unto this Last*, and from it worked out the idea of *Sarvodaya*, universal service or benevolence, thus giving a name and substance to something that had been implicit in the Hindu mind. The idea was taken up and developed by one of the Mahātma's most faithful disciples, Vinoba Bhave, India's walking saint (b. 1894).[16] Bhave travelled on foot far and wide through India, developing the *Bhūdan* (land-giving) movement; landlords were encouraged, not without success, to give up some of their lands to their landless peasants, and thus to develop the idea of equality and fellowship in the village. He regarded it as his task 'to establish a classless, casteless society, in which every individual and group would get opportunity and means for an all-round development'. Such is part of the modern face of Hinduism.[17]

The way in which men act has changed. The change would seem to demand a restatement of the religious beliefs on which Hindu society rests. It is at this point that we encounter the third and in some ways the most important of the three great creators of modern Hinduism, Dr Sarvepalli Rādhākrishnan.

Rādhākrishnan studied at the Madras Christian College, and thus at a very early age was brought into contact with the Christian faith as represented in men of stainless integrity and notable intellectual power. He was disturbed to realise that the west was strong and that India was weak; he discerned that one of the major causes of India's weakness was Hinduism as it had come to be believed and practised. What should he do? Some of his predecessors in the nineteenth century had decided that the regeneration of India could come about only through Christian faith and had therefore become Christians. Rādhākrishnan took a very different decision. Hinduism must be rethought and restated in such a way that it would become a source of strength

---

[16] This is the title of the book by Hallam Tennyson (New York, 1955), in which the actions and ideas of Bhave are sympathetically portrayed. This venerable disciple of the Mahātma was still alive at the time of writing, but has since passed to his reward.

[17] On the continuing influence of Gāndhi's ideas, see Judith M. Brown: *Men and Gods in a Changing World* (1980), pp. 140-41.

and not of weakness. To this task he set himself, and carried it forward with unfailing vigour for the next sixty years. He had studied the Bible and knew it well.[18] Not merely so; he had an extensive acquaintance with contemporary Christian writing in the field of dogmatic theology, and could turn this knowledge to his advantage in contrasting the confusions and contradictions of Christian thinking with the lucidity and certainty of eastern thinking based on the Vedānta.

In a whole series of books Rādhākrishnan set himself to commend eastern wisdom to the materially-minded peoples of the west. With a perfect command of English and an attractive style he was almost the ideal showman for the purpose. Yet, for all the attitude of generous tolerance which Rādhākrishnan assumes and attempts to maintain, the careful reader can hardly fail to receive the impression that much of what he writes is the expression of a dislike and disapproval of Christianity.[19] Christianity must not be allowed to score a single point; all the trumps must be in the hands of the eastern thinker. Thus, for instance: 'The emphasis on definite creeds and absolute dogmatism, with its consequences of intolerance, exclusiveness and confusion of piety with patriarchism are the striking features of western Christianity.'[20]

The implication is that the religion of the east is free from all these defects. The title of the book *Eastern Religions and Western Thought* is revealing. It appears that the west, by defining religion, has lost its true nature, since religion is experience and therefore indefinable; if the west wishes to rediscover religion, it is to the east that it must turn. This attitude represents what is perhaps the final stage in the reaction of the east against the west.

It was a cardinal principle with Rādhākrishnan, as with Swāmi Vivekānanda, that every form of religion is a manifestation of genuine human striving after God, and that none therefore may be condemned as false and useless. This is not to say that all religions are equally true or equally useful. And in fact

---

[18] He is not, however, always happy in his interpretation of it. For a curious and elementary misunderstanding of Romans 1: 14, see *The Brahma Sūtra* (1960), pp. 250-1.

[19] This is the view of Dr Hendrik Kraemer: *Religion and the Christian Faith* (London, 1956), pp. 99-136.

[20] S. Rādhākrishnan: *East and West in Religion* (1954), p. 58.

Rādhākrishnan himself seems prepared to classify religions in a descending scale of validity.

At the summit stands the perception that the Ultimate and Supreme as it is in itself is impersonal, for personality is a form of limitation such as may not be attributed to that which by definition is unlimited. The Supreme is unknown by man, and is in fact unknowable. This humility of approach is expressed, better than anywhere else, in the Upaniṣads and in Hindu wisdom generally. Not all men can attain to this austere comprehension of reality. For those whose feet grow weary in this steep ascent there is the possibility of belief in a personal God. There is good authority in the Hindu tradition itself for this attitude. The man who needs a personal object of worship may choose for himself his *ishtadevatā*, his own preferred deity. Each should choose that deity which best corresponds to the image or reflection of reality that he is able to grasp, and that is most suitable to him at this level of being. In this category of faiths Rādhākrishnan is able to find a place for Judaism and for Islam.

On a lower level still are the believers in incarnations. One who stands so low in the level of spiritual perception as to be unable to apprehend the deity in itself, even in a personal form, may need the help of some human figure to which he may cling as the only means by which on this level the divine can penetrate his spirit. This is not wrong, though from the standpoint of Hinduism it is at a very long remove from the true nature of reality. Christians are not wrong in worshipping Christ or in considering him as a revelation of God; they are wrong only in supposing that the whole of truth could be incorporate in a single manifestation, in their failure to see that there are other realms of Spirit of which Christianity knows nothing, and in the intolerance of the demand that others to whom the Christian medium may be quite unsuited should adapt themselves to it.

Even lower come the worshippers of idols and spirits. Highest of all is the man who has no need even of a mental image for the purposes of his worship. Lowest is he who cannot form a mental image and therefore needs the outward and visual image to help him form some concept of the divine. Yet even this level must not be despised; even here there are gleams of divine truth, and this too is to be taken as one of the roads that lead to God.

All this is set forth in terms of the most candid and engaging tolerance. Hinduism is a broad and all-embracing sea: 'As a result of this tolerant attitude, Hinduism itself has become a mosaic of almost all the types and stages of religious aspirations and endeavour.'[21] For a true Hindu there are few places dedicated to God in which he may not silently worship, few prayers in which he may not reverently join.'[22] Rādhākrishnan was himself as good as his word. He has left it on record that he had preached or lectured not only in Hindu temples but also in Sikh gurdwārās, Muslim mosques and Christian churches. During his Oxford days he was known at times to read in chapel services the lessons from the Christian scriptures.

This tolerance is possible only because of the underlying conviction of the relativity of all religion and of all human religious experience. The truth is essentially unknowable, and all our approaches to it are marked by imperfection and error. The recognition of our weakness should lead us to gentleness and tolerance with one another:

> The truth which is the kernel of every religion is one and the same; doctrines, however, differ considerably since they are the applications of the truth to the human situation . . . Rites, ceremonies, systems and dogmas lead beyond themselves to a religion of utter clarity and so have only relative truth. They are valid so long as they are assigned their proper place. They are not to be mistaken for absolute truth. They are used to communicate the shadow of what has been realized. Every word, every concept is a pointer which points beyond itself. The sign should not be mistaken for the thing signified. The signpost is not the destination.[23]

Such doctrine, sedulously propagated in charming English over many years, has undoubtedly exercised deep influence on many western minds. The sense of mystery which to so large an extent has been lost in pragmatic western religion, the call to the freedom of a quest in place of the inhibiting reliance on dogma, the broad genial tolerance which is prepared to find a place for

---

21 Eastern Religions and Western Thought (1939), p. 313.
22 Ibid.
23 East and West, the End of Their Separation (Harper, New York, 1954).

everything, the respect for the individual which encourages him
to find his own spiritual way – all these correspond to certain
moods and tendencies which are widespread in the west of the
twentieth century.

Vedānta for western man has been expounded by Christopher
Isherwood with the help of Indian colleagues. Some Christian
thinkers have tried, with perhaps limited success, to incorporate
the doctrine of reincarnation into schemes of Christian theology.
Transcendental meditation attracts a number of young people in
search of an inwardness which they have failed to find in various
western forms of Christianity.[24] Classes in yoga are to be found
in many cities in the west. The slightly bizarre forms and
practices of Hare Krishna, based on a selective understanding of
Hindu Scriptures, have drawn in young men and women
rebellious against the trammels of the society and the traditions
in which they have been brought up. So the east has flowed back
upon the west and challenged the west to change its attitudes to
the unchanging east.

★

In fact, the east is not as unchanging as is often thought.
Independence has brought new life to India. It seemed almost
inevitable that Indira Gāndhi should step into the succession of
her father Jawaharlal Nehru as prime minister of India; but that
India, which has accepted for many centuries the relegation of
women to the background of life, should have a woman prime
minister is a startling phenomenon. At least in the cities the old
iron chains of the caste system are being relaxed. It is not perhaps
as widely recognised as it should be that 'reform in social *practices*
required a restatement of corresponding underlying religious
beliefs'.[25] But subtly and almost unobserved the Hindu outlook
has become different from what it has traditionally been.

Hinduism has through the centuries been a religion of destiny
and submission. A man's future was written on his forehead at
his birth, and this is something that cannot be changed either by

---

[24] Judith M. Brown refers vividly to the 'eruption of TM into the world of
students and business men' (*Men and Gods in a Changing World*, p. 126).
[25] P. D. Devanandan: *The Gospel and Renascent Hinduism* (1959), p. 8.

God or man. This calm acceptance of destiny can be a source of inward strength; the Indian peasant shows amazing courage in the face of suffering, poverty, the death of loved ones and his own death. Those who speak of the misery of India do a great injustice to the Indian people. There is indeed poverty and hardship; but Indians, especially when they are young, get a great deal of enjoyment out of life, and show astonishing resilience in the face of hardship and bad times. Yet there is all the time an underlying melancholy in the belief that nothing can be changed; and this for many has brought about a passivity and lack of enterprise even when things could be changed.

This will not do for young India today. The modern Hindu believes that, within limits at least, man's destiny is in his own hands, and that he is called to strive and to achieve. He will find in Rādhākrishnan a prophet able to give vivid expression to his new aspirations:

> Man is not at the mercy of inexorable fate. If he *wills*, he can improve on his past record. There is no inevitability in history. To assume that we are helpless creatures caught in the current which is sweeping us into the final abyss is to embrace a philosophy of despair, of nihilism.[26]

This is fine bracing doctrine. But who is it that is speaking? Is this the sage of the Upaniṣads? Or is this the voice of Thomas Carlyle in *Sartor Resartus*?

The traditional doctrine is that misfortune and suffering are the penalty for sins committed in a previous life. But can this be unconditionally asserted today? One of the striking features of contemporary Hindu life is the deep reverence in which Jesus Christ is held by many Hindus. Jesus Christ ended his life on a cross. Was this the fruit of ancient deeds? I have never heard any Hindu suggest that this shameful death came to Jesus in expiation for great sins committed in a previous existence. That is an ancient tale; but a parallel can be found in much more recent history. The tragic death of Mahātma Gāndhi at the hands of an assassin might be fitted into the traditional framework of suffering in this life as retribution for sins committed in a previous existence. But the veneration for the Mahātma felt by

---

26 *Recovery of Faith* (1956), p. 4.

millions of his fellow countrymen makes it seem to me unlikely that they would see in his death anything other than suffering endured as the consequence of, or as expiation for, the sins of others. One of the great Hindu concepts that is due for reconsideration is that of *māyā*. This ancient Sanskrit word is generally translated 'illusion', and this is perhaps as near as a western language can get to representing one of the ideas associated with *māyā*. But careful definition is needed. It seems that there is here a difference between the Buddhist and the Hindu ideas. Buddhism seems to hold that the visible and the temporal lack reality. This is all sheer illusion; man cannot be saved until he is delivered from the illusion of existence. Passages can be quoted from the Hindu Scriptures in support of this view; but the more general understanding of *māyā* would seem to attribute to it a kind of minimal existence.

If this is true, then *māyā* would seem to be rather like matter, *hylē*, as understood in late Greek philosophy. *Hylē* is as near non-existence as anything existent can be; it is that potentiality on which form can for a brief space be impressed, and thus it can serve as a substratum for a kind of reality. But it belongs to the world of becoming and can never have a share in true being.

Here once again Rādhākrishnan is the courageous interpreter, who will open out to the modern Hindu new fields of possible achievement. His exposition is not perfectly clear; but he seems to come near to the Christian idea of contingent existence, except that his thought finds no place for a Creator God. To suppose that the visible universe has true reality is indeed to dwell in a world of illusion. But *māyā* is not mere illusion; it has existence, though a very limited and partial existence. The only finally valuable achievement is still that illumination of the spirit, which sets man above all temporal goals and releases him into union with the source of all being. But the possible values of *māyā* are not to be despised: 'though the world has not absolute reality, it is not to be compared with illusory experiences ... Embodiedness has positive value for the evolution of the soul and every form of life should be respected.'[27] The world of *māyā* is a field in which men can serve and in which real and valuable achievements are

---

[27] *The Brahma Sūtra* (1960), p. 140.

possible. Rādhākrishnan is far from being alone in his view. Some modern interpreters would go even farther in attributing reality, albeit conditional or contingent reality, to the world. For instance, Professor S. Sengupta, in a paper entitled 'The Misunderstanding of Hinduism',[28] affirms that of the six Hindu systems of philosophy only one, the Vedānta, and not even the Vedānta in all its forms, puts forward the doctrine of *Māyāvāda*, of the unreality of the world: 'Sri Aurobindo, the most noted of recent Hindu philosophers, in his *The Life Divine*, bases his interpretation of Hinduism on the extensive and effective refutation of *Māyāvāda* ... the world is characterised as an expression or manifestation of the supreme reality, and it is evident that an expression or a manifestation of the real cannot be unreal.'

If the strict Vedānta doctrine that the visible world is illusory, and that no great achievement within it is possible, is maintained, history can have little meaning, and the writing of history can hardly be regarded as a serious occupation. It is remarkable that Sanskrit literature, so rich in every other field of literary art, has no great tradition of history writing.[29] This extensive neglect of history will not do for the modern Hindu.

The writing of Indian history by Hindus has become something like a major industry in India. Research is being carried on in a great many directions, and some of the results, as they appear in learned dissertations, are of great value, calling for the correction of many errors and the reconsideration of many earlier judgments. Conspicuous among the achievements is the great synthesis set out in the eleven stately volumes of *The History and Culture of the Indian Peoples*. Not all the chapters of this composite work are of equal value, though the general standard is high. Nor is this strictly impartial history. History is here written to a thesis – that there has been a steady continuous stream of Indian, and that means primarily of Hindu, history in which the basic principles of Indian, that is of Hindu, life have found expression.[30] Invaders have come and gone; but they have

---

[28] *Truth and Dialogue*, ed. J. Hick (1974), pp. 96–110.

[29] History writing on the major scale came in with the penetration of India by Muslim influences.

[30] It is to be noted, however, that there have been a number of Muslim contributors to this notable work. Rewriting of Indian history from a Muslim point of view is also a considerable industry, especially, naturally, in Pakistan.

touched and affected only the surface and never the heart of the story. There is truth in this, but it is not the whole truth. The story is complex, many of the complexities having been introduced by foreigners, and particularly by five centuries of contact with Europe and with a partially Christian civilisation. The contribution of the stranger to making India what it is today is not to be underestimated.

The modern Hindu, however, is concerned not just with writing history but with making history. He is convinced that he made history in the long process of the struggle for Indian independence. He believes that India, as the largest of the unaligned nations, has a great part to play on the stage of world history, and that, in the Gāndhian doctrine of non-violence, rightly applied, he has available a force that may lead the nations to a better and more peaceful manner of co-existence than they have ever known in the past. Friends of India are well aware of the elements of fantasy that are present in this assessment of present and future; they cannot but wish their Indian friends well in their search for historical reality and significance.

In the past, history has played little part in the thinking of Indian philosophers, but the problem of history and its meaning plays a considerable part in the philosophical work of some at least among the younger Indian thinkers. It will be interesting to see what happens, if they turn their minds to the relationship between history and religion.

Hinduism has presented itself on the whole as a religion of ideas, which would be true anywhere and everywhere, regardless of the particular situation in which they came to birth. It would not seem to matter very much whether there ever was such a person as Krishna, and, if there was, whether he bore any resemblance either to the heroic Krishna of the *Bhagavadgītā* or to the amorous Krishna of the *Purāṇas*. If these thinkers are now led to consider the nature of religion from the historical angle, they may find themselves on a path which their Christian brethren have trod before them.

For more than a century Christian thinkers, bewitched by the remark of Lessing that 'the contingent truths of history cannot serve as proof for the unchanging truths of the intellect', tended to present Christianity also as a religion of ideas, and to regard the history as of secondary importance. Of recent years there has been a reaction against this purely rational approach; it has come to be seen that the history is part of the revelation, which would have been wholly other, if it had come in any other way than through a particular history, and a particular historical person. The historical had seemed to be inferior; Christians are now coming to agree with what was said a good many years ago by a Christian philosopher –

> a religion which involves as part of its essence a sacred history is . . . at a higher level than one which, while setting forth certain universal principles, moral or metaphysical, is ready to symbolize them by anything that comes to hand, as it were, and is comparatively indifferent to the particular symbol chosen.[31]

So the title of an old book, *India's Problem – Krishna or Christ?*,[32] might take on a new significance in the modern world.

★

So far we have considered reconstructions to which the Hindu may feel himself led by analysis of what he himself really believes today, and on the basis of which he acts in the world. We may now go on to a certain number of questions which the Christian may respectfully present to him as relevant to the reconstruction in which he is engaged.

First, we may raise the question of personality, both in relation to God and in relation to man.

Indian thinkers have tended to regard personality as a limitation, such as may not be imposed on God who is by definition the unlimited.[33] But Christians understand personality as a principle not of limitation but of freedom. The living being has a freedom denied to the non-living. The rock will remain for ever where it is, unless some force from outside moves it. The animal is freer than the plant, since it has the capacity for movement. Man, with his gifts of experiment and creativity, is freer than the animal. In Jesus we see the full reality

---

[31] C.C.J. Webb: *Studies in the History of Natural Theology* (1915), pp. 29-30.
[32] By J.P. Jones (New York, 1903).
[33] But not Professor Sengupta, who asserts confidently that 'Hindu religious believers . . . reject the Advaita ontology to the extent that they affirm the infinite as divine person, having moral attributes such as goodness, justice, love, etc.' in *Truth and Dialogue*, p. 105.

of human freedom, unhindered by the inner dividedness which is the lot of all other human beings. The risen Jesus is free from the limitations of time and space to which he was subject in the days of his incarnation. He leads us upwards to God who is perfect freedom, except in so far as he has limited himself by accepting relationship to the beings whom he himself has created and to whom he has given a measure of freedom.

Human personality is, so far, the highest thing we know in this three-dimensional universe. Teilhard de Chardin in his remarkable book *The Phenomenon of Man* emphasises the central significance of *reflection* – 'no longer merely to know, but to know oneself; no longer merely to know but to know that one knows . . . Because we are reflective, we are not only different but quite other. It is not a matter of change of degree, but a change of nature resulting from a change of state.'[34]

Is all this to be lost, as we move higher in the evolutionary scale? Man, the reflective being, may have to move out into far wider fields of relatedness, and, as religion teaches him, to an indefinite enlargement of his reflective self by its apprehension of the whole. But would it not seem paradoxical, and contrary to everything that we know of ourselves and of the universe that we inhabit, to suppose that the most crucial thing that has yet appeared on this planet, individual awareness, is destined simply to vanish and to leave no trace in a total re-absorption into the impersonal? We may rightly look forward to a transcendence of personality, to a state that is as different from our present consciousness as that consciousness is from the consciousness of the animals. But such a state should be regarded as the fulfilment of personality rather than its disappearance.

We may believe that the Hindu, by returning to his own origins, may find himself nearer to Christians than at times he thinks.

Professor R. C. Zaehner of Oxford has analysed with great subtlety three kinds of mysticism, all of which are present in Hinduism in varying degree.[35] Any mystical experience is an

---

[34] P. Teilhard de Chardin: *The Phenomenon of Man* (Eng. trans. 1959), pp. 165–6.
[35] *At Sundry Times* (1958), pp. 30–133. In his Gifford lectures, *Concordant Discord* (1970), pp. 200–4, Zaehner has expanded three to four – cosmic consciousness, transcendence of time, the experience of absolute oneness, the infinite love of God.

experience of total absorption, in which for the time being individual existence is forgotten and the sense of identification is complete. Since such experiences, as described by those who know them from within, all seem to manifest the same 'feeling-tone', there is a tendency to assume that they are all in essence the same experience. But this is a simplification. We have to ask what it is with which the subject feels himself to be so wholly identified as to be unaware for a time of himself as a separate existence. Professor Zaehner identifies three distinct types or fields of mystical rapport.

The first may be called, for convenience, cosmic consciousness. This is most familiar to English readers in the nature mysticism of Wordsworth. Wordsworth finds peace in the sense of his identification with all other things. He loved to think of himself as 'clothed with the heavens and crowned with the stars';[36] and in two of the most familiar lines in all his writing he refers to himself as

> Rapt into still communion that transcends
> The imperfect offices of prayer and praise
> ('Excursion', book I, 214-15)

This experience is a genuine experience of one particular kind of reality. We are of the dust of the universe, and its smallest particle is of our kin. It is good that at times we should feel this kinship, and that the whole movement of all that is should for the time being deliver us from our restless gyrations in the pettiness of our own orbits.

Secondly, there is that experience in which a man finds himself at one with all the depths of his own being. A large number of yoga techniques seem to be directed towards the liberation of the self into such an experience. The whole of modern psycho-analytic method rests on the belief that it is possible to bring into consciousness those deeper levels of human life, which may represent earlier and forgotten stages of the individual's own pilgrimage, or, like some palaeozoic strata cast up from the depths of the sea, may represent the vestiges of some memory within him of the whole age-long pilgrimage of the human race.

---

[36] Basil Willey: *The Eighteenth Century Background* (1950), p. 287.

We are composed of many layers of being, and there is no limit to the depths of human personality. It is good that we should be aware of the whole of ourselves and reconciled to it.

Thirdly, there are traces, in Hinduism as in other religions, of the possibility of ecstatic union, through love and devotion, to a god personally conceived. The earlier part of the *Bhagavadgītā* consists of rather jejune argumentation, starting from the duty of Arjuna to engage in the battle with the *Pāṇḍavas* which is about to begin, and wandering through many questions of philosophy and psychology and ethics. Many European readers must have wondered why so flat a book has received such absorbed reverence from so many generations of Hindu readers, and why Gāndhi declared that he found deeper revelations in it than in the pages of the New Testament. Then suddenly the tempo changes. Krishna, serving as the charioteer of Arjuna, is transformed before his eyes, and in a long passage of great rhetorical splendour reveals himself as the supreme reality, as the ultimate unity of all that is. 'The real message of the *Gītā* does not lie in its philosophy, but in its teaching that God is not a passionless Absolute but the love of man's soul, indeed love itself.'[37] Confronted with this manifestation of terror Arjuna cries out 'Bowing down and prostrating my body before thee, I implore thy grace, adorable lord. Bear with me, I pray thee, as a father with his son, friend with friend, lover with beloved.'[38]

This notable passage confronts both Hindu and Christian with the problem of the nature of the oneness of man with God, the supreme experience after which the adherents of both religions strive. In classical Hinduism it is, on the whole, the austere *advaita* of Śaṅkara which has prevailed. *Tat tvam asi*, 'that art thou'. The *ātman*, the hidden inner reality, in men is identical with the *brahman*, the hidden inner reality of the universe. So the unity of man with God may be considered as total. It may be compared with that which happens to a drop of rain-water when it falls into a pool; it is totally absorbed and has no further separate existence of its own. But there is another tradition in Hinduism, especially in the *bhakti* religion of South India. Here, as in the theophany of the *Gītā*, is a profound sense of the nearness of the divine, a

---

[37] R.C.Zaehner: *Concordant Discord* p. 30.
[38] *Bhagavadgītā*, 11: 44.

delighted awareness of the favour of the god resting on his
devotee, a sense of oneness in which separate existence is no
longer felt. But it is made clear that this is oneness of will and of
desire, and not an ontological oneness in which the self of the
worshipper simply ceases to exist. There must be a twoness in
the oneness, an everlasting I and Thou; otherwise the true
nature of deliverance will not be understood. 'If they become one,
both disappear; if they remain two there is not fruition; therefore
there is union and non-union.'[39]

It is in studying the literature of this movement that the
Christian feels himself to come nearer to the Hindu than
elsewhere.[40] It is not for him to attempt to teach the Hindu his
own religion. He may perhaps be permitted respectfully to ask
the Hindu to consider whether the kind of revelation set forth in
the theophany in the *Gītā* and expounded in other *bhakti* writings
may not more truly set his feet on the way towards an intimate
understanding of the divine than the more abstract philosophy
which has so long been set before him as the highest
manifestation of the truth.

In an entirely different realm also the Christian has his
question to ask.

One of the new things that has come into Hindu life has been
an enriched sense of the value of the individual man. Social
reform is in the air,[41] and the aim of all these reforms is the
removal of everything that hinders the individual from finding
the fullness of his being. It must, of course, be said that the sense
of community and of responsibility for the community is by no
means lacking today. Yet there is a real and significant change of
emphasis in the direction of individual concern for the individual.

Why is the individual significant? In the past he has been
regarded as little more than a link in the chain of being. On one
hand, he is connected with the mysteries of birth and succession.
He must marry and bring forth children, and so secure the
continuity of existence and of human frames in which souls can

---

[39] Unnāpathi: *Tiruvarudpayan* (AD 1307), couplet 75.
[40] A notable contribution to this debate is by an Indian Christian, M. Dhavamony
SJ: *Love of God According to Śaiva Siddhānta* (Oxford, 1971).
   See also S.C. Neill: *Bhakti, Hindu and Christian* (1974).
[41] On social reform in India, see Judith M. Brown: *Men and Gods*, pp. 44–8, 97–9.

take up their residence. On the other hand, he is merely the moment, the atom, in his own chain of endless existences, as he passes from birth to birth in the search of final release. So it has come about that traditionally the individual has been almost completely subordinated to the needs of the community and the race. Now this is no longer taken as a self-evident assumption; the individual is beginning in a new way to win recognition as having rights and deserving consideration and because he has an intrinsic value of his own. It is not merely that he is a voter who must be considered for secondary and interested reasons; he is coming to be seen as a fitting object for the serious concern of human beings other than himself.

But what gives him this value? On what intellectual or spiritual foundations does this new conviction rest? Here, once again, the challenge to the Hindu is to analyse and to become fully conscious of the principles that underlie his actions. To the Christian the answer to this question is obvious. The human individual is of value because he is the object of the unremitting care and interest of God. This the Hindu may not experience great difficulty in admitting, if it is squarely put to him. He may find it more difficult to proceed to the Christian corollary from this affirmation.

God is concerned with the individual as individual. What is of special interest about him is just those things that make him different from every other member of the human race. But, if that is true, will not his disappearance as individual, his re-absorption into the undifferentiated unity of the One, involve the whole universe in loss, in a diminution of the richness of its variety? Is the Christian belief in personal immortality necessarily to be considered as a form of selfishness, a desire for individual achievement and perfection? May it not be that God himself delights in individuality, that he has deliberately made a universe in which it can exist, and that he intends it to continue in other realms of being, as part of his delight in his chosen people and as part of the delight of his chosen people in him?

It will be interesting to observe the extent to which Hinduism in the coming years is able to make clear to itself certain concepts that seem to be implicit in its present day practice. And, with the absorptive capacity of the Hindu tradition, all these ideas could be absorbed as ideas without disrupting the majestic fabric of Hinduism. The next Christian challenge, however, comes as a much more serious shock. The Christian believes that such ideas must find expression in a community which is appropriate to them, and that this must be a community of a particular kind. It must be a community, ultimately, of freedom, of choice and decision, of total loyalty and commitment, and therefore in certain directions necessarily intolerant since it cannot hold that all convictions are equally and indifferently of value. This is where the Hindu meets a challenge that it is particularly difficult for him to face. The discussion between Hindus and Christians in India has been taking on sharper and less mellow tones in recent years. The stumbling-block for the Hindu is the church.

The Hindu is accustomed to reckoning with two poles of religious existence.

He is perfectly familiar with the idea of 'the flight of the alone to the alone'. Ultimately every man has to find his way to God in splendid isolation. Ultimately he has to be responsible for his own salvation. There may be teachers and guides – there is in Hinduism a magnificent tradition of spiritual teaching reaching right back to the time of the Upaniṣads. There can be intellectual discussion and even some exchange of spiritual experience. But, if the moment of enlightenment comes, it comes to the individual in his aloneness. There are in Hinduism only rare examples of corporate worship or of the fellowship in the approach to God of which corporate worship is the expression.[42]

At the other end Hinduism is perfectly familiar with the *given* community, which is held together among other things by religious sanctions. Every Hindu is born a member of a caste and, unless formally excommunicated, remains a member of that caste until his death. He will on occasion worship its gods, and every stage of his life is marked by the appropriate religious ceremonies. Even if he wished, there is no means by which he could transfer himself to another caste. Here everything is social, in contrast to that other field in which everything is individual. Here everything is determined by the iron law of custom whereas in that other field everything is free.

---

[42] Even at great festivals, where crowds assemble round the shrine, there is no corporate worship as this is understood in Christianity and in Islam. But the movement in South India for the revival of Hinduism does seem to resemble, or perhaps even to have borrowed from, the Christian experience of corporate fellowship in teaching and worship.

The one thing that the Hindu finds it hard to understand is the idea of a community to which a man attaches himself of his own free will and in permanence, to which he totally commits himself, in which he involves himself in a completely new set of responsibilities for his fellow-members, and by life within which his own character and being undergo extensive modification. Here, then, is the paradox. The Hindu does not object to people being Christians – after all the Thomas Christians of Kerala have been there for at least fifteen hundred years. He does object very strongly indeed to anyone becoming a Christian. The idea of conversion is anathema to him. Even Mahātma Gāndhi, in spite of his friendship with many missionaries and his deep respect for Jesus Christ, harshly criticised what he called proselytism; why can missionaries not be content to render service, as they have so splendidly done, to express in action the ideals of Jesus without trying to separate people from that community in which alone they can feel at home? To Hindus his message was that, if God has caused you to be a Hindu, that is where you ought to stay; to attempt to go elsewhere is disobedience to the divine will. Some missionaries became so sensitive to this kind of criticism that they came to see their task as helping Hindus to be better Hindus and Muslims to be better Muslims. Some Hindus, who had come deeply under the influence of Christian teaching, felt it to be their vocation to live as Christians among their Hindu relations and so to make known to them the reality of Christ.

If Christianity meant simply the adoption of good and new ideas about God and man, this would be a simple and acceptable solution of the problem; for some this might be the best expression they could attain of their devotion to Jesus Christ. But this falls very far short of what a Christian understands by the word 'conversion'.

In the Christian sense of the term, conversion involves commitment to a particular Person. On this follows self-dedication to a particular manner of life, in which every detail must be organised in relation to the central loyalty. Such a life can be lived fully only within a community of which every member is ideally inspired by equal loyalty to the divine Head. Thus we come to apprehend that the doctrine of the church is not an appendage to the Gospel but an integral part of it. Such an idea is completely foreign to Hinduism:

The idea of the Church is essentially incongruous, and therefore repugnant, to the Hindu believer. The reason is obvious. Religious maturity in Hinduism is the result of individual achievement in self-discipline, towards which others like-minded can only help by the inspiration of example or through wise counsel. The idea of a transforming community is alien to the Hindu genius because of its basic belief about the nature of God as the eternal Brahman, and of the nature of man as essentially that of Brahman itself. There can, therefore, be no such community as the Church claims itself to be, where there is an inflow and outflow of personal influence which is transforming, because the real bond of fellowship therein is provided by the Holy Spirit which draws the members of the Church together in communion with God as revealed in Christ Jesus.[43]

The Christian comes to his Hindu friend with just one more question, and this is perhaps the most important of them all.

We have seen the central significance in Hindu thinking of the idea of *avidyā*, ignorance. Salvation is understood in terms of enlightenment; once the darkness of *avidyā* has been dissipated by true knowledge, the man is free. So at the very end of the *Gītā* Arjuna says almost enthusiastically to Krishna, 'Destroyed is the confusion; and through your grace I have regained a proper way of thinking; with doubts dispelled, I stand ready to do your bidding.'[44] All this is reminiscent of much Christian language; there is a great deal in the New Testament about light and darkness, about ignorance and knowledge – 'Ye shall know the truth, and the truth shall make you free.' But is the New Testament not right in bringing in a further dimension – the distortion of the will? When a man has been set free, may he simply forget the harm that by his wrong-doing he has done to others in the course of his pilgrimage, and disclaim responsibility for it?

It is perhaps not surprising that the word 'forgiveness' is rarely found in Hindu writings. Everything is neatly tied up in the doctrine of *karma*, retribution. Rādhākrishnan writes that 'the law of *karma* tells us that as in the physical world, in the mental and moral world also there is law. The world is an ordered

---

43 P.D.Devanandan: *The Gospel and Renascent Hinduism* (1959), p. 37.
44 *Bhagavadgītā* 18: 73 (trans. R.C. Zaehner).

cosmos... The universe is ethically sound.'[45] The ordinary Hindu regards forgiveness as impossible – the iron law of *karma* cannot be broken. If God were to forgive transgression, this would be immoral, since the inviolable eternal order of the world would be violated. This would be a conclusive argument, but for one factor of which account has not been taken. It may be possible to calculate the gravity of offences against law, and to determine the exact penalty earned. But what if the calculus by which sins against love can be measured? Are they not infinite in gravity? Such sins always involve the disturbance of a personal relationship. The relationship can be restored only through action taken by the one who has been wronged, and at great cost. The Hindu understands the Cross of Jesus as an instrument of spiritual power; the idea that the heart of God could be broken by the transgressions of man is one to which he finds it hard to bend his mind. 'Forgive us our trespasses' is a petition which does not come readily to his lips. He knows that man needs to be enlightened; he does not so readily admit that what man needs is to be saved.

So in the twentieth century the two great forces of Hinduism and the Christian Gospel confront each other. Nor is it possible to foresee what the issue of the dialogue is likely to be. On the whole Hindus do not feel serious anxiety about the future, as they tended to do in the nineteenth century. 'Christian and Muslim propaganda is now no longer a serious threat', writes A.L. Basham.[46] Similarly, one of the most notable of modern Hindu apologists, Professor D. S. Sarma, writes:

> It is obvious that we cannot absorb Islam or Christianity as we once more or less absorbed Buddhism. Our *Kabirs* and *Keshubs* must remain isolated phenomena and, at best, could give rise only to small sects. Therefore our policy should be not one of absorption but of fraternization. In this great country all of us have to live in peace, each community following its own *Dharma*.[47]

The Christian must be prepared to recognise that the task of

---

[45] *The Brahma Sūtra*, p. 194.

[46] *Concise Encyclopaedia of Living Faiths*, p. 260.

[47] D.S. Sarma: *Hinduism through the Ages* (Bombay, 1956), pp. 276-7.

Christian witness in India is likely in the future to be more difficult than it has been in the past. On the credit side must be placed the almost universal respect accorded by Hindus to the person of Jesus, and the development of friendly and open dialogue in a number of places. The Indian Constitution includes generous provision for the protection of religious liberty; as long as the Nehrus are in power this is likely to be carefully observed. On the other hand, there lingers resentment at what was felt to be Christian aggression in the past, and deep suspicion of any attempt to convert anyone to the Christian faith. This has found expression in various ways. Soon after independence, in the 'Nyogi report', a long list of charges against missionaries of using devious and unworthy methods to secure conversion was made public. The National Christian Council of India had little difficulty in showing that many of these charges were baseless, and that others referred to practices which may once have obtained but had long since been abandoned. More recently a bill was brought forward with the innocuous title of a bill 'for the protection of religious freedom'. What lay behind it was clearly the intention to make conversion to the Christian faith so difficult as to be nearly impossible. It is unlikely that such a measure will come into force during the lifetime of the present government; it is, however, a warning that the Christian witness must be scrupulously careful in the methods that are used, and also evidence of the strength of anti-Christian feeling in many quarters.

So what is the Christian witness to do? Primarily the Christian task is to live out the life of Jesus Christ before the eyes of men. They cannot see him. They will not see him, unless they can see him in the lives of his followers. If Christians are as different from others as they ought to be, questions may arise in the minds of those who watch them. This may give the Christian the opportunity to sharpen up these questions in the enquiring mind, to suggest that perhaps the answers to such questions as are given in the Hindu system are not entirely satisfactory, and lovingly to point those who are willing to listen to the one in whom all human questions can receive their all-sufficient answer, the Lord Jesus Christ.

CHAPTER V

The Doctrine of the Lotus

To many in the west Buddhism is the most attractive of the great religions of the east.

On a superficial level, there are considerable resemblances between Buddhism and Christianity. Buddhism has its origins in Hinduism, but more by way of reaction than of acceptance. It is, however, unlike Hinduism and like Christianity in having a known and identifiable founder: Gautama the Buddha is certainly an historical figure.

At once, however, differences assert themselves. The earliest accounts of the life of Jesus were written down while many people who had seen him and heard him speak were still alive. The Buddha, like Jesus of Nazareth and the prophet Muhammad, did not write anything down, as far as we know; for our knowledge of him we are dependent on the recollections of his disciples. But nothing was written until long after the first generation of his hearers had died out, and four hundred years were to pass before the Southern (Pāli) Buddhist canon (the *Tipitaka*, the 'three baskets') began to take on its present form. In the intervening years the historical data were overlaid by a mass of legendary and mythological material. Great critical acuity has to be used in the handling of the sources. One of the triumphs of western critical scholarship has been the enucleation of the historical from the legendary, and the emergence of a recognisably historical figure.[1]

On the general outlines of the story there would be much agreement. Siddharta, later known as Gautama the Buddha, was

---

[1]My favourite among the many accounts of the Buddha is still the work of H. Oldenberg: *Buddha*, which, though first published in 1881, continues to be reprinted in German in edition after edition; it is satisfactory that the work is again available in English translation, New York, Intl. Pub. Service 1971.

born about the year 562 BC (though this date is still doubted by some) in Kapilavastu in the borderland between India and Nepal. He was of quasi-royal stock. Till the age of twenty-nine Gautama had lived the ordinary life of a Kṣatriya prince, luxurious, sensual, though perhaps not to grave excess, and completely sheltered from the darker side of life. Then, in a few hours of crisis, this darker side forced itself upon him in a sense of the transitoriness of all things: all that is grows old and feeble and dies; what lies behind the mystery of suffering by which all life is conditioned and limited? Impelled by the imperious need to know, the young prince, leaving his sleeping wife and his little son, slipped out at dead of night to launch himself upon the pilgrimage of enquiry.

He was not alone in his quest. Many ascetics were wandering about India in search of truth. Gautama was exceptional among them only in the ardour of his pursuit, and in the austerities which for six years he sedulously practised. Then one day it came home to him that, weakened as he was by excess of fasting, he was in no promising condition for the reception of a revelation; he modified his rule, and regained a measure of physical strength and mental lucidity. Then, as he was sitting engaged in meditation under a *bo* tree at Bodh Gaya, the revelation came. He who had been a seeker now became the Buddha, the Awakened One, and, as such, in Buddhist estimation the centre of human history.[2]

He had long since realised that suffering was the dominant element in human life. But whence comes suffering? He now saw that the origin of suffering was in desire, in that eager grasping self that holds men chained to the wheel of insubstantial things. If desire could but be eliminated, release from suffering would be possible and then the human quest would be at an end. The very centre of the doctrine of the lotus is the elimination of desire. So this doctrine does not deal, like the Gospels, equally with joy and sorrow, with life in all its variegated complexity. It directs attention to one aspect of life to the almost total exclusion of all others.

Gautama is now the Awakened One. What is he to do next?

---

[2]'Enlightened One' seems a less accurate rendering of the word; all other men are asleep: he alone has been awakened to reality.

What follows is marked by an almost uncanny resemblance to the story of the temptations of Jesus in the Gospels, most unlikely as it is that there is any dependence of one upon the other. Māra, the tempter, the negative counterpart to the Buddha, draws near to the exhausted sage and tries to lure him away from his vocation. The Buddha has now overcome everything that holds him in thrall to the three-dimensional world. Why should he not quietly withdraw and enter into *nirvāṇa*, timeless and endless bliss? This temptation is overcome. The Buddha cannot withdraw 'until this holy manner of living which I teach is approved and makes progress, and is spread abroad among all people, and enters into currency, and is well proclaimed by men'. So the second temptation arises. This new teaching is hard to understand. Men who are sunk in earthly concerns will not find it easy to grasp these truths which only the wise can apprehend. If the Awakened One proclaims this teaching and is not understood, this will mean for him only weariness and trouble.

Buddhist thought in early days embraced the possibility of the existence of a hidden divine being, to whom the ancient Vedic name Brahman Sahampati is given.[3] The vivid traditional narrative at this point brings in this divine figure:

> Brahman Sahampati came to understand what was in the mind of the Holy One, and he said to himself: 'The world will go to destruction. The world will certainly be destroyed, if the heart of the Perfected One, the holy highest Buddha, is inclined to abide in rest, and not to proclaim the teaching'... So Brahman Sahampati... lifted his folded hands to the Exalted One, and spoke to the Exalted One: 'Lord, may the Exalted One proclaim the Teaching, may the Perfected One proclaim the Teaching. There are beings which are free from the dust of the earthly; but, if they do not hear the proclamation of the Teaching, they will go to destruction. There are those who may come to an understanding of the Teaching.' Three times the request is repeated. At last the Exalted One is prepared to accept the challenge, and gives expression to the gospel of deliverance: 'Let the door of eternity be made open to all. Let him who has ears hear the Word and believe. In order to avoid fruitless trouble, have I not as yet made known to the world the noble Word.' So Brahman Sahampati

---

[3] The interpretation of the term Sahampati is uncertain.

understands that his plea has been accepted; he bows down before the
Exalted One and disappears.

This passage makes clear the extent to which the Buddhist
doctrine in its early stages is dependent on the Hindu past.
Perhaps it is possible to see already in germ the tension which led
later to the development of the widely divergent schools – the
austere rationality of the Theravāda (southern school), and the
complex and luxuriant mythology of the Mahāyāna (the
northern school of Nepal and Tibet).

So, temptation ended, Gautama accepted the mission of an
evangelist and before long delivered to the five ascetics, who had
long awaited his coming, the famous Benares sermon in which
the main outlines of the teaching were clearly set forth. Then,
like Jesus, Gautama set out on the life of a wandering preacher.
Like Jesus, he soon gathered around him a group of disciples,
whom he organised into a religious order with increasingly
elaborate rules and precepts. Unlike Jesus, he did not welcome
women as readily as he welcomed men to be his disciples, so that
it is only towards the end of his life, and then grudgingly, that he
allowed the monastic order to be supplemented by an order of
nuns. This strenuous life was carried forward for more than
forty years, and was ended only by the death of the Founder.

The Buddhist classical writings are an almost shoreless sea. The
Pāli (Ceylonese) canon consists of three main groupings. The
central grouping has five sections. One of these sections is made
up of 152 sub-sections, and these together fill a thousand pages
of the excellent German translation. Clearly, like the ḥadīth of the
Muslims, these have grown up over the centuries and represent
in part the development of Buddhist scholastic thought as a
result of controversy between Buddhists and those of other
persuasions.

The Buddha plays the leading part in all the dialogues and
discourses. Buddhist scholars accept the whole as almost verbally
inspired Scripture, and have shown little interest in the western
concern to apply the methods of historical criticism to the long
process of the development of the material. These historical
methods ascribe greater value to some sections of the material

than to others. But out of the sifting process certain clear results emerge. We seem at some points to hear the authentic voice of the Master, and to find ourselves face to face with a teacher who has left his mark on the history of the human race for more than two thousand years.

The quest of the historical Buddha bears some resemblance to the quest of the historical Jesus, which has so strongly exercised Christian scholars for a century and a half. Perhaps an even closer parallel is to be found in the *Fioretti*, the little flowers of St Francis. This great classic of the Middle Ages is not so much history as the expression of a vivid historical and religious imagination. It is hardly likely that the Little Poor Man of Assisi spoke exactly as he is here represented as speaking, or that he actually converted the Wolf of Gubbio. But who has ever read this triumph of the literary art without feeling that he has been brought very near to Francis in his simplicity and power? The man who created the most powerful movement of the medieval period must have been very like the figure who shines out of the pages of the *Fioretti*. In the same way, even when we have questioned as legendary and mythological a great deal of the material in the Buddhist writings, we are left with a real historical figure, who has left his impress on the whole. In all the ocean of the Buddhist classics, there is one figure that stands out, the figure of the Founder himself.

The reference to the ocean of Buddhist literature is apt, in as much as it takes up a metaphor which the Master himself seems to have used. One of the most certainly authentic of his sayings is this: 'As in all the seven seas there is but one taste, the taste of salt, so in all the *dhamma* (teaching) there is but one taste, the taste of deliverance.'

It is possible to dig almost at random into the many volumes of the *Dialogues of the Buddha*, and to encounter the endlessly repeated emphasis on the exclusion of the irrelevant and the concentration on the essentials of Buddhist teaching. For instance, in a dialogue with a mendicant named Potthapādu, which turns on the doctrine of the soul, the Buddha says, 'That . . . is a matter on which I have expressed no opinion.' To a number of other questions he gives the same answer; when asked the reason for his refusal to give an answer, he replies: 'This question is not calculated to profit, it is not concerned with the *dhamma*, it does not resound even to the elements of right conduct, nor to detachment, nor to purification from lust, nor to quietude, nor to tranquillisation of heart, nor to real knowledge, nor to the insight, nor to *nirvāṇa*. Therefore it is that I have expressed no opinion on it... I have expounded... what pain is; I have expounded what is the origin of pain; I have expounded what is the cessation of pain; I have expounded what is the method by which one may reach the cessation of pain'... 'That is so,' admits Potthapādu, 'O Excellent One, that is so, O Happy One. And now let the Exalted One do what seemeth to him fit.'⁴

If one writing is to be chosen to make plain the essential teaching of the Buddha, in relation to his life as a teacher and his death, the choice is likely to fall on the *Mahāparinibbāna-sutta*,' the Exposition of the Mighty Entrance into *nirvāṇa*'. The Buddha is now eighty years old. He knows that death is not far away, and he himself chooses the place where he would like to die. Like Jesus, the Awakened One has a beloved disciple. Ānanda, feeling that the death of the Master was drawing near, withdrew into the little house and stood weeping. The Awakened One, noting this, sent for him and said: 'Not so, Ānanda, do not weep, do not lament... For a long time you have honoured the One who has been made perfect, in love and kindness, with joy, without deception, without ceasing, in thought and word and deed. You have done well, Ānanda; strive only, and soon you will be free from all that is corruptible.'

Later he said: 'It may be Ānanda, that you are thinking: The Word has lost its Master, we no longer have any Master. So you must not think, Ānanda. The *dhamma* [teaching] and the order which I have taught and proclaimed to you, that is your Master, when I have departed from you.' To the disciples he said: 'All things that have form are transitory; strive without ceasing.' Those were his last words.

The impression left upon the mind by the figure of the Buddha is one of graciousness. Here is a man filled with concern for his fellow-creatures; fired with a sense of mission, but always calm, always serene, always reasonable, even with the unreasonable, always gentle though not without sternness, and not without a sense of humour. In him compassion breathes and takes form.

---

⁴ T.W. Rhys Davids: *Dialogues of the Buddha* (Part I, edn. of 1906), pp. 241–65. Later in the study we shall come again to these four 'noble truths'.

Men suffer and live in darkness; it is the task of the Awakened One to remain among them and to show them the way to deliverance. To this task he will be faithful to the end.

★

Buddhism manifested great fertility in thought and writing for a thousand years after the death of the founder. The elaboration of the Pāli Canon was the work of centuries. The greatest classic of the second, Mahāyāna,[5] tradition of Buddhism, the *Saddharmapundarīka-sutta*, the lotus of the good law, seems to have been written in its earliest form about AD 200. Almost contemporary was the greatest philosopher of that tradition, Nāgārjuna, the apostle of the *sūnyatā*, the void, who went farther even than traditional Buddhism in the destruction of the ordinary categories of human thinking. In China and Japan, from about the seventh century on, the school of Zen Buddhism began to take hold, and developed over a number of centuries. But then, as a Buddhist scholar has placed on record, 'the creative impulse of Buddhist thought came to a halt... Buddhists have merely preserved, as best they could, the great heritage of the past'.[6] The twentieth century has seen the stirrings of new life. The birth of new nations and the end of colonialism have brought about a resurgence of Buddhism, as of so many other religions of the ancient world.

Thailand, uneasily poised between the British empire and the French zone of authority, never became a colony of either. But it could not but be deeply penetrated by influences from the west. When the royal family, which provided much of the staffing of the civil service, decided to send its scions to be educated at Eton and Harrow, the door was thrown wide open to the entry of western ways of doing things, very different from the traditions of the past. Now Buddhism, of a rather conservative kind, seems to be once again firmly in the saddle. It is laid down in the constitution that the monarch must be a Buddhist. The king himself has accepted the duty of serving his Buddhist apprentice-

---

[5] The Theravāda is in the main southern as the Mahāyāna is in the main northern Buddhism.
[6] E. Conze, quoted in *The Revolt in the Temple* (1953), p. 25.

ship, and of experiencing during part of his adolescence the life of a monk. Thailand claims to represent the Theravāda tradition in a purer form than any other country.

In Sri Lanka (Ceylon) the majority of the inhabitants are Buddhists. The Buddhist priests form an extremely strong corporation with extensive influence in political as well as in religious affairs. Their aim is uncompromising – to make Buddhism the national religion and the supreme influence in every aspect of the nation's life. An attempt was made to do away with Sunday, as a western importation, and to replace it by the Buddhist sacred days determined by the lunar calendar. This proved impracticable for a variety of reasons. The week, with its tradition of one day's rest in seven, has proved widely acceptable even in non-Christian countries.[7] So the Buddhist experiment had to be abandoned within a few years of its introduction.

Nevertheless Sri Lanka is the scene of intense intellectual activity among Buddhists, both in the study of the ancient Pāli texts and in the production of literature on a variety of levels, directed both at local Buddhists and to those of other religious professions, who may be open to the presentation of what to Buddhists is truth in religion. This is also the area of the most active and vigorous contact between Buddhist and Christian thinkers. If one name is to be mentioned, it should probably be that of Dr G.P. Malalasekera, scholar and diplomat, and the first president of the World Fellowship of Buddhists. In all his writings this notable scholar gives attention both to the re-formulation of the traditional Buddhist categories, and to the integration of Buddhist thought into the development of scientific discovery.

Burma moved out of the Commonwealth on attaining its independence in 1947, and since then has not known much of peace and quiet. The country is divided between the government, the bandits, and the Marxists, whose forces are still strong and enemies to peaceful order. For some years after independence Burmese Buddhists, the great majority of the population, set before themselves the task of making Buddhism the official religion of the country. U Nu, prime minister of Burma until 1962, put forward a ringing declaration in this sense:

---

[7] In Muslim countries Friday is the day of rest, and Saturday in Israel.

If any Marxist comes out with the statement that Karl Marx was a very wise man, it is not our concern to question it. But if he encroaches on our sphere and ridicules Lord Buddha whom we all adore and revere and if he has the effrontery to say that Marx was wiser than Lord Buddha, it is up to us to retaliate. It will be our duty to retort in no uncertain terms that the wisdom or knowledge that might be attributed to Karl Marx is less than one-tenth of a particle of dust that lies at the feet of our Great Lord Buddha.[8]

A bill enforcing Buddhism as the national religion was brought forward, but was dropped after the fall of U Nu from power. Since that time, Buddhists in Burma have been quieter. But a new feature of their activity has been the development of missionary work among the non-Buddhist tribes and peoples of the hills and the frontier, among whom Christian missions have recorded successes far greater than those which have attended their efforts among the Buddhist peoples.

Japan is of special interest in the revival of Buddhism, not merely because of Japan's political power in the new Asia, but also because of the variety and vigour of its manifestations. Japanese Buddhism has always tended to take on new and sometimes aggressive form, as in the sect founded by Nichiren (1222–83), in the thirteenth century,[9] which still has many adherents in Japan.

The defeat of Japan in 1945, and the renunciation by the emperor of his divine status, anxiety about the future and the need for widespread reconstruction of the national life, left deep traumas in the Japanese mind. One result of this was an extensive revival of religion, finding expression in the creation of a large number of sects to which the only parallel is the proliferation of independent churches in Africa. Classification of these sects is difficult. Almost every one of them claims some relationship to the Buddhist tradition, usually in one of its Japanese forms. But there are also elements from the older Shinto tradition, in which Japanese national sentiment and religious feeling were closely allied. And there are evident traces

---

[8]Quoted in A.C. Bouquet: *Christian Faith and Non-Christian Religions* (1959), p. 290.
[9] A useful note on this sect in T. Ling: *A History of Religions East and West* (1968), p. 316. Ling quotes the remark of E. Conze that 'all this is very un-Buddhistic'.

of movement resulting from the contacts and conflicts of Japan
with the west and with western influences in religion. By far the
largest of these new religions is the Soka Gokhai, 'the Creation-
Value-Study-Society', founded in 1930, which like others claims
to have origins in the Nichiren form of Buddhism, but is strongly
nationalistic in character and oriented towards a future to which
all strive. Its basic principles are faith, activity, organisation.
Organisation in recent times has included political organisation,
including the election of members to the Japanese parliament.[10]

★

With this inner resurgence has come a renewal of the Buddhist
sense of missionary obligation. Buddhist expansion had almost
ceased. Now the sense of world mission has been vigorously
activated. There have always been a few Buddhists in the west;
but now what had been no more than sporadic enterprises of
conversion are taking on the lineaments of an organised
campaign. The Buddhist World Council, which met in Rangoon
for two years and was brought to an end in 1957, turned its
attention to this matter. By a decision of the council Germany
was allocated to Sri Lanka as its special field of activity. It was
reported that in Buddhist 'Sunday schools' children were
bringing their small offerings towards the conversion of 'the
heathen' in Europe and America.

It is difficult to obtain accurate information concerning
Buddhist enterprises outside Asia. The first Buddhist Society in
England was formed in 1906. After this had faded out, it was
reconstituted in 1943 by a vigorous and highly intelligent English
Buddhist, Christmas Humphreys, whose Pelican book *Buddhism*,
a manual of Buddhism adapted to the needs of modern western
man, has sold well over a hundred thousand copies. Buddhist
societies flourish in various centres in Britain and in the United
States. One of the new developments is the sending of young
western neophytes for periods of study in monasteries in Asia; it
is said that these novices come back from their sojourns burning

---

[10] These Japanese religions really need a section, if not a chapter to themselves.
But even in a very brief section on contemporary Buddhism, some reference to
them must be made.

with zeal for the propagation of their new faith. Results so far
may be numerically small; but this Buddhist missionary presence
is something of which the Christian churches should be aware,
and which they should take seriously.[11]

★

What, then, is the Gospel with which the contemporary Buddhist
approaches the western world?

In the first place, it is to be noted that modern Buddhism, like
modern Islam, claims to be a religion for reasonable people, and
to have less difficulty than Christianity in accepting the
conclusions of science. Of the Buddhist in Germany it has been
written:

> It is regarded as the special privilege of Buddhism that, 'as the oldest
> world religion, some six hundred years older than Christianity, it
> stands, as no other religion does, in complete harmony with scientific
> thought, and fulfils all the demands with which reason and feeling can
> confront a man in his power of discernment and in his conscience'. It
> can thus never be in disagreement with the findings of science, the
> most recent achievements of our modern research-workers having
> been already known by the Buddha over two thousand five hundred
> years ago, even, for example, the parliamentarianism of modern
> democracy going back to the earliest days of Buddhism.[12]

So the Buddhist witness approaches western man with the
assurance that Buddhism can give him the answers to all the
questions that he may ask, and is a religion which he can accept
without doing violence to convictions reached through other
approaches to reality. The starting point is simple recognition of
the fact that the dominant element in all experience is suffering.
'Birth is suffering, old age is suffering, sickness is suffering,
death is suffering, to be united with that which one does not love

---

[11] *The World Christian Encyclopaedia* (1982) indicates roughly 120,000 Buddhists in
the United Kingdom, 180,000 in the United States, 5,000 in Germany, but does
not distinguish between immigrants from Buddhist countries and converts
among citizens of the western countries.

[12] W. Holsten in *IRM* 48 (October 1959), p. 412.

is suffering, to be separated from that which one loves is suffering, not to obtain that which one desires is suffering.' Everyone knows that he suffers. It is possible to paraphrase the famous saying of Descartes, 'I think, therefore I am' in the terms 'I suffer therefore I am'. This was the problem with which the Buddha wrestled under the *bo* tree in Bodh Gaya, where to him the moment of enlightenment came.

How can suffering be eliminated? The cause of suffering is desire, thirst for the impermanent, the unsatisfying. From this thirst man must be set entirely free. How is this to be accomplished? Here the Buddha, or the later Buddhist tradition, takes the most radical of all possible solutions; abolish the entity, and therewith we shall abolish the sufferer; abolish the ego which believes that it suffers, and there will no longer be anything that can suffer.

Man appears to be a unity; but this is a misunderstanding. All apparent existence belongs to the realm of the *anicca*, the impermanent and perpetually changing, in which there is no abiding reality. But such a realm is necessarily *anatta*, 'without soul'; there can be no place in it for a permanent centre of human consciousness.[13]

The apparent existence of man is simply due to the coalescence of five *khandhas;* the word is sometimes translated 'aggregates', but this hardly represents a concept which is not easily grasped by the western mind, and which indeed it is not easy to define. Under one aspect the *khandhas* can be described as 'individual moments of consciousness, following each other in a constant succession, which light up all moments with intense immeasurable velocity and then immediately disappear for ever ... short-lived, existing forces which burst out in functional dependence and disappear again'. To put it more scientifically, they seem to resemble centres of tension in a diffused field of magnetic energy. When the five come together, they bring about a brief appearance of existence, which is in fact illusory.

The five *khandhas* may be briefly described as follows. The first is *rūpa*, a familiar Sanskrit term meaning 'shape' or 'form' – all

---

[13] Clearly at this point the teaching of Gautama diverges radically from that of contemporary Hinduism, which regards as essential the existence of the *ātman*, the real self of man.

that presents itself to us as the visible properties of the apparently existent. The other four are grouped together as *nāma*, the immaterial properties of the apparently existent. Of this the first is *vedana*, feeling or sensation, arising out of contact with the apparently existing external world. The second is *sanna*, perception, or recognition of the similarities and differences between phenomena. The third is *sankhara*, a term which even the experts in Buddhism find it difficult to define. Perhaps the best term is synthesis, the capacity to bring together different aspects of experience into a whole; it may be thought to resemble the western idea of conceptual thinking. Finally there is *viññana*, sometimes translated 'consciousness', but perhaps better self-consciousness, inner reflection, man's ability to think about himself, to ask questions about himself. Modern writers have praised the acuteness of this Buddhist analysis of human awareness, and have recognised how closely it corresponds to a modern understanding of consciousness.

The *khandhas* come together, but then they separate, and the 'illusion of existence comes to an end'. Can they come together again? Here we encounter the acceptance in Buddhism of the ancient Hindu doctrine of *karma*, the deed and retribution. 'Not in the realm of the air,' says one Buddhist classic, 'not in the midst of the sea, not if you hide yourself in caves of the mountains, can you find or enter a place where you can escape from the fruits of your evil deeds.' Elsewhere it is said that the might of our deeds leads us through the five realms of transmigration – 'through the existence of men and gods, through the realm of the ghosts, the world of the animal, and through hell'. This ancient doctrine does not fit easily into the general Buddhist scheme. When poetry is abandoned for plain prose, it is explained that, when the *khandhas* give up their temporary cohesion, they wander in separateness through the vast abyss of nothingness, the endless universe. If in the infinite expanse of time they come together again, the same experience of apparent existence will be born. But is the continuity sufficient to justify the statement that *I* have been reborn? The many *Jātaka* stories, memories of previous births, suggest that it is possible to speak of such continuity. The meaning of the doctrine is that it is hard to escape from illusion, from the bonds of corporeality, that this can hardly come about within the span of one single period of time; enlightenment is likely to come only as a result of seeking through an innumerable series of existences. 'Strive without ceasing.'

The Buddha has abolished the self; has he also abolished God? A single passage can be quoted from one of the sermons attributed to him, which seems to imply that he did in some sense recognise the existence of God, or at least of something that has permanence amid the flux of that which never abides in one stay:

> There is, monks, an unborn, not become, not made, uncompounded, and were it not, monks, for this unborn, not become, not made, uncompounded, no escape could be shown here for what is born, has become, is made, is compounded. But because there is, monks, an unborn, not become, not made, uncompounded, therefore an escape can be shown for what is born, has become, is made, is compounded.[14]

Very little is said on such subjects in the range of the teaching which stands nearest to the Buddha himself. He found the teachings of the Hindus cluttered up with such ideas, and perhaps thought them better avoided, as leading only to doubtful disputations. He may have thought that to dwell on the idea of God would distract his disciples from that reliance on themselves for deliverance which it was his concern to inculcate. However that may be, the Theravāda form of classical Buddhism is a doctrine which finds no place for God, and in that, as it seems to me, is true to the spirit of the Founder. Buddhists do recognise the existence of beings known as *devas*, which in some respects are above the human level. Many English-speaking Buddhists translate the word *devas* as gods. But *devas* are all still in *saṁsāra*, the bondage of existence. 'In no sense is a *deva* a creator, omnipotent or omniscient, but simply a denizen of a deva-world.'[15] The deva-world could have no place for 'God', as that word is understood in the Bible and in Christian theology. In Anselmian language, that than which nothing greater can be conceived is God. What is that in Buddhism than which nothing

---

[14] *Udāna-Sutta* VIII. 3. This is a good example of the endless repetition in which the Buddhist discourses abound. I am inclined to think that the reference is really to the *dhamma*, the teaching, rather than to a supposed divine being.

[15] I.B. Horner in *Concise Encyclopaedia of Living Faiths*, p. 295. The *devas* are rather like the other gods of which the Old Testament speaks – their existence is not denied, but they cannot enter into comparison with the one true God whom Israel is called to worship.

greater can be conceived? The answer is *nirvāṇa*, that state of perfection after which the Buddhist monk most earnestly aspires. God or *nirvāṇa*? Here is the central problem of Buddhist-Christian dialogue.

If there is a certain ambiguity in what the Buddhist scriptures have to say about God, the same is true of what they have to say about *nibbāna*,[16] final deliverance. In itself the word means simply 'extinction'. Who or what is it that is extinguished? And, when extinction has taken place, what if anything remains? What can be left other than nothingness? Many orthodox Buddhists draw this conclusion. Extinction, *nirvāṇa*, is like the flame of a candle when it has been blown out. Is there any sense in which it can be said to exist? Any kind of existence is associated with suffering. So, if it be claimed that *nirvāṇa* is some kind of existence, it must also be some kind of suffering, and so deliverance proves to be no deliverance at all; the chains of bondage have once again been superimposed.

Even the Christian, in time of great distress, may be inclined to think that there could be no destiny so blessed as that of everlasting and dreamless sleep – sleep that will never end and in which there is no possibility of waking. Yet this is not the Christian hope. In the same way, many Buddhists are unwilling to lie down under the thought that ultimate destiny is no more than ultimate nothingness. *Nirvāṇa* is so utterly different from three-dimensional existence in time and space that anything that is said of it in human words must be false and mistaken. That is why the wise who speak of it do so almost always in negative terms; but the negations must not hide from us the positive realities which are hidden under them. What has been blown out is man's desiring, and it is this extinction which sets us free from the bonds by which we have bound ourselves to circumstances. If we are free from personal desire, it follows that resentment, anger, pride, fear, impatience, all these limiting emotions have been blown out like so many candles. That is why *nirvāṇa* is also spoken of in highly positive terms – as Highest Refuge, Safety, Absolute Purity, Supramundane Security, Emancipation, Peace.[17]

Nor need it be supposed that *nirvāṇa* is a mysterious something

---

[16] This is the Pāli form of the word, which in Sanskrit appears as *nirvāṇa*.

[17] See Paul Clasper: *Eastern Paths and the Christian Way* (1980), pp. 41–2.

to be attained the other side of death. It could become the great reality here and now, as it did for Gautama himself:

> Its unspeakable bliss cannot be described, it has to be experienced. It is for the here and now rather than a kind of heaven to be entered into by a virtuous man when he dies. Perhaps it has therefore become less difficult now to answer the question that many people find perplexing: Who is it that enjoys *Nirvāṇa* if there is not much left of the man so-and-so after he has died? The question framed thus is inept and does not fit. Rather should it be asked: Who enjoys *Nirvāṇa* here and now? The answer is the adept in meditation. For *Nirvāṇa* may be seen in this very life.[18]

The Christian should not be too much perplexed by this apparent clash between the idea of emptiness and the idea of fullness.[19] The philosophy of Plotinus has had immense influence on mysticism – Jewish, Christian and Muslim. There is the same demand for the stripping off of all the accretions of material existence, for the ascent of man through the worlds of soul and spirit, until he comes to the final experience of the One, beyond which there is nothing. And if I make the steep ascent and reach the goal, what shall I have attained? Is it Nothingness, or is it the perfect Fulfilment? Do I then cease to be, or do I begin for the first time in any real sense to be? The experience, for the Christian mystic, may come as a sense of total denudation, even inanition; or it may come with a sense of the plenitude of existence, in comparison with which all other existence seems as nothing. And, like the Buddhist, the Christian who has attained to this experience will declare that it is impossible to convey its reality in any form of human speech.

The attention of many western students of Buddhism has been concentrated on the perplexing and elusive idea of *nibbāna*, total deliverance or emancipation. But this should perhaps be balanced by a complementary idea, which is certainly present in early Buddhism, that of the *nibbūta*. Who is the man who has attained to the state of 'coolness' (this seems to be the literal meaning of the word)? He appears to be rather like the picture of the devotee in

---

[18] I.B. Horner in *Concise Encyclopedia of Living Faiths*, pp. 292-3.

[19] See Appendix to this chapter: 'Christian Approaches to Buddhism' (pp. 156-8).

the *Bhagavadgītā* - free from passion and desire, tranquil, undisturbed, master of himself and of his soul. He is, we are told, 'one who cannot be provoked, whose mind is unclouded, who is free from all the lower and baser desires, free from indolence, guide to those who are still enslaved to the passions, master of life and death'. Where is such a man to be found? Surely the answer is that the only one who has attained to the perfection of the *nibbūta*-state is the Buddha himself; but this he has left behind as an ideal after which all men should strive.

Clearly this ideal is related to that of *nirvāṇa*; but it seems to present deliverance in a rather more accessible form, available to those who are still living in the world. If all the fires of greed, hate and illusion have been extinguished, then the devotee has attained to holiness. 'But this plainly does not mean the extinction of life or annihilation. The *nibbūta*-man continues to live, to move about in the world, to proclaim the truth, as, for example, the Buddha did from his enlightenment until the age of eighty.'[20] It remains, however, true that this is not the highest form of deliverance, important as it may be in practical terms; beyond it lies the final *nibbāna*, the total cessation, the total liberation from all that holds fast. This is recognised in the *Abhidhamma*, the third of the 'baskets' of which the Pāli canon is made up; a distinction is drawn between the *kilesa nibbāna*, the dying away of all moral defilements, and the *khandha nibbāna*, the dying away of the 'aggregates' out of which the appearance of existence in this illusory world is made up.

★

The figure of the Founder of Buddhism, a little romanticised by time, is full of charm. It is replete with that quality, of which modern man in his sorely troubled world feels himself most to stand in need - serenity. In most of the countless statues by which the Buddhist world is adorned, the One who has been made perfect is depicted as calm and tranquil, lifted high above the tumult and squalor of human life and that 'unrest which men miscall delight'. It might be thought that Buddhism, with its endless emphasis on suffering, should be a sorrowful religion,

---

[20] T. Ling: *A History of Religions East and West*, p. 93.

but this is not the case. The quality which the monk in greater or less degree evinces is precisely serenity. He may not yet have attained *nirvāṇa*, but he believes that he is on the way; if he follows the injunction of the Master, 'strive without ceasing', he is convinced that one day he will attain.

Modern man finds much to attract him in a religion in which we are to be entirely cast back upon ourselves and upon our own endeavour. The Buddha won through to *nirvāṇa* by his own efforts, without calling upon the help of any God or saviour. 'Therefore, O Ānanda, take the self as a lamp; take the self as a refuge. Betake yourselves to no external refuge. Let the truth be your light and your refuge. Seek no other refuge ...' So the *Mahā-parinibbāna-sutta*, from which we have already quoted. So it was with the Master, so it must be with the disciple. A teacher may be of the utmost value; but in the last resort the achievement of the aspirant must come from within himself, from his apprehension of the Buddha, and the Teaching, and the Order.

'Man for himself.' This fits in very well with the modern mood. The last thing that modern man wants to be told is that he needs to be saved or that he requires the help of a Saviour. Many of our contemporary psychologists criticise the Christian faith as keeping the believer always in the state of infantile dependence; if we are ever to be real people, we must emerge from this infantile state, we must grow up and learn to be ourselves. This is how a highly regarded Buddhist teacher has expressed it:

> All through the Buddha's teaching, repeated stress is laid on self-reliance and resolution. Buddhism makes man stand on his own feet; it arouses his self-confidence and energy... Understanding that neither a god nor ceremonies can help or save him, the true Buddhist finds no place for prayer; he feels compelled to rely on his own effort, and thus gains self-confidence. He sees that the tendency to rely on a god or other imaginary power weakens man's confidence in his own power and lessens his sense of responsibility; he sees that blind faith in any authority leads to stagnation and spiritual lethargy.[21]

Buddhism has always claimed to be a religion which introduces the seeker to the world of reality. Western man has become over-

---

[21] U Tittila, in K.W. Morgan (ed.): *The Path of the Buddha* (1956), pp. 76–7.

intellectualised; by thought he has imposed a veil of unreality between himself and things as they are; Buddhism tears away the veil, and opens the door by which the aspirant can enter into the real world. The particular form of Buddhism which has proved most effective in demonstration of the non-intellectual way, and therefore most attractive to many western men and women, is that which is called Zen.

The purpose of Zen is to penetrate to reality. The method is the way of meditation, in which all earthly holds, even the dhamma and nirvāṇa itself, are let go, and there is nothing left but the I and the It, and gradually the I and the It become identical:

> Sitting quietly, doing nothing
> Spring comes, and the grass grows by itself.

Zen is a world of paradox, of the apparently irrational – deliberately so in order to draw the mind away from that rationality which interposes itself between the world and the mind. We are familiar with the sound of two hands clapping; what are we to make of it when we are asked to ponder the sound of one hand clapping? Here is a specimen, less illogical than many, of Zen dialogue:

> 'Am I right when I have no idea?' asked an enquirer.
> 'Throw away that idea of yours,' replied the teacher.
> 'What idea?' asked the pupil in perplexity.
> 'You are free, of course, to carry about that useless idea of no idea.'

The intellect divides and orders, defines and describes. But how would it be, if we were suddenly to apprehend all things at once and simultaneously? This is illumination, when thought ceases and something else takes its place. This is the experience which in Zen is called satori – 'that condition of consciousness wherein the pendulum of the Opposites has come to rest, where both sides of the coin are equally valued and immediately seen'.[22]

Satori can come only when thought ceases; it exists only on the other side of thought. This is what makes it so hard for western man to understand. Am I then to stop thinking? We live in a

---

[22] C. Humphreys: 'Buddhism, p. 185.

Cartesian world; we have been taught to take as our starting point *Cogito ergo sum*, I think, therefore I am. If I stop thinking, I shall stop existing. Exactly, says the *Zen* master; because you cannot stop thinking, you can never attain to enlightenment. If you would take the trouble, and for you especially this is not easy, to enter on the path of non-thinking, you would discover a far more beautiful and satisfying reality than you have ever known. Thought covers reality with a veil which makes impossible any direct contact between observer and reality. Because reality is terrifying in its lack of form and meaning, the observer who wishes to understand or to control reality, or even simply to make it endurable, imposes on it some kind of order. But this order exists only in the thinking mind; thought leads not to the understanding of reality but away from it. Elimination of thought is the way to immediacy of experience.

It is not surprising that many psychiatrists are deeply interested in *Zen* Buddhism, and find its message attractive. A great deal of mental illness can be diagnosed in terms of a withdrawal from reality, an unwillingness to face things exactly as they are. It is the aim of the psychiatrist to restore to the sick person the immediacy of experience. If I learn to accept myself just as I am, and to accept other people as they are and not as I would like them to be, and the external world as it is in its untidiness and uncouthness and recalcitrance to my ideas of what a nice world would be, I can be well.

The Enlightenment of the eighteenth century believed that strict rationality is the way to happiness; a great many people today seem to have come to the opposite conclusion – that things have been 'sicklied o'er with the pale cast of thought', and that the recovery of the immediacy of experience would do us all the good in the world. It is unlikely that the way of *Zen* will be the way for everyone; some may come to wonder whether it offers a way of escape rather than a way of acceptance and achievement. But the Christian who can say with the blind man in the Gospel, 'I was blind and now I see', will be able to understand and to some extent to appreciate what the *Zen* teacher is trying to do.

★

The main attraction of Buddhism in the modern world, however, would seem to be that it offers a high and noble ethical ideal, and a reasonable discipline unencumbered with dogma and directed to the attainment of that ideal. Ethical excellence is, in Buddhism, only a stage on the way to deliverance, but it is a stage that must be passed through. And minute instructions, based on the experience of many centuries, are offered to the aspirant to guide him in thought and action at every point along the way.

This unquestionably chimes with the mood of many men in the present world. They are weary of uncertainty and are glad to be given rules, even very exacting rules, by which to live. They are weary of the clash of dogmas and sects and philosophies, and relieved to be told that all such can be forgotten in the accomplishment of a law that is itself the highest wisdom. This is the way to freedom, this is the way to peace. In the words of an old Buddhist classic, 'Immaterial things are more peaceful than material, cessation is more peaceful than material things.'

The general outline of Buddhist philosophy and of Buddhist method is so familiar that it can be very briefly sketched in.

The aspirant to wisdom is first taught the principle of seeking refuge: 'I take refuge in the Buddha; I take refuge in the Teaching (dhamma);[23] I take refuge in the Order (sangha).'

These principles once accepted, the pupil will be introduced to the first principles of doctrine, and these have hardly changed at all since the four Āryan (noble) Truths were announced by the Buddha himself in the very first of all his discourses.

The first Āryan Truth is the Truth of Anguish. Birth, age and death are anguish, and so are all the states of mental suffering which men may experience. This is the truth of human experience.

The second Āryan Truth is the Truth of the Arising of Anguish. This comes only from desire – the craving for the experience of the senses, for the process of becoming and of existing in the world of illusion. No one English word will exactly represent the Pāli word tanha:

> It is the desire for what belongs to the unreal self that generates suffering, for it is impermanent, changeable, perishable, and that, in

---

[23] Many experts complain that 'Teaching' is an inadequate rendering of dhamma; they would like to compare it with the flexibility of the Greek logos. See a useful note in A Dictionary of Non-Christian Religions, s.v. 'Dhamma', and s.v. 'Dharma'.

the object of desire, causes disappointment, disillusionment, and other forms of suffering to him who desires. Desire in itself is not evil. It is desire to affirm the lower self, to live in it, cling to it, identify oneself with it, instead of with the Universal self, that is evil.[24]

The third Āryan Truth is the Truth of the Stopping of Anguish; this involves the complete stopping, abandonment and rejection of this desire, this craving for existence.

The fourth Āryan Truth, which is the means to the attainment of the third, is the Āryan Eightfold Way or Path. This is defined in terms of right understanding, right aspiration, right speech, right action, right mode of livelihood, right endeavour, right mindfulness, and right concentration.

Right understanding means the apprehension of the four noble Truths.

Right aspiration is the aim of renunciation of all desire. It includes also ahiṃsā, the purpose of not harming any living being.

Right speech is abstention from lying and slander, from unkind words and foolish talk.

Right action is abstention from stealing, and from wrongdoing in the world of the senses.

Right mode of livelihood forbids the earning of one's living by any trade that causes bloodshed, by the sale of intoxicating liquor, or by anything that causes harm to other beings.

Right endeavour aims to prevent the arising of evil mental states, the elimination of evil mental states that have arisen, the bringing into existence of good, or 'skilled',[25] mental states, and the development of good mental states that already exist.

Right mindfulness means to be clearly aware of the body as body (and therefore of the dangers that necessarily attend our existence in the body), to be aware of feelings as feelings, of the mind as the mind, and of mental states as mental states.

Right concentration makes possible the entry on the four-fold

---

[24] Edmund Holmes: *The Creed of Buddha*, p. 68, quoted in C. Humphreys, *Buddhism*, pp. 91-2. Some Buddhist authorities distinguish three forms of *tanha* – *kāma-tanha*, desire for pleasures of the material world; *bhāva-tanha*, clinging to existence; and *vibhāva-tanha*, craving for immortality.

[25] The word *upāya*, generally translated by the English word 'skill' constantly recurs in Buddhist writings. N. Smart defines it as 'spiritual adaptation to the conditions of the hearer' in *Beyond Ideology* (1981), p. 139. See also pp. 161-2.

way of meditation, which is open to the aspirant after perfection when he has overcome the five 'hindrances' of sense-desires, of ill will, of sloth, of restlessness, and of doubt or questioning. Such is the way to *nirvāṇa*. Together it comprises an impressive complex of psychological intuitions, of ethical and moral self-discipline, and of meditative aspiration. All these things are but the portal – beyond lies the goal of ultimate liberation.

★

We have not yet come to that claim which perhaps gives Buddhism its strongest appeal to the modern world. It claims to be the true gospel of peace.

The Buddha took over almost unaltered the old Hindu, or perhaps rather Jain, doctrine of *ahiṃsā*, harmlessness, abstaining from injury to any form of life. This has its roots in the doctrine of *karma*, of retribution in later lives for sins committed in the earlier, which itself is inextricably involved in the doctrine of transmigration. Souls can wander through every form of being; therefore life, even in its lowest form, is to be respected and preserved; no sin is greater than the taking of life, even though it be only the gnat or the worm that perishes. If only all mankind would accept this simple gospel of gentleness and respect for life, strife, contention and war would cease for ever from the earth.

At this point the Buddhist, armed as he is to reaction against the west, can make a devastating attack on the supposedly Christian nations: 'You have controlled the greater part of the world for fifteen centuries. What have you done with it except to produce one devastating war after another? Christians have not even been able to keep the peace with one another. Not content with that, they have drawn millions of innocent Asians and Africans into their quarrels. Christianity has no effective gospel of peace for the world today. Is it not time that the Christian stood aside and gave the Buddhist a chance?'

The great World Buddhist Conference held in Rangoon came to an end in 1957. It was claimed at the time that the world was beginning to show the influence of the healing streams of 'peace and reconciliation' which flowed forth from the Conference. This may have been so. But the twenty-five years which followed were years of tragedy for many parts of the Buddhist world. Sri Lanka was torn by internal strife between those of different races, languages and faiths. Burma was unable to overcome the forces of disorder which had long divided the country. Cambodia, an entirely Buddhist country, was the scene of devastating civil war and of massacres as terrible as those perpetrated by Hitler and his men in the attempt to exterminate the Jews. The Buddhist world has not been a scene of peace and goodwill.

The Buddhist would, I think, maintain that these tragedies have come about because so many in these areas, where Buddhism is the generally accepted faith, have not seriously accepted that faith, and at many points have been seduced and led astray by siren voices from the materialistic west. Christians would say much the same about the failures of the so-called Christian west – it has been at a time of widespread repudiation of the Christian Gospel that the west has plunged itself and much of the rest of the world in war upon war, disaster upon disaster.

Nothing is to be gained by recrimination. It is clear that all who sincerely believe in peace, and especially Christians and Buddhists, should get together, and co-ordinate their efforts in the cause of peace.

In recent years there have been many more meetings between Christians and Buddhists with a view to mutual understanding than had taken place in earlier years. There has been a considerable amount of writing by Buddhists on Christian themes. But, when allowance has been made for the difficulty of arriving at mutual understanding, there seems to have been less progress than might have been hoped for in the direction of a real meeting of minds.

One of the ablest Buddhist contributions to the debate is the book *A Buddhist Critique of the Christian Concept of God* by a learned scholar from Sri Lanka, Dr Gunapala Dharmasiri.[26] The aim of the work is frankly polemical; the writer wishes to show that, whereas Buddhism is a wholly rational religion which makes no appeal to the supernatural or the superstitious, Christian faith is wholly irrational, involved in self-contradiction and based on

---

26 Lake House Investments Ltd, Colombo, 1974.

presuppositions which a rational thinker is hardly likely to accept. The writer sets to work to demolish a number of convictions which are basic to western thought, and which also generally underlie Christian theology. First and foremost is the conviction that there is a self, an ego, 'the centre of my sinful earth', as Shakespeare calls it, which is the experiencing centre of all that happens to this strange thinking, feeling existent, which remains constant through all the changes and chances of the years, and is still itself – though a self which has grown and changed through contact and conflict with a world outside itself. Through a great number of quotations from Christian thinkers, though few from the Christian scriptures themselves, the learned writer has little difficulty in showing the variety of definitions of the self and the soul which have been given, and the difficulty which Christian writers have experienced in explaining exactly the subject about which they have been speaking. The Buddhist answer to the problem is quick and ready to hand – the problem arises only because we think that something exists; if we realise that there is no such existent, the problem simply disappears.

There is no self, there is no soul. These are simply illusions to which a name has been given. It is true that the Buddha did not deny the existence of mental states, but 'this does not mean that one can speak of the mind or consciousness as the persisting principle of continuity' (p. 13). Consciousness is not be thought of as a continuously flowing stream. We are not even to think of it as a line; when what appears as a line is placed under a microscope it is seen to be in reality a series of dots, each separate from that which comes before and from that which follows. We may rather think of a set of billiard balls each of which is set in motion by the one which preceded it in the line. Each is discrete and separate from every other; motion is passed from one to another only by physical contact.

Now this dissolution of self and soul cannot be dismissed as wholly impossible. It must be noted, however, that it is based neither on logical necessity nor on actual observation. It rests on unproved assumptions, and no rational evidence in its favour is adduced. We have no experience of entirely detached moments. Even to hear a single note of music is not in fact a momentary experience; and to hear and recognise a tune is an experience entirely different from that of hearing a detached and individual note; the reality of the tune lies in its pattern, and it is the pattern which is retained in the mind and recognised.

An explanation must, in the phrase of Plato, 'save the phenomena', account for what is there and take probability into the reckoning. Buddhism does not deny the existence of memory – 'here one's continuity is felt through one's memory' (p. 13) – but it seems hardly to have taken the existence of memory seriously or to have analysed it in depth. It is a mysterious reality. It is just the fact that I can clearly recollect events which took place seventy years ago; I can recall vividly the emotions by which some of these events were accompanied. How this is possible I may not understand. Scientists tell me that every particle of my body has changed ten times over in my lifetime; if that is true, it is hard to understand what continuity there can be. But no amount of sophisticated rhetoric can argue me out of my awareness that these events did happen, that they happened to me, and that I am still the same self to which, or to whom, they happened. This takes seriously all the facts that can be observed, though it falls far short of explaining them all.

The Buddhist faith took over from Hinduism the idea of reincarnation and rebirth. No evidence based on reason or observation is adduced in favour of this doctrine. Buddhism abounds in *Jātaka* stories, tales of memories of previous births; indeed one of the excellences of the Perfected One himself is stated to be that he alone among mortals has the capacity to remember all his previous births. But most Buddhist scholars recognise that, in retailing the *Jātaka* stories of previous births, the Buddha was using mythological material to make difficult truths accessible to simple minds; such tales are not to be taken as verifiable history. But, if so, on what does the doctrine of reincarnation rest? It is affirmed that, if the *khandhas* separate at the moment of death, they will surely at some later date be reunited to re-establish at least some kind of continuity with the past. But what evidence can be produced in favour of this view?

The Buddhist affirms belief in countless universes and endless time, and looks with some contempt on Christianity which is content with one universe and a miserably short span of time:

according to Buddhism the universe evolved ... out of the dispersed matter of a previous universe, and when this universe is dissolved, its dispersed matter – or its residual energy which is continually renewing itself – will in time give rise to another universe in the same way. The process is therefore cyclical and continuous. The universe is composed of millions of world systems like our solar system, each with its various planes of existence.[27]

This may be so; but direct evidence in its favour is not available. The Christian has no objection whatever to the idea of many universes, existing now or to exist later in the unimaginable span of future time. But this is because he believes in the inexhaustible energy of a creator God; he prefers to maintain a modest silence on things which he does not know and cannot know.

There is a third area in which the Christian feels entitled to ask his Buddhist friend to reconsider his position – the nature of suffering. Is it wholly evil, or can it have significance? To put it more directly, what are we to think of the suffering and death of Christ? Dr Dharmasiri is immediately ready with his answer:

A Buddhist cannot make any sense of Christ's sacrifice, or he would say that Christ did the wrong thing when he allowed himself to be taken. If the idea of sacrifice and divinity are taken away as not very essential, then Christ becomes *primus inter pares* with many other moral teachers (p. 98).

That he is not alone in his inability to make any sense of what is central in Christian faith is confirmed by reference to other Buddhist thinkers. A Roman Catholic writer Aelred Graham reports that 'the depiction of an almost naked figure being nailed to a cross as an object to be reverenced is unintelligible, with its presentation of barbarous cruelty, to a devout Buddhist, who is disposed to regard violent death in any form as the result of "bad karma".'[28]

This is echoed by D.T. Suzuki, one of the pioneers in the interpretation of Buddhism, especially in its *Zen* form, to the western world:

This is where Buddhism differs from Christianity. Buddhism declares

---

[27] U Tittila, quoted in K.W. Morgan, pp. 76-8.
[28] *The End of Religion* (1971), p. 164.

that there is from the beginning no self to crucify. To think that there is the self is the start of all errors and evils ... As there is no self, no crucifix is needed, no sadism is to be practised, no shocking sight is to be displayed by the roadside.[29]

The same writer, strangely, contrasts the Buddha who dies lying down with the Christ who dies in a vertical position. This he understands as indicating the contrast between the serenity of the one who accepted things as they are and the agony of the one who tried to change things and thus brought about his own destruction. The terrible sight of the crucified Christ one cannot 'help associating with the sadistic impulse of a physically affected brain'.[30]

On this strange, indeed perverse, misunderstanding, Bishop John Robinson aptly comments:

the sadism is in the world itself, and to say that 'no crucifixion is needed' is to blind oneself to the fact that there were, and have since been, countless crosses set up by man's inhumanity to man before ever Jesus took his place between two others. Rather, what Calvary shows is God, through a completely real man of flesh and blood, entering right into the depth of that evil and refusing to burke it. And that is the price of resurrection and of the transfiguration of this entire very material body of history. This I believe is the *real* difference between Buddhism and Christianity.[31]

It is pleasant to turn from these areas of disagreement, even harsh disagreement, between the Buddhist and the Christian, to some aspects of the teaching on which it may be much easier to reach at least a measure of understanding.

One of the noblest concepts in the vocabulary of Buddhism is *mettā*, a term which is usually translated 'benevolence' or 'good

29 *Mysticism, Christian and Buddhist* (1957), p. 136.
30 *Ibid.* p. 137.
31 *Truth is Two-Eyed* (1979), p. 94.

will'.[32] The classic exposition of this theme is the *Mettā-sutta*, in which the Master himself is represented as saying:

As a mother, even at the risk of her own life, protects her son, her only son, so let him cultivate goodwill without measure towards all beings. Let him cultivate goodwill without measure toward the whole world, above, below, around, unstinted, unmixed with any feeling of differing or opposing interests. Let a man remain steadfastly in this state of mind all the while he is awake, whether he be standing, walking, sitting, or lying down. This state of heart is the best in the world.

We must not let these noble words carry us farther than their strict meaning will bear. The attitude of *mettā* is part of Buddhist meditation; it cannot in any way disturb the tranquillity which it is the purpose of the monk to attain. He stays where he is, and lets his thoughts of goodwill go out round all the points of the compass to the beings which are in each area. But he is not personally engaged, and there is no suggestion that his thoughts of goodwill might lead to any kind of action.

For that reason it is misleading when Buddhist or Christian writers render the word *mettā* as love. In biblical language the word *agapē* means engagement: the one who loves makes himself vulnerable – he does not isolate himself from the suffering of one who is loved, he takes it into himself, suffers with it, makes it a part of himself and of his own suffering. *Agapē* is anything but passionless contemplation; it is for this reason that in so many biblical contexts the word 'love' can be translated 'redemptive action'. But the aim of the Buddhist ascetic is not the same as that of the student of the Bible. A passion of sympathy, and still more redemptive action arising out of it, would bind him fast to the *saṃsāra* from which it is his most dearly loved intention to escape.[33]

What carries us nearer to the Christian understanding of the

---

[32] *Mettā* is one of the four *Brahma Vihānas*, heavenly states of mind, the others being compassion, joy, and serenity.

[33] So the statement of Humphreys that 'Buddhism is as much a religion of love as any on earth' (p. 124) is misleading, unless the meaning given to the word 'love' is clearly expounded.

nature of love is the concept, developed mainly in the Mahāyāna tradition, of the *bodhisattva*.[34] The *bodhisattva* is the man or woman who has made such progress towards perfection as to be at the point in which it is possible to enter into final *nirvāṇa*. But just at this point the *bodhisattva* resolves, for the sake of other struggling, suffering entities, to remain a little longer in the *saṃsāra* to help them on their way. Out of compassion he resolves to become a kind of saviour:

> The merit I achieved by all these pious actions, may that make me
> Quite able to appease the sufferings of all beings . . .
> Heedless of body, of good, of the merit I gained and will gain still,
> I surrender my all to promote the welfare of others.

So Śāntideva, a seer and poet probably of the seventh century AD. In another passage he goes even farther:

> I take the sufferings of all beings on myself . . .
> For I have taken the vow to save all beings . . .
> I am not concerned only about my own salvation
> Since with the resolve to attain to perfect knowledge
> I must save all beings from the flood of the *saṃsāra* . . .
> And why? Because it is better that I alone should suffer than that all these beings should sink down into the places of torment. I give myself as a ransom.[35]

Fortunately even those religions which claim to be most logical are not logical at every point. But it is hard to see how utterances of this kind can be fitted into the structure of Buddhism, as it appears to have been taught by the Founder and as it developed in the early centuries after his death. Are we reading a Buddhist classic or a Christian meditation? Some have been so impressed by the similarities as to posit a dependence of the Gospels on Buddhist tradition, or an infiltration of Christian influences into Buddhist developments. Neither of these is very likely. But at

---

[34] For a good exposition of the *bodhisattva* ideal, see N. Smart: *Beyond Ideology* (1981), pp. 142-9.

[35] Quoted by M. Winternitz: *History of Indian Literature*, vol. II (German edn., p. 261; Eng. trans., pp. 368, 371.

least such passages as these encourage the Christian to be bold enough to invite his Buddhist brother to look again at certain things in Christianity which he had found hard to understand, and also to look again at some of his own deepest convictions. We have passed beyond the realm of rational discourse and of the attempt to convince by the arguments of reason. Below reason lies the realm of existential decisions, and these are hard to change.

The Christian has made his existential decision in one direction. Existence is better than non-existence; it is good that God, for reasons known only to himself, has decided to create a universe. It is good that, when he looked on all that he had created and made, he saw that it was very good. Of course there are problems in this universe that God has made; the art of theodicy, the justification of God for having made such a world as he has made, is one that all theologians at all times have found very difficult. But the Christian is able to say in faith with Julian of Norwich (c. 1342-after 1413): 'All shall be well, and all shall be well, and all manner of thing shall be well', though he will further agree with her that 'What the deed shall be, and how it shall be done, there is no creature beneath Christ that knoweth it, nor shall wit it till it is done.'

Buddhism has made its existential decision. Non-existence is better than existence, at least in any ordinary sense of these terms. He would be ready to say, 'Oh, why did I awake? When shall I sleep again?' Deliverance is deliverance from life and not deliverance into life. The Christian's desire for eternal life is necessarily strange to him – it seems to him to be a part of that *tanha*, thirst, from which it is his great desire to be delivered. Even if it is explained to him that the Christian desire is not just a wish for the endless continuation of life as we know it, but for uninhibited and unbroken fellowship with the God whom we know in Jesus Christ, he is not likely to be brought very much nearer to understanding.

These two views of the nature of existence naturally spill over into two radically different views as to the nature of suffering.

The Buddhist has made his existential decision. Suffering, anguish, is bad, undesirable. Therefore suffering must at all costs be extirpated, even at the cost of destroying the sentient being that suffers. We must cut off the branch that we sit on, even though we should fall to destruction with it. We must root up the very tree of life itself. 'The door is open,' so runs the Buddhist invitation, 'why suffer?'

Why suffer? That is the ultimate question. It comes to sharp and challenging expression in the contrast between the serene and passionless Buddha and the tortured figure on the Cross. In Jesus we see One who looked at suffering with eyes as clear and calm as those of the Buddha. He saw no reason to reject it, to refuse it, to eliminate it. He took it into himself and felt the fullness of its bitterness and horror; by the grace of God he tasted death for every man. Others suffer; he will suffer with them and for them, and will go on suffering till the end of time. But he does not believe that suffering is wholly evil; by the power of God it can be transformed into a redemptive miracle. Suffering is not an obstacle to deliverance; it can become part of deliverance itself. And what he was he bids his children be – the world's sufferers, in order that through suffering the world may be brought back to God.

The Buddhist ideal is that of passionless benevolence. The Christian ideal is that of compassion. When argument has done its best, we must perhaps leave the two ideals face to face. We can only ask our Buddhist friend to look long and earnestly on the Cross of Christ, and to ask himself whether, beyond the peace of the Buddha, there may not be another dimension of peace to the attainment of which there is no way other than the Way of the Cross.

APPENDIX: Christian Approaches to Buddhism

A number of Christian thinkers take the view that Christianity and Buddhism are the most vital and most adaptable of the great religions of the world, and that some coalescence of the two is essential if we are to arrive at a 'global civilisation' suited to 'the human development of the global city'.

A somewhat clumsy effort in this direction was made by the historian Arnold Toynbee in two books, *A Historian's View of*

Religion, and *Christianity Among the Religions of the World.* But, if two religions seek unity by each abandoning that which is most characteristic of itself, the result can only be either an ungainly amalgam, or a fusion so deprived of essential content as to lack that vitality which each had in separation. It seems clear that this way is not a way forward.

A much more elaborate attempt has been made by Professor Ninian Smart in his book *Beyond Ideology: Religion and the Future of Western Civilisation* (London, 1981). The argument is pursued with great subtlety through chapters 3 to 7 of the book; two of the chapter headings – 'Reflections on Buddhism and Christianity' and 'The Buddhist Meaning of Christianity; the Christian Meaning of Buddhism' – may serve to indicate the depth and intensity of the thought that the writer has devoted to his theme.

Professor Smart is right in seeing, as has been suggested in the text of the chapter, that if Christians and Buddhists are to talk at all, they must talk about ultimates. In Christianity the Ultimate is God; in Buddhism the Ultimate is *nirvāṇa*. Is there any possibility of reconciliation between the two?

It would seem at first sight that there is no possibility of reconciliation. Smart is honest about the differences and the difficulties:

> The ultimate in Buddhism ... is not the source, still less the living source, of the cosmos. This of course represents a genuine conflict between Christianity and Buddhism (p. 191).
>
> The Christian has all the infinite substance and power of God to sustain him ... If he has God's blessing, how can he fear anything in this hard and suffering world? The power of God is ultimate security, and in its operation as motivated through sacraments the Christian is assigned a kind of fearlessness, a transcendental destiny, a new glory, a transfiguration of his life (p. 204).

Has Buddhism anything to correspond with this? Does it offer anything more than emptiness? But is the contrast as deep as we at first imagine?

> For [in Christianity] God's path is that of the sufferer, of the self-emptier. And there is at the heart of Christianity the paradox that God is self-emptying, in that the Christian receives in the same breath of the spirit the promise of the highest, transcendental power and

glory and the imprint of human emptiness, losing one's life, maybe with a sense of tragic despair (p. 255).

If this is recognised 'the two faiths may serve ... as mutual critics and give one another new resources of insight and symbol' (p. 205).

Short quotations cannot give a fair impression of the strength and subtlety with which the argument is maintained. The writer has been almost desperately honest in the attempt to be fair to both traditions, to see and to set forth the strengths of each. The book is certain to remain for a long time the subject of careful study and debate as experts from both the Buddhist and the Christian camps try to assess the writer's understanding of their respective faiths, and his success or failure in the attempt to achieve what he calls 'complementarity of Buddhism and Christianity' (p. 309).

I have to admit that, after several readings of the book, I am not yet convinced that the argument has been brought to a successful conclusion. I can see clearly in the two great faiths a certain similarity of concern – the central concern is with the Ultimate – and in the kind of questions asked. But the answers given still seem to me so divergent that I do not see the way to the complementarity which Professor Smart desiderates. I share the perplexity of a not unfriendly reviewer, Bishop Lesslie Newbigin:[36]

Granting the legitimacy of a methodological suspension of belief for specific purposes, can there be any encounter with the real while that suspension is maintained? Can we find what is true by considering what is desirable for the future of our planet? Does not the method in effect rule out the possibility of an actual revelation? Does not this explain why – in the end – experience of the transcendent becomes fused with experience of the void?

36 In Theology (September, 1982), p. 383.

CHAPTER VI

The Primal World

Few of the books on Christianity and the other faiths contain a chapter on the religions of the primal world. This is to be regretted, not only because of the interest of the subject in itself, but also because so large a part of the inhabitants of the world still live on the level of this very ancient form of religion. It is commonly said that India is in the main a Hindu country, and that everyone who is not registered as Muslim, Christian, Parsi or Jain is to be reckoned a Hindu. But, in point of fact, the inhabitants of the villages, who still make up 70 per cent of the population. – some 350 million people – have very little contact with Hinduism as this is set out in the books; the very names of the Hindu gods are unknown to many of these peoples, the world of thought they inhabit is not that of their Hindu neighbours, the sacrifices they offer in their little village shrines would not be acceptable in any of the larger temples. The same is true in many other areas of the world. Indonesia is reckoned to be the most populous Muslim country in the world; but it is evident that in many areas the Muslim crust is very thin, and that under it a much more ancient form of religion survives.

Africa with its more than five hundred peoples, languages and cultures, is the continent in which man has been allowed to live longer, and with less disturbance, in the ancient ways than in other parts of the world. Even making allowance for the incursion of Islam and Christianity in recent times, there are probably more than a hundred million people still living according to the traditions of their ancestors. And when the African is transported far from the place of his origin and has been taught alien ways, the old has astonishing power of survival in uneasy co-existence or conflict with the new. Everyone has heard of the Voodoo cults in Haiti and other Caribbean countries; in these the old Africa is still very much alive.

Even more surprising is what can be observed in Brazil, in many ways one of the most sophisticated societies in the world. In Rio de Janeiro on Christmas Eve all along the sea-beaches of that beautiful capital little fires are lighted and exotic African rituals are performed, with the burning of a black cock's feathers and other such strange survivals from the ancient African heritage. Those who come to look on, driving up in their expensive limousines, are by no means all of African lineage. One of the features of the Brazilian scene is the very rapid growth of the spiritist movements, in which perhaps 5 per cent of the population are involved: there may be Christian elements in these associations, but initiations and spirit possession and many other ceremonies are the expression of feelings and impulses that are very ancient and belong to a different world from that of Christianity.[1]

One of the most remarkable examples of the survival of the old world among those who have long been exposed to Christian influences is to be found among the Indians of the United States of America. Some of the Indian peoples, such as the Navajos, live in considerable numbers in their reservations, where they are to some extent protected from the ravages of the modern world. It is natural for them rather self-consciously to maintain their association with the ancient ways. Smaller groups seemed to have been completely Christianised and assimilated into the American pattern. Yet during 1959 the writer and literary critic Edmund Wilson published in the New Yorker an extraordinarily interesting series of articles based on his contacts with the remaining fragments of the 'Six Nations', the Iroquois in the north of New York State and over the Canadian border. The studies made it plain that even among these peoples, which for two centuries and more have been overwhelmed by the surging tides of an alien civilisation, something survives that belongs to a far more ancient pattern; it is this underlying structure that keeps the Indian from ever feeling quite at home in the world in which he spends the greater part of his life, and in which he earns his living.

'You but not me', western man in his arrogance is inclined to

---

[1] See F. Houtart: Art: 'Spiritism' in Concise Dictionary of the Christian World Mission, with bibliography, and World Christian Encyclopaedia (1982), p. 187.

say, overlooking the fact that there may be many pagan survivals in his own way of living. In the names of his weekdays he commemorates the pagan Thor and Freya; the most important festival of the Christian year, Easter, is associated with a pagan goddess. The yule log, so faithfully lighted on the hearth of many Christian homes, in the days when we still had hearths, was almost certainly of pagan origin; the same may be true of the apparently innocent Christmas tree introduced into England by Albert the Prince Consort.

★

We know a great deal more of these ancient forms of religion than was known a century ago.

Through the learned researches of the scholars who have recovered for us long-forgotten languages we can now acquaint ourselves with religion as it was four thousand years ago in Sumer and Akkad, and among the Assyrians and the Hittites. We find that all those ancient forms were nature religions, closely associated with heat and cold, with the wet and the dry, growth and decline, and with the endlessly recurring seasons of the year.

Now that we read the Old Testament against the background of the other eastern nations, we are not surprised to find in it elements of much more ancient forms of faith. In Numbers 19 we find set out at length the ritual of the ashes of a red heifer, which mixed with water and sprinkled with hyssop availed to take away the defilement incurred through contact with a dead body. As a modern writer has expressed it, these ashes serve as 'a conducting vehicle of a dangerous spiritual electricity'.[2] By the time that the account in the book of Numbers was written, these ancient symbols had become demythologised, and simply expressed in vivid form the fact that holiness and purity are essential characteristics of the people of God.

Everyone is familiar with the classic dignity of the gods whom the Athenians worshipped. Professor E.R. Dodds, in a remarkable book, *The Greeks and the Irrational* (1951), has shown up for us the other side of things. There were the great Uranian gods of the sky and the bright air; but there were also the Chthonian

---

[2] L.R. Farnell: *The Evolution of Religion* (1905), p. 95.

deities, the gods who live below ground and emerge from time to time not to the advantage of human beings.

There is the same duality in the religion of the Romans. Cicero could plan and write such eloquent books on philosophy and religion as *De Natura Deorum*, on the nature of the gods. But in his day, on 9, 11 and 13 May the Lemuria, the festival of the dead, was celebrated, when the good Roman householder walked nine times through his house, spitting black beans from his mouth, and saying 'with these beans I redeem me and mine', and at the end saying 'Ghosts of my fathers, be gone.' What are we to call this – superstition or survival? And did the civilised Roman really take such things seriously? The historian of Roman religion, R.M. Ogilvie, expresses himself rather cautiously on the point: 'At first sight it is difficult to imagine Livy or Horace or Agrippa solemnly getting out of bed and going through this ritual. And yet they probably did – at least in a modified form.'[3]

It is commonly said that missionaries in the nineteenth century were not interested in the rites and ceremonies of the people among whom they dwelt, and desired nothing so much as to sweep them all away. No doubt there were some among them who despised the life of these people as being, in the words of Thomas Hobbes, 'nasty, brutish, and short'. There were, however, others who recognised the importance of understanding what they saw, and faithfully recorded it. The French missionary Eugène Casalis (1812–91) wrote about *The Basuto*[4] – he had served for years almost as the prime minister of the great chief Moshoeshoe. The Anglican R.H. Codrington wrote down what he had learned in twenty-four years among *The Melanesians* (1891),[5] and only regretted that he had not had longer to acquaint himself with their ideas and their ways; it was he who made known the useful word *mana* for the mysterious power which is believed to reside in people and places and things. Another

---

[3] R.M. Ogilvie: *The Romans and their Gods* (1969), p. 85.
[4] Eng. Trans. 1861; reprint, Cape Town, 1965.
[5] Reprint, London, 1972.

Anglican, John Roscoe, wrote of *The Baganda*[6] and other peoples of the territory we now know as Uganda. Best of all, the Swiss missionary H.A. Junod among the Batonga people of what is now Maputo wrote *The Life of a South African Tribe* (1913),[7] stimulated by a remark of Lord Bryce, regretting that the Romans in Britain had taken so little interest in their neighbours that we know very little indeed about the religion of the Britons of that time.

These works are criticised, by the more sophisticated descendants of those about whom they wrote, as being at certain points imperfect. It could not be otherwise; no one can ever fully understand a culture other than that in which he has himself grown up. But missionaries of that earlier generation had the advantage of making the acquaintance of these peoples before they had been deeply corrupted by western men. As a result these books are being reprinted today not by the churches and missions but by the ethnological societies. They are found to be irreplaceable, as giving us a generally faithful picture of an age that has for ever passed away.

★

Anyone who approaches the subject of the primal religions is likely to be almost overwhelmed at the start by the extraordinary complexity of the material. How in the world are we to make any sense of it all? He will be well advised to take careful note at the start of four cautions set before us by those who have a right to be heard.

The first caution comes from H.H. Farmer of Cambridge:

> The fact is that we have no direct knowledge of the earliest beginnings of religion, of the true chronological primitive. The observation of present-day backward tribes plainly does not obviate this difficulty, for such tribes are after all our contemporaries, with as long a history behind them as we have ourselves, and the possibility of degeneration cannot be excluded; it is obviously illegitimate simply and uncritically to equate the backward with the chronologically primitive.[8]

---

6 Reprint, New York, 1977.
7 London, 1911; reprint, London, 1965.
8 H.H. Farmer: *Revelation and Religion* (1954), p. 44.

The other three warnings come to us from the immensely learned Arthur Darby Nock, one in a paper on 'The Study of the History of Religion', which though it was written fifty years ago is still a classic; the others in a shorter paper on 'Mana and Roman Religion'.[9]

Primitives... as a whole... differ from civilized men mainly in that they lack the art of writing, ie the use of convenient symbols sufficiently narrowed in meaning... and employed not only to transact ordinary business and to implement the use of magical formulas, but also to fix and preserve traditions and ideas... Without it, man's mental horizon seldom extends more than three or five generations backwards (p. 603).

Here Nock has put his finger on one of the essential points. The invention of writing, which cannot be put back more than six thousand years in human history, and probably less, marks the watershed between culture and civilisation. Culture is very ancient; civilisation, as it grew up in the valleys of the Nile, the Euphrates and the Tigris from 4000 BC onward, depends on the new form of communication which itself is dependent on the preservation of written records. This does not mean that religion without writing is always in flux. In point of fact these forms of religion among pre-literate peoples tend to be very conservative. Change does take place; but the powers of memory of these simpler peoples are astonishing, and, especially in matters of ritual and custom, change is eschewed as diminishing the value of that which has been inherited. Dr Nock continues:

Nevertheless the primitive is not a different biological animal; he is by no means necessarily less sophisticated or less prone to make elaborate social and religious patterns; and his problems of subsistence and self-adjustment, physical and moral, are not altogether diverse from those of civilized man.

Here the crucial words are 'religious patterns'. When evolutionary ideas were much in the air, about a century ago, it was assumed that religion was a sign of advanced development,

---

[9] A.D. Nock: *Essays on Religion and the Ancient World*, pp. 331-40, 603-5.

and had appeared rather late in the evolution of the human species. So ethnologists wandered round the world looking for peoples without a religion, and periodically reported that such a people had been found. In every case later investigation disproved the first assertions. It is evident that religion, in the broad sense, as 'the history of the human spirit in its relations with everything outside itself which it conceives as not merely material and fully understood', goes very far back in human history, and some of those peoples who are generally regarded as the most 'primitive', such as the Australian aborigines, have in fact a liturgical and ceremonial life of almost unbelievable complexity.

So we are warned to beware of simplification. Man is unwise and curiously planned. If we approach these pre-technical and pre-literate religions, we must be prepared for confusion and complexity:

> The key to all religions and to all mythologies has been sought in various theories... Each time the key has opened certain doors, but no amount of filing has enabled it to open all doors... Life does not happen like that. If any domain of the history of man and of his thought seems to us quite straightforward, we may be fairly certain that we are ill-informed about it or view it from a particular standpoint (p. 333).

We have been warned. Generalisations about this amazingly wide and varied world of the pre-literate religions must all be viewed with great suspicion. But some phenomena meet us in so many areas that they may be taken, with a good deal of hesitation, as characteristic of religion at this level.

1. In the evolutionary days, introduced in 1871 by E.B. Tylor's great book *Primitive Culture*, it was widely held that belief in spirits preceded belief in gods, and that out of belief in many gods belief in one god slowly and painfully emerged. Monotheism is, therefore, to be taken as a late appearance in the development of the religious spirit of man.

Later research has cast doubt on the universal validity of the thesis. The first to expose it to damaging criticism was Andrew Lang, who in his book *The Making of Religion* (1898; 2nd edn., 1900) affirmed that among the Australian aborigines there were clear traces of belief in one high god. The learned world found it extremely difficult to accept this view; Tylor himself put forward the idea that, if such beliefs existed, they must have come in as borrowings from the teachings of Christian missionaries, who for a number of years had been active among the aborigines. A later anthropologist, Pater W. Schmidt of Vienna, devoted the whole of a lifetime of laborious research to the investigation and elucidation of the idea. In the twelve volumes of an immense work *The Origins of the Idea of God*,[10] Schmidt brought under scrutiny the least developed peoples he could find, such as the pygmies of the eternal rain forest of Zaïre, and remote peoples in Siberia. In almost every case he was able to find at least traces of a primitive monotheism, which he believed to be part of an original revelation given by God himself and later defaced by the ignorance and sinfulness of man. In many cases, though not in all, this god is believed to have withdrawn far away from this world; worship is not offered to him, and he does not interfere in the affairs of men. But it is worth noting that many Africans object strongly to the use by western anthropologists of the term 'ancestor-worship': 'We do respect the ancestors, but the word we use for the worship of the one high god is quite different, and used only in relation to a single object' (Zululand). From a quite different part of Africa (Togo), 'We knew about God before the missionaries came, but we did not know that he is our father.'

2. This first aspect of religion leads on naturally to the second, the immense importance of the ancestors in the life of many peoples. This deep conviction of the continued existence of the ancestors and their influence in the life of the people presents considerable difficulties to the organisers of Christian churches, for instance in Africa; what place can be found in the life and worship of the church for non-Christian ancestors? This perplexity is delineated in fascinating fashion in a study carried out by Roman Catholic Sisters in a girls' training college in Lesotho.[11] From these it became clear that it was natural for

---

[10] *Der Ursprung der Gottesidee* (Münster i.W. 1926–55), has not been translated into English. For a shorter work by Schmidt, see Bibliography.

[11] *Ancestors, as seen by Teacher Training College Students in Lesotho*, ed. Sister Jocelyne Michaud SNJM. Essays presented to the Department of Theology at UBLS (1972).

these students to pray to the ancestors, especially for help in time of need, and that it did not make very much difference whether these ancestors were Christian or non-Christian. Ancestors are seen as powerful mediators; they are near God, 'next to him', and because of this 'God shares his power with them' (p. 6). 'I like to pray to my ancestors, because even though they were pagans, they served God, so I think they entered the Kingdom of God, and will be able to listen to my prayer as they are closer to God' (p. 9). It also became clear that ancestors who belonged to long since departed generations have no great meaning to these young people; of far greater importance are those whom they can remember, and among these it is the grandmother who seems to play the greatest part.

This makes it easy to understand that, for many peoples, not all the dead become 'ancestors'. Some were so feeble in life that no serious account need be taken of them after their death. Some left no descendants to keep alive their memory. Some who were notoriously bad in life may even be classed as dangerous or harmful spirits. In that case certain rituals are performed in order to prevent such a dead person from ever having any relations with the living, or from becoming 'incarnate' again in some member of the tribe in a later generation. In some cases, the corpse of the dead person may be disinterred and burned; as a result of this he is now totally dead, and has no longer any share in the life of his people.

The 'great ones', on the other hand are generally beneficent spirits, who have laid down the ordinances of their people, and whose behests must be obeyed. Only if these ordinances are most carefully observed will the favour of the great ones rest upon the people, and enable them to continue in prosperity. But, if the people are dependent upon the ancestors, the ancestors may also be in some sense dependent on their descendants. Their life-force has to be perpetually renewed. Unless the people do their duty in inviting the ancestors to be present at their feasts, and give them their due share of libations and gifts and offerings, they may lose their power to help, or may withdraw their favour from those who have failed to do their duty by them.

This sense of continuity with the past has great value in maintaining the unity and cohesion of the people. On the other hand dependence on the past may inhibit the spirit of adventure, and hinder change at points at which change is greatly needed.

Shortly before this chapter was originally written, I had the privilege of a long conversation with the aged Christian Keysser (1877–1961), a German missionary who had penetrated perhaps more deeply than any other into the recesses of the minds of the peoples of New Guinea. A point on which he laid greater stress than on almost any other was the tyranny of custom in the inviolability of what the ancestors were believed to have laid down. If any rule is infringed, the consequences will be terrible. When a mother is out of the house, a child has sat in a place in which he is not entitled to sit. The child must be killed. Why? Because the ancestors have said so; if retribution is not executed they will withdraw their favour from their people, and everything will fall in ruins. And why did the ancestors lay down that particular rule? That kind of question it is impertinent to ask.

★

E.B. Tylor in his *Primitive Culture* used the term 'animism', belief in spirits, to express the pre-literate man's understanding of the life of the human race and the forces which control it. 'All things are full of gods' said the ancient Greek philosopher. 'All things are full of spirits' says the African in Tylor's interpretation of his mentality. The word 'animism' has gone out of favour, as it has come to be realised that 'spirits' implies too narrow an understanding of the forces by which man on this level of development regards himself as being surrounded.

A wider interpretation of the African outlook on that world was given by a Belgian missionary Fr Placide Tempels in his book *Bantu Philosophy*.[12] Is there such a thing as a Bantu philosophy? Certainly not, if we think of a system worked out by a process of pure ratiocination and systematised in categories of ideas. But, if we look for a central concept round which a number of others are grouped, we may be able to find it. Tempels fixes on power, energy, life-force as the central Bantu idea. He has been criticised as having generalised too widely from experiences with one African people among whom he had worked in Zaïre. This may

---

[12] The original work in Flemish was published in Elisabethville (now Kisangani) in 1945. Eng. trans. 1959.

be valid criticism; but, if we do not tie ourselves down too inflexibly to the details of his formulations, the ideas that he puts forward are found to be illuminating in many parts of the world. All people and all things are possessed of force. This life-force can be diminished or increased. Man finds himself surrounded by certain 'natural forces placed by God at the disposal of men for the reinforcement of their natural energy'. If a man's natural force is on the increase, he feels well. If he is tired, he says 'I am dying.' This sounds to European ears absurdly exaggerated; to the African it sounds sensible, the man is giving expression to an awareness of the diminution of vital powers, which if not checked will lead in the long run to his decease. So says an African Roman Catholic priest, who naturally has an exceptionally clear understanding of the point of view of his own people: 'The duty of the increase of the vital forces, which can only be accomplished in community, is the primal duty of our Muntu ['man'; singular of Bāntu, people], and the point on which all his efforts converge.'

This will help the foreigner to understand some things of which he is inclined to form a possibly unfavourable judgment. Cannibalism is to the western mind wholly repellent; it is taken as evidence of barbarism and degradation. To the African or the Melanesian it could appear in a very different guise. You have successfully killed your enemy; the next thing may be to eat his heart or other important parts of his anatomy, in order that his life-force may not escape and be wasted, but by being absorbed into you may contribute to the strengthening of your life-force, an end which is greatly to be desired.[13]

A man's life-force may be diminished not only by what happens to him, but by what happens to anyone or anything with which he is intimately concerned. Fr Tempels gives a touching example of the extent to which this principle may hold. One African had entrusted to another the care of a lamb. Not long after, the guardian's dog was found feasting on the unfortunate lamb. It was hardly likely that the faithful dog had itself killed the lamb; no one could deny that he had been seen eating it. The guardian started by sending a lamb to the injured man to take the

[13] Many examples in the still valuable article 'Cannibalism' (J.A. MacCulloch) in Hastings: *ERE*, III, pp. 194–209.

place of the one that had been eaten; he then sent a second and a third, and finally a gift of Fcs 100, a considerable sum for an African to pay. No trial had been held, the guardian had not been sentenced to pay a fine. He had simply recognised that his friend had suffered a diminution of his life-force, and he wished to repair the loss. Only when all these payments had been made was the friend able to say 'Now I am happy; now I am a *living man* again'.[14]

There are innumerable forces in the world. Everyone knows that he is able to manipulate some of these and use them to his own advantage. But it is believed that there are certain people who have special knowledge, and that this gives them the ability to control the hidden forces in a way that goes beyond what is possible for one who does not share their special gifts. Pre-literate society is familiar with magic both black and white, with the use of powers to help and to heal, and of powers to hurt and destroy.

The old term 'witch-doctor' is not now in favour, since it has sinister connotations.[15] But there can be no doubt that many of the practitioners of these arts can effect cures of sickness which baffle those trained in western science. Combining a considerable knowledge of the local herbs with a deep understanding of the psychology of their people, they set to work. Many of the sicknesses that afflict these people, especially in areas where the tensions of modern life weigh heavily upon them, are what would now be called psychosomatic. By understanding and easing the tension the practitioners perform what appear to simple people to be miracles and leave the western observer uncertain and astonished.

There is, however, the other side. Almost everyone on this pre-literate level is firmly convinced of the power of the evil eye, and of the harm that can be done by those who are skilled in the black arts. He has evidence of the power of this dark world which to him is completely convincing. In some areas to this day it is taken for granted that no death is natural; it can only have been caused by magic. So the one who understands these things is

---

[14] Tempels, pp. 117–18.
[15] All the same, quite recently a student in Kenya started an essay with the words 'My parents are both witch-doctors.'

called in to discover who it is whose magic has brought about the fatal result. In such areas, many go about afraid that they may have this destructive power and be exercising it unawares. This will not seem surprising to those who are familiar with the witch-trials of a not so very distant date in Europe and America, and with the confessions of many of those who were put on trial for witchcraft.[16]

The world in which pre-literate man lives is not the world of western man, but for him it has a logic of its own by which things are held together. Things, however, always have a tendency to fall apart. If order is threatened, still more if it has been impaired, action must be taken to restore order, to bring things together that ought never to have been separated. Among many simple peoples there is this proud sense that it is their solemn prerogative and responsibility to restore the threatened order of the universe.

The Dyaks of Borneo had a firm belief that to them had been given the privilege of maintaining order in the affairs of the universe. Head-hunting seems to western man to be pure savagery. Not so to those who practise it. Natural forces have been disturbed. To restore and increase the fertility of the fields, a head is needed – naturally the head of a man of another tribe. Head-hunting is not an enterprise to be lightly or wantonly taken in hand; among certain peoples it was carried out only as the climax of ceremonies that had lasted for several years. The practice played so central a part in the life of the people that the prohibition of it by a western colonial power has been identified as one of the causes that led to the decay of a people and a decrease of population. The vital forces had been touched and diminished at what was literally a vital point.

Some such idea seems to have dominated the Aztec civilisation of Mexico, at the time that stout Cortes and his men first made contact with it. The gods demanded a steady tribute of human hearts torn from living human bodies. If this tribute failed, the sun would cease to rise and ruin would fall not only upon the Aztecs but upon the whole human race. Montezuma and his

---

[16] See a fascinating essay by H.R. Trevor-Roper: 'The European Witch-Crazes of the Sixteenth and Seventeenth Centuries', in *Religion, the Reformation and Social Changes* (London, 1967), pp. 90–193.

lords seem to have been on the whole kindly and reasonable people. But, when strife began, the Spaniards knew very well what would be the fate of those who were taken prisoner. For a time they would be cared for by their captors, well fed and supplied with everything that they needed. But, when the appointed time had come, on the top of the high pyramid the sharp stone knife would tear open the victim's belly, the heart would be plucked from the still living body, and the needed offering would be made to satisfy for a moment the insatiable gods. That the death of the victim came to him as a privilege was more evident to those who carried out the sacrifice than to the one who endured it; the priests were shocked when the carrying out of what they clearly saw to be their duty was stigmatized as murder.

★

Over the last fifty years intensive study has been directed to the minds and to the ways of almost all the peoples of the world who still live in the pre-literate stage of human existence. What has emerged from these many studies is the unquestionable fact that such peoples have on the whole made a remarkably good job of adaptation to the perhaps unfavourable circumstances in which they live. The Eskimo, in the trackless white wilderness of the north, learned through centuries of experiment to make use to his advantage of everything yielded by that grim and un-promising world, managed to hold on to life through generation after generation, and even to maintain himself at a modest level of comfort. The logic of such peoples is not the same as the logic of western man. Yet it holds all things together in a unity of experience. Even the simplest peoples have made for themselves a world which is complete, rational by the standards which they accept, and well ordered. Each individual knows where he stands in the ordered hierarchy of the tribe, what his station is, and what are the duties which he must fulfil. Every member of the group, larger or smaller, lives supported by all the members seen and unseen. There is much in this ordered way of life that is attractive; some western observers go so far as to compare it favourably with the haste and fret, the intense competitiveness, the vicious self-assertion, which are seen in so much of 'civilised' life as they have known it.

This positive attitude towards the ancient ways is far to be preferred to the ignorance and arrogant disregard with which the foreigner all too often swept aside cultures which he was too lazy to attempt to understand, and the excellences of which he did not care to appreciate. But there is one aspect of life in the old order to which the anthropologists rarely refer and to which they seem to have paid less attention than it deserves. That is the element of fear. The old way of life was not as carefree and joyful as it is sometimes represented as being. It was not exempt from the darker shadows of shame and guilt and fear, and especially the last of these three. Many spirits are good; and the ancestors, if treated with proper respect, can usually be relied on to be helpful. But there are other forces in the world, dark forces the aim of which is to injure and to destroy.

A young Christian convert in the beautiful island of Bali, where the tourists flock together, when asked what his feeling was about the shadow side of the life in which he had grown up, replied, 'Those things no longer mean anything to me. But no woman or child in Bali very much likes to go out after darkness has fallen.' Naturally it is in the dark that these evil forces are most active and most dangerous. One observer has expressed this reality in vigorous terms:

> The native aboriginal is above all fear-ridden. Devils haunt to seize the unwary; their malevolent magic shadows have waking moments, he believes that medicine men know how to make themselves invisible so that they may cut out his kidney fat, then sew him up, and rub his tongue with a magic stone to induce forgetfulness, and thereafter he is a living corpse devoted to death.[17]

All this is true, and should not be passed over without mention. Yet within this world of possible or actual danger, pre-literate man has managed to create for himself a world in which he can feel at home, surrounded by familiar things and people, ancestors and animals and human friends. That world may be very small. Many of the tribes in Papua New Guinea number no more than a

---

[17] S.D. Porteus in *Reader in Comparative Religion* (1979⁴), p. 273.

thousand people. Since many of these small nations lived in a state of continuous hostility with their neighbours, one who strayed beyond the narrow limits of the territory recognised as belonging to his tribe was immediately putting himself at risk. But within those narrow limits there was safety and warmth and a sense of being protected.

All over the world this unified and coherent life is being threatened and shattered by forces which pre-literate man is unable to control. In many areas the missionary was first in the field, with his strange talk of unknown gods, and a style of life which was at first terrifying but gradually came to seem attractive. The explorer was not far behind. The trader began to find profitable markets in unexpected places. Colonial and imperial powers stepped in, in many cases to put a stop to the destruction of whole peoples unable to protect themselves against the white man's fire-arms and the white man's diseases. Finally the tourists arrived, all too ready to gaze upon specimens of humanity that they regarded as barbarous and uncouth, and to pauperise by indiscriminate giving those whose poverty contrasted painfully with their wealth. The reaction of the weaker peoples has not in all cases been the same. Some, like the unhappy Tasmanians, simply disappeared. Others, like some of the Indian peoples in the United States, have been reduced to the shadow of a shade. Yet others, by a skilful process of adaptation, have managed to maintain a somewhat uneasy existence, in which the gains have not in every case been adequate to compensate for the loss of old skills and capacities.

We may wish that none of this had ever occurred. But this sorry picture of the conflict between the stronger and the weaker races goes back far into human history, much farther than the beginning of the contacts between the white man and the peoples of Africa, the Pacific and the Americas. The Spartans had their helots, the Romans their innumerable slaves. One part of the population of Japan is regarded as unclean. India has the problem of the scheduled communities and the tribal peoples. What the Christian is called to do is to attempt to understand what is going on, and to co-operate with those who are trying to save what is good from the past and to create a future where the hope of a future had apparently ceased to exist.

We may note three ways in which, almost everywhere, the forces of disintegration have broken up the older orders, and painfully affected the lives of both societies and individuals.

1. What has affected human life perhaps more than any other factor in the last hundred years has been the growth of cities. This phenomenon can be observed all over the world; urbanisation can be seen as a torrent which gains rapidly in speed and violence. To take one single instance: where today Nairobi stands there was in 1894 nothing but a river. Those who were building the fantastic railway which crosses the equator at 9,300 feet needed water for their repair station, and found what they needed. Now Nairobi has a population of more than half a million. Cities seem to act as magnets; they draw in new inhabitants in a steady stream, holding out the lure of hopes which can never be fulfilled. 'Detribalisation' is perhaps the most acute of the many problems by which Africa is faced today.

One result of detribalisation is the emergence of the individual as individual. In the earlier form of existence, everything fell into a pattern; the occasions for personal decision were few and far between. Of course every human being differs from every other. Even in the most fully integrated society there are differences of gifts and powers. One hunter is more skilful than another. The hunter has to decide on each expedition in which direction he will set out to look for game. But the occasions of choice are limited, and deliberate individual decision is comparatively rare. Even in so important a matter as marriage, decision is more often taken by the parents or the elders of the community than by the boy and girl concerned.

When a young man comes into the city, everything seems to be different. If he is lucky he will find groups of his own people to whom he can turn. But many of the old familiar rules seem to be inapplicable. At home almost everything was shared; here individual possession seems to be the rule. At every point decisions have to be taken, for which there seem to be no precedents, and without assurance that the right decision has been made. Gradually the new freedom, which at first seemed terrifying, comes to be accepted. The individual has emerged.

South Africa depends for its prosperity largely on manpower derived from Mozambique, Malawi and other adjacent countries. The young men come to the mines or other industrial areas, spend part of the year at work, and then return home for a period of leave. They find it extraordinarily difficult to enter again into the life of their people. They have become accustomed to a freer kind of existence, in which many of the old restrictions no longer operate. They find that they are expected to accept with docility whatever is laid down by the elders. If they do so, they feel that they have betrayed their integrity, and a smouldering resentment grows up between the older and the younger generations. If they assert their independence, the older men complain of the arrogance of the young, and deplore the idea they seem to entertain that they possess a wisdom greater than that of the ancestors who laid down lines for the behaviour of their people.

2. This is one sign of the breakdown of the ancient structure of the African peoples. Another sign is the conflict between two types of aristocracy. On the one hand there is the aristocracy which is hereditary, and is manifest in the person of the chief or chiefs. This is countered by the aristocracy of the book, which depends not on heredity but on individual efforts to learn, and so to acquire knowledge and power denied to those who have been dependent only on the traditional education given within the tribe. Sometimes the two coalesce. A number in the first generation of Anglican clergy in Uganda were chiefs by birth, but also had been educated by the missionaries during the first period of almost unlimited enthusiasm for education which accompanied the appearance of the first printed books in the Ugandan languages. In other cases the divergence is wide and deep.

Much of the recent history of the African peoples can be understood in terms of this clash between the old and the new.

In Ghana, the heir of the former kings of Ashanti was the Asantehene, the great chief who lived in the old capital Kumasi. Under British rule the Asantehene had little or no political power, but he had immense influence among his own people. Dr Nkrumah, the popular leader, could make no such claims. He was simply a school teacher, who had spent some time in America (whether he ever actually acquired the title of Doctor is doubtful), and came back with clear ideas as to the way in which a revolution could be staged in his own country. The presence of the old aristocracy was almost as much an obstacle in his way as the presence of the white man. Sometimes the chiefs have found themselves in alliance with the white man as a defender of the old ways against the greater threat from the revolutionary forces. A similar and more tragic history can be read in Uganda. In that composite territory, there were four African kingdoms, the largest and most powerful of which, Buganda, was ruled over by the Kabaka, who was regarded by the Baganda as almost divine. There was also a large northern area, bordering on the Sudan, which had never known true kingship. This did not at all suit Dr Obote, a representative of the younger and less conservative school. During his first period as prime minister Obote managed to abolish the four African kingships; the Kabaka fled from Uganda, and died in England in sad circumstances. Now Obote is back in power, but the young Kabaka is still alive, and resident in England. It appears that many of the Baganda are devoted to him, and still hope to see their divine king back in his inherited position as ruler.

3. Other instances could be cited, and from areas other than Africa. Those who think, and some of those who feel without being able to speak articulately of their feelings, are aware of what is often called a loss of identity, a crisis of identity. Who am I? What does it mean to be an African? How, in this perplexing world, do I relate myself to my past and to my inheritance? Perhaps it is French-speaking Africans such as Léopold Senghor who are most vocal on this subject. He speaks of *négritude*, though he might be hard put to it to explain exactly what he means, and is confident that as an African he has great gifts, which are to be used for the benefit of the whole world.

How, then, is a people which has lost its past to recover its identity, that wholeness of which it believes itself to have been deprived by powers that it was unable to control?

Five forces seem to be contending today for the soul of Africa, as of other regions still inhabited by pre-literate peoples.

First, there is the strong pull of the old, of the simpler life of the past, rather idealised, as it was before the coming of the white man. This was expressed in moving terms by a young Kenyan, who had passed through a mission school and been baptised, but startled a group of his Canadian fellow-students by speaking of his attachment to his earlier and pre-Christian life:

On the whole I am more a pagan than a Christian, and is that such a bad thing to be? In the tribe I learned discipline and the law of the tribe. The old women told me that I was always being watched, in the day-time by the big light, the sun, and in the night by the small lights, the moon and the stars; whatever I did would be known, and, if I broke the law of the tribe, what I had done would certainly come to light. Was that a bad way of educating the conscience of a boy? And what have I gained in Christianity that is better than what I had in the tribal system?

This same nostalgia speaks out strongly in the writings of the Ugandan poet Okot p'Bitek.[18] In the song of Lawino, an African woman looks back to things as they were, with a profound sense of loss and not of gain. It is impossible not to feel deep sympathy with those who have suffered under such experiences. There was in the ancient ways much that was beautiful and of value; all that can be done to preserve and to recover these valuable things is to be encouraged. But it is just the fact that in history the clock cannot be turned back. That old life was a life of illiteracy and monotony. It was marked by recurrent tribal wars, and to such the modern educated African, or Papuan, or Indonesian, is strongly opposed. The old ways can contribute to the recovery of identity; unaided they cannot bring it about.

Some educated Africans are deeply interested in what technology can do, and in the material benefits which it can bring. Africa was poor; the African today is convinced that he can become rich. The mineral wealth of Africa is as yet only partially disclosed, but it is already known to be immense. Nigeria has become one of the world's great producers of oil. Botswana, till recently regarded as mere desert, is now known to be rich in diamonds and probably in a great many other things. The copper of Zambia and Katanga seems to be almost inexhaustible. Zimbabwe shares with Cuba and the USSR a near monopoly of the valuable mineral chromium, widely used in the production of stainless and alloy steels.

It is right that the African should share in the good things that God has hidden beneath his soil, that he should aspire to life more affluent, or less oppressed by poverty, than he has previously known. But it can hardly be expected that the African will be

---

[18] Since this chapter was rewritten, the death of Okot p'Bitek was recorded, in an accurate and perceptive obituary notice, in *The Times* of London.

satisfied with mere materialism. He seems to be by nature a religious person; as one of his most fluent spokesmen, Professor John Mbiti, has stressed again and again, the African in his own natural circumstances is religious all the time. If one religion does not satisfy him, it is almost certain that he will find another. Another form of materialism is making strenuous efforts to capture the heart of Africa. A number of Africans who have been sent to study abroad have been deeply influenced by Marxism – by its philosophic and economic thought, and also by its intense hatred of the west. The Chinese were well installed in Burundi, until the king of that country decided that he had had enough of them and sent them all packing. The Chinese also built the long railway from Zambia to the coast in Tanzania; but, when they had finished this task, they were not encouraged to remain. With Russian and Cuban help Marxist governments have been established in two African countries, Mozambique and Angola, and these have made deep water ports available to the Russians on the Indian Ocean and on the Atlantic. Marxists are making convulsive efforts to establish a permanent hold on Ethiopia. Yet it does not seem that African, or Indonesian peoples in any large numbers have been enamoured of materialism in the form developed by Lenin and Stalin and their successors. One reason for this may be the unfavourable report brought back by students who have been sent for training in Marxist countries. One student from Uganda on his return expressed the opinion that he had enjoyed more freedom in his own country in British colonial days than had been permitted to students in Moscow. But deeper is the reason already given – the African needs religion; a system which dispenses with it is not likely to make a strong and lasting appeal to him.

For centuries Islam was a great power in Africa. It claimed to be a natural religion for the African, and to offer him a higher culture than he possessed without too greatly disturbing customs such as polygamy which were well-established in African society. Its influence was steadily moving southward, and seemed to carry all before it. Many Muslims believe that this process is still going forward; but, as we have seen, there is reason to think that the influence of Islam has reached its peak and is declining in many of the countries south of the Sahara.

In addition to the reasons mentioned in a previous chapter, two others may here be mentioned.

Africa, especially in its eastern regions, has been newly alerted to the share of the Muslims in the devastation of the continent through the slave trade. African young people had been taught in school that slavery was the white man's crime. Closer contact with history has made it plain that in East Africa, apart from a measure of participation by Portuguese in Mozambique and Frenchmen in Mauritius, the white man had very little to do with it; the trade was almost exclusively in the hands of the Arabs, who were pressing farther and farther towards the very heart of the continent. In Malawi anyone over the age of fifty is likely to have met people who had actually been carried off by Arabs into slavery. The wounds went very deep and are still felt. One interesting result is that that highly independent country has more or less adopted David Livingstone as an honorary Malawian, because of his services to the country in its time of greatest need.[19]

There is little doubt that the slave trade in one form or another still maintains a surreptitious existence. It is true that Saudi Arabia has in recent years abolished slavery. But not many years ago two men in Nigeria were sentenced to long periods of imprisonment for kidnapping; the evidence strongly suggested that the persons thus kidnapped were to be conveyed across the continent, and across the Red Sea to some port on the Arabian coast.

Except for a very small minority which is totally embedded in the past, all Africans believe in development, and are aware that the services of technology must be called in, if poor Africa is ever to become rich. But the Muslim countries as a whole are backward in the field of technology, and do not offer that of which the less developed countries feel themselves to stand in need. An investigation of the countries to which African students go for higher education is revealing. Apparently Western Germany tops the list in the contest for popularity, followed at varying distances by the French- or English-speaking countries. Russia and other countries under communist domination are less popular than they were. Muslim countries are near the bottom of the list. Arabic is one of the great languages of

---

[19] I had the honour of delivering in Blantyre the first Livingstone Memorial Lecture at the time of the centenary of his death (1973).

the world – but who wants to learn it? Will one who has studied in Egypt come back well qualified to contribute to the social or economic progress of his country? Islamic religion and philosophy seem to offer inadequate compensation for Islamic imperfection in the field of technology.

*

We are left with Christianity as the fifth and as yet unidentified power among those which are contending for the future of Africa.

In a quarter of a century the number of Christians in tropical Africa has increased twofold, and in some areas considerably more. The history of these years has as yet hardly been written.[20] Attempts to account for so vast a movement must at present be somewhat provisional, even conjectural.

It is clear that in some cases a change in social and economic order is accompanied by a felt need for a new religion. For a century the Masai in Kenya and Tanzania had been extremely resistant to the Gospel. Now this seems to be changing. Over many generations the tall and elegant Masai had been a purely pastoral people, moving here and there with their flocks, subsisting on a diet of blood and milk, and devoutly believing that at the creation God had given all the cattle in the world to the Masai as their possession. Now, with the increasing pressure of population on soil, the Masai can no longer live as they used to; they are having to take to a more settled existence and to agricultural pursuits. If the old God has failed them, perhaps they should be prepared to exchange him for another. This seems to be happening especially among the women.

When the African peoples became independent, it was thought that there would be an extensive redrawing of boundaries, as peoples, such as the Ewe in Ghana and Togo, which had been split up by harsh action on the part of European masters, coalesced in the recovery of their lost unity. This has hardly occurred at all. To a large extent the peoples are maintaining themselves within the boundaries fixed in the nineteenth century. Awareness of a

---

[20] Though a good first attempt has been made by Fr Adrian Hastings: *A History of African Christianity* (Cambridge, 1979).

common citizenship of Kenya, of Nigeria, or wherever it may be, is gradually, though in many cases slowly, replacing the tribal loyalty which was decisive in earlier days. A religion adapted to these larger units naturally enters into competition with the traditional religion of earlier times.

In many schools it is fashionable for young people to be baptised between the ages of thirteen and seventeen. In many cases this does not mean very much, and a good many of those so baptised fall away in after years. But this tendency does seem to express a rather vague sense that Christianity is better suited than the traditional religions to the modern world in which these young people expect to pass their days.

These are superficial reasons. Much more important is the question as to the Gospel which was preached to primal man, and as to the way in which it came home to him.

The missionaries, strictly orthodox as they were, preached salvation through Jesus Christ and his death. But what is actually heard is not always exactly the same as what is preached. On this Bishop John Taylor has wise words to say: What the missionaries preached was Christ; what the Baganda heard was a message about God the Father. They knew of Katonda, the supreme God, but he was to them an unknown and scarcely heeded creator. Now he was proclaimed as the focus of all existence, and yet not confined within it:

> The revelation of a transcendent, personal and righteous God was not relevant, but revolutionary to the Baganda, yet that was the Word which they heard. The fact that they did hear it, and did not at this stage, for the most part, hear the message of the Saviourhood of Christ or the power of the Spirit, though these were the themes that were being preached, suggests that this was the Word of God to them, and it was independent of the word of the preacher.[21]

The Baganda are a highly intelligent people. The missionaries had made plain to them that the distant and unkown Katonda was not at all distant – he was deeply interested in the Baganda, and had sent the missionaries to make known to them the truth about himself. From this the Baganda drew the correct inference

---

[21] J.V. Taylor: *The Growth of the Church in Buganda* (London, 1958), pp. 252-3.

that, if Katonda is interested in them, he must also be interested in the Batoro and the Banyoro, and the other neighbouring peoples with whom they had often been at war. If this is so, the message must also be passed on to them. The result of this was the astonishing wave of evangelistic activity on the part of those who had themselves only recently become Christians.

The best known of these is Apolo Kivebulaya, who went beyond what are now the boundaries of Uganda, penetrated the forest where the pygmies live, made friends with the pygmies and translated the Gospel of Mark into their language.[22] But Apolo was only one of many. Others have come to life for us in the pages of the work of Louise Pirouet.[23] This writer also has clear and pertinent things to say about those early witnesses for Christ:

> The modern preoccupation with indigenizing Christianity has led some people to suppose that Christianity was most acceptable where it could most easily be understood in terms of the old religion, and where it caused least disruption to traditional life. There is some evidence which suggests just the opposite: that it was welcomed because it offered something new. If it offered nothing radically different, why bother to change from the old way?[24]

All true Christian preaching is Trinitarian. The Baganda had discovered the Father; it was necessary that they should discover also the Son. But their discovery was not quite that which was intended and expected by the missionaries.

We have noted the element of fear by which the life of primal man was beset. To primal peoples in many areas of the world, Jesus has come as the conqueror of the demons.[25] And this is exactly as it should be; that was the way in which he came to a great many people in the ancient world. We know today, from magical papyri and other sources, much more than our fathers

---

[22] A. Luck: *African Saint: The Life of Apolo Kivebulaya* (London, 1963). The charming photographs of Apolo were taken by his friend Dr A.T. Schofield.

[23] *Black Evangelists* (London, 1978), based on deep, extensive and sympathetic research, seems to me one of the most important books on Africa ever written.

[24] *Black Evangelists*, p. 198.

[25] This is the title of a chapter in T.R. Glover's book *Jesus in the Experience of Men* (1921).

knew about the popular religion of the apostolic age. That too was an age in which men's minds were oppressed by fear. The stars could exercise malign influence on human destiny. There were eerie spirits abroad and these could take possession of the human spirit. It is for this reason that there are in the Gospels so many stories of the casting out of demons. A more critical age may see in the diseases that Jesus cured recognisable sicknesses such as epilepsy. But over all these powers, whatever they may be, that distort the life of man and inhibit development, Jesus shows himself supreme. His miracles are not works of magic; they are great acts of liberation, in which the world is restored to what in the purpose of God it was intended to become.

It is no use telling the simple, third world believer that evil spirits do not exist or that magic has no power. He has what is to him convincing evidence to the contrary. Those who have lived closest to him are not always prepared to admit that he is entirely wrong. What he can be told is that Jesus has vanquished all those hostile powers, and that the one who has put on the whole armour of God can walk without fear because no evil power can touch him.

The believer who still lives in the primal world also needs Jesus the Son in another way. Jesus came as a lawgiver, claiming the right to say 'I say unto you'. His law is a law of liberty, but it is more exacting than any law which has gone before it. The old laws and customs of the tribe are crumbling; the powerful restraints of the old corporate life are vanishing. What is to take their place? It is a consolation to the one who wishes to walk in the new way to learn that there is a yoke of the Gospel, and that the freedom which he has been promised is to be exercised within the framework of a structure which Jesus has indicated in his teaching, and carried out to perfection in his life.

Herein lies also a danger, through the inveterate tendency of the human mind towards legalism. Men and women are great inventors of laws and regulations. Take away one law, and they will quickly find another. Missionaries are often blamed for having imposed on simple societies laws which they could not understand, and which did not fit in with their understanding of life. This is true in part. But it is also true that sincere converts, just because they have had a tremendous experience of liberation from the past, tend to forget that that was an experience of grace, and to hide the joy of the new life under a somewhat uninspiring veil of rigorous and legalistic judgment. Their friends of a longer Christian tradition are compelled at times to admit that those who have become Christians have lost something of the spontaneity and gaiety of their old way of life. The remedy for this is a discovery of the meaning of the Spirit in the life of the new fellowship. The old world was a world in which the African, the Papuan, felt at home. When that old world collapses around him, he feels like Housman's rebel – 'I a stranger and afraid/In a world I never made'. Can the church of Jesus Christ provide such a believer with a fellowship larger and richer than that which was experienced before? Where the Spirit is love, there is no doubt that it can. Not all churches are spirit-filled; not all hold out the right hand of fellowship to all who come. Precisely where this quality of fellowship is most needed, in the cities where detribalised man feels loneliness in all its bitterness, there are few churches in which the stranger can feel certain of being taken in and made welcome. Even in church the newcomer may be left to feel himself an individual rather than a member enriched by the corporate life of the whole body into which he has entered.

*

A place to feel at home. This phrase expresses the regret of the new Christian for the spiritual home which once he had, and which he has not yet been successful in replacing by another. It is also the title of a notable book in which two scholars, one African and one European,[26] describe the life of one of the independent churches that are springing up in such numbers in every part of Africa, in India, and in the isles of the Pacific.

Some of these new cults or religions are bizarre. The Cargo-cults of Papua New Guinea were based on the idea that the white man had a secret which enabled him to live richly on the cargoes that came endlessly with the big ships, without apparently ever doing any work or ever paying for anything – the mystery of the cheque and the bank-draft was naturally unknown to those simple peoples. Many believed that this secret was written on the first page of the Bible, which the missionaries had carefully

---

[26] F.B. Welbourn and B.A. Ogot: *A Place to Feel at Home* (Oxford, 1966).

concealed from their converts; if this could be learned, the messianic days would come, when the black man would be on top, and the white man would deservedly be reduced to servitude.[27] Others among these churches are, however, making a serious attempt to encounter the Gospel independently of the foreigners, and to find out its true meaning for the peoples of the third world today.

Missionary opinion was in the beginning very hostile to these movements, regarding their prophets as charlatans who would bring division where there had been peace, and who would use their charismatic gifts to reintroduce old pagan customs, to the rejection of which the missionaries had with great labour attained. In recent times the point of view has considerably changed. It was discovered that some among these charismatic leaders, so far from countenancing old ways incompatible with Christian standards of conduct, were proclaiming an austere doctrine involving rejection of much that had been tolerated in the past. This became plain in, for instance, the Alice movement in Zambia. Those who came under the influence of Alice Lenshina, the remarkable woman who headed the movement, were required to give up all fetishes, amulets and charms and everything which belonged to the dark realm of non-Christian survivals. The quantity of objects delivered up was enormous. It was clear that neither missionaries nor African pastors had any idea of what was going on, and that they were startled to observe the standing in the church of some of those who had been led to make known their secret ways. The consternation cannot have been greater in Ephesus when those who had been practising curious arts came forward and confessed their deeds, and brought their secret books.[28]

It became clear that some at least of these movements were perfectly orthodox in doctrine. They had come into being simply through the desire of Africans 'to be ourselves', not to be subject to the domination of foreigners and to the restrictions that they imposed, to enjoy the freedom to express the Gospel in a more spontaneous fashion and according to an understanding of it which they had discovered for themselves. The largest of these

---

[27] G.F. Vicedom: *Church and People in New Guinea* (London 1961), pp. 58-62.
[28] Acts 19: 18, 19.

churches is the Kimbanguist Church in Zaïre, the full name of which is 'the Church of Jesus Christ upon earth through the prophet Simon Kimbangu'. Simon Kimbangu was a charismatic figure, who was imprisoned by the Belgians on the flimsiest of charges, spent thirty years in prison, and died without ever being released. The movement, now directed by the three sons of the founder, claims three million members,[29] and has clearly come to stay. When one of the leaders was asked, 'What is the status of Simon Kimbangu in your church? Is he your African Messiah?' the answer was, 'Certainly not; Jesus Christ is the Messiah, Simon Kimbangu is the prophet through whom God has given to us an understanding of the Gospel which is neither Catholic or Protestant, but simply African.'[30]

In these churches there was for a long time deep suspicion of the main-line churches, with their colonial antecedents and their links with the western churches. This seems to be passing away. Students from these churches have begun to attend theological seminaries attached to the main-line churches. The Kimbanguist church has made foreigners welcome to help in the training of its ministers, and has successfully applied for membership in the World Council of Churches. This new attitude has been reciprocated by many in the main-line churches, who are far more willing than they were to take these movements seriously and, without exaggerating as some do their numbers and their importance, to think that they may be able to contribute some things that will be of value to the whole world-wide church of Christ. If asked to indicate the salient characteristics of the Christian faith as expressed by those who have come in from the primal background, many observers would fix on the terms spontaneity, endurance, joy. If asked to specify one area in which the theology of these groups might enrich that of the older churches, they would point to the experience of wholeness – the unity of all things in Christ, and the ability to transcend the dichotomy of the secular and the religious by which the western world is afflicted.

Some are alarmed at the prospect of these younger and in many ways inventive churches going off in the pursuit of new

---

[29] Six million, according to the *World Christian Encyclopaedia* (1982).
[30] M.-L. Martin: *Kimbangu: An African Prophet and his Church* (Oxford, 1975).

experiences in religion and theology. Is there not a danger of the Christian substance being hidden or absorbed by survivals from an earlier period of existence? Is there any guarantee that they will remain within the limits of responsible Christianity? It is true that no such guarantee can be given; it has already been admitted that some of these groups are marked by aberrations, and even by regression away from Christian faith and in the direction of paganism. Of the larger and more stable movements this cannot be said. If they can hold fast to their biblical convictions and not despise the help that they can receive from other churches, time may prove that the fears were exaggerated, and that the anxieties were inflated beyond what was necessary and reasonable.

This chapter ends with a personal reminiscence. During my first period of teaching at the University of Hamburg (1956-7) I was lecturing on this theme, and in the course of my lecture dropped the remark, 'Better an African heresy than a European orthodoxy.' At that one point only, my students applauded. How right they were!

CHAPTER VII

No Faith and Faith Implicit

The word 'faith' can be used in a great many different senses. The term is used in the subtitle of this book, and it will be taken for granted by most readers that it deals with that area of human experience, or illusion, which is commonly regarded as the field of religion. From very early times there have been atheists in the world – in the book of Psalms, the fool, that is to say the man of arrogant insensitiveness, says 'There is no God' (Ps. 14: 1) – and in more recent times there have been those who, following the example of T.H. Huxley (1825–95), call themselves 'agnostics'. But, until recent times, it could be taken for granted that the vast majority of human beings, if they were not Christians, would be adherents of some identifiable religion, such as Hinduism or Buddhism, or perhaps of one of those systems which do not lend themselves so readily to definition or identification; or that, at least, if they made no definite religious profession, would manifest in action certain ideals and standards bearing a relationship to what is commonly known as the sphere of religion. This is no longer the case. Many, especially in the west, have not merely abandoned religion in any recognisable form, but have settled down happily to live in a purely three-dimensional world, and would not admit the applicability of the term 'faith' to the basis on which they build their manner of living.

For the sake of clarity it will be well to pause and ask what it is that the man of no faith believes himself to have been rejecting, and whether his understanding of faith would be acceptable to the Christian. St Paul (2 Cor. 5: 7) tells us that we walk not by sight but by faith. Faith here is related to that which is invisible but need not for that reason be any the less real. Sight does not mean in this context the act of seeing or the capacity for vision, but the thing seen, that which can be observed by the senses and made the object of intellectual analysis. Modern man would probably express the contrast differently, but this is essentially what the religious debate is all about. Such a man is prepared to accept affirmations made on the basis of observations and experiments which are accessible to all, and conclusions which are based directly on the evidence or on inferences from that evidence. Assent to such affirmation seems to him the only assent worthy of a reasonable man. Faith, as he understands the word, seems to deal with that which is accepted on authority, because someone said it a long time ago, and other people have since repeated it a great many times; or on faulty deductions from inadequate evidence; or on a 'leap of faith' made in defiance of such evidence as there is; or on sheer fantasy related to a world entirely different from that with which the reasonable man has to do.

An eminent scholar has recently written a book with the impressive title *The Secularization of the European Mind*,[1] to which we might add also the Asian, the American and the African mind. We are dealing with a world-wide phenomenon, in which the development of scientific knowledge and the growth of technological skills seem to set themselves firmly in opposition to all the traditional forms of religion. This has led to a society described by a thoughtful writer as 'That society in which those who govern justify themselves by appeal to technical experts who, in turn, justify themselves by appeal to scientific forms of knowledge. And beyond the authority of science there is no appeal.'[2] To this he adds by way of explanation: 'That the vital needs of man are purely technical in character. If a problem does not have a technical solution, it is not a real problem.'[3] As a fairly accurate definition of all that is implied in secularisation, this may be regarded as useful. But secularism is a complex phenomenon. Before we consider it in its purely negative aspects, it will be well to consider three aspects of it, in which a possibility of faith still exists though not faith in the specifically religious sense of the term.

---

[1] W.O. Chadwick (Cambridge, 1976, 1978).
[2] T. Roszak: *The Making of a Counter Culture* (1970), p. 8.
[3] T. Roszak, p. 15.

Ask a Christian from where he thinks that the greatest danger to religion threatens and he is likely, especially if he is an American, to answer 'from Marxism'.

This is by no means an implausible answer. It is claimed that religious liberty exists in Russia, but this is understood to mean that there must be the fullest possible freedom for anti-religious propaganda as well as for the practice of religion. Anti-God campaigns are launched with the full approval of 'the party'. No secret is made of the fact that the Marxist regards religion as a mere survival from the capitalist past, that he is perplexed by the toughness with which religion refuses to accept its dissolution before the advancing power of science, and that he looks forward with hope and expectation to the day when religion will finally disappear. It is not only Christianity which is threatened: Judaism and Islam are equally under the ban. But Christianity is perhaps more suspect than others because of its international character and its close connection with the hated world of capitalistic power. Religions can continue to exist, in a Marxist-controlled economy, only if they limit their concerns rigidly to what happens within their place of worship, and make no attempt to intervene in the social, political and international affairs which the state has claimed as belonging exclusively to itself.

All this is true. But Karl Marx must not be held responsible for everything that passes as Marxism today. Lenin, Trotsky and Stalin made Marxism their own, but as it emerged from their hands it had taken on forms which Marx is hardly likely to have foreseen. A distinction must be drawn between what the Marxists have made of Marxism and what is actually found in the teachings of the founder. In the latter, Christians will find much to interest them, and some features which seem to hold out a possiblility of Christian-Marxist dialogue.[4]

In the first place, Marx has brought us back firmly to the terrestrial realities, which religious people have been inclined to overlook or to treat with less than the seriousness which they

---

[4] For a well-informed and perceptive account, from a Christian point of view, of what Marx actually taught, see N. Lash: *A Matter of Hope: A Theologian's Reflections on the Thought of Karl Marx* (DLT 1981).

deserve.[5] There is no authority in the Gospels for this kind of 'religious' attitude; Jesus is much concerned with loaves and fishes and other very material entities. He tells us that we are not to take anxious thought about such things. But, though he reminds us that man shall not live by bread alone, he never for a moment doubts that man shall live by bread. 'Give ye them to eat' still stands as his command to his church. If at any time the church has been inclined to spiritualise this command, to think that it has fulfilled its duty by providing man with spiritual food and so preparing him for life in heaven as a compensation for poverty and hardship on earth, the word of Christ is there to rebuke it. If we had ever been inclined to forget the words of Christ, Marx is there to make sure that in the modern world we cannot do so. It matters immensely that man should have enough to eat and to wear, and a reasonable home to live in, and such social and economic conditions as favour genuinely human life. When these things are lacking, man becomes alienated from himself, he loses the truly human quality of life.[6]

Secondly, Marx had been responsible for a new understanding of history which is today almost universally accepted. We are all Marxists to a far greater degree than is generally recognised. The *Communist Manifesto* was first published in 1848. It took about a generation for its significance to dawn on historians. But, if we contrast history as written before 1878 with history written since that date, we cannot but become aware of the change. Earlier history was written in terms of dynasties and wars and political changes, and little attention was paid to economic and social factors. Economic history is a comparative newcomer in the field of history writing. The English pioneer William Cunningham published his first great book, *The Development of English Industry and Commerce in Modern Times*, just a century ago, in 1882. Now it is taken for granted that we cannot understand history aright unless we recognise that changes in methods of production, distribution and communication affect the lives of men and the movement of history more than all but the most

---

[5] The title of an interesting book by Professor G. Thils of the university of Louvain is *Théologie des réalités terrestres* (Louvain, 1946[2]).

[6] Alienation, *Entfremdung*, is one of the great Marxist ideas, though Marx seems to have used the word much more frequently in his earlier than in his later works.

revolutionary of political organisations. This is true of almost all history writing, and not only of those areas which are specifically labelled 'economic'.

Thirdly, Marx claimed, not without reason, to have made Hegel's dialectic stand on its head, and to have established the principle that the business of the philosopher is not to understand the world so much as to change it. Marx held that history advances according to irreversible and immanent laws; but he also believed that, through scientific understanding of these laws and a willing 'acceptance of necessity', it is possible to serve the inevitable revolution and to advance its cause, just as the refusal of necessity may slow down the progress of the revolution, and this is the unpardonable crime.

It is sometimes said that, at a time at which the churches were deaf to the cry of misery that arose from the new industrial proletariat, Marx heard that cry and was moved by compassion to champion the cause of the so-called working class. Two arguments can be brought to bear against the accuracy of such a statement. Recent research has shown that the church was very far from being deaf, at least in England, to the needs of the poor, and that in some of the worst affected areas an overwhelming majority of the clergy were behind the great Lord Shaftesbury in his campaign for the better conditions provided by the Factory Acts.[7] And compassion is hardly a virtue which one would associate with the real Karl Marx. He was an angry, contentious, authoritarian man, who managed to quarrel with almost all who had at one time or another been his associates.

But on the duty of the man of vision to see to it that society changes and is changed the Christian can heartily concur with Marx. There has been a strain of pessimism in Christian theology, a concentration on the eschatological hope and the second coming of Christ, which is easily compatible with a laissez-faire attitude towards politics and economics, and the supposition that in these regions nothing can really be changed for the better. It is not surprising that much attention has been attracted by the book of Professor Jürgen Moltmann: *The Theology*

---

[7] All this is plainly set out in J.G. Gill: *The Ten Hours' Parson, Christian Social Action in the Eighteen-Thirties* (London, 1959); and *Parson [G.S. Bull] of Byerley* (London 1963).

of Hope.[8] Moltmann is one of the German scholars who has made a deep and sympathetic study of Marxism, and is much concerned about the possibility of Marxist-Christian dialogue. He came to his views on Christian responsibility perhaps by way of Karl Marx rather than by way of the New Testament; but the challenge he has thrown out can only be welcomed by those who have long believed, with Frederick Denison Maurice and all his disciples, that society can in a measure be transformed and that it is the business of Christians to transform it.

So far Christians can go with Karl Marx himself. But even in Marxism as it has further developed they can discern something that it is hard to describe by any other word than 'faith'.

Marx was a Jew who had been baptised. He was well acquainted with Christianity and seems to have found it hard to get away from it. His system sounds at times almost like a parody of New Testament teaching. Here too there is an innocent victim, the proletariat, through whose suffering the world is to be redeemed. Here is the eschatological hope, the coming kingdom – only here it is the kingdom of man, and not the kingdom of God. But the eager expectation with which the convinced Marxist looks forward to the coming of that kingdom, his absolute certainty that he has the clue to the future and that that future is in his hands, is something that the Christian can understand, since it is no more than a transcription into another key of the certainty which he entertains himself.[9]

Moreover, the Marxist conviction, no less than the Christian, has shown its capacity to breed martyrs. We in the west are more aware of the massacres for which the Marxist has been responsible, of the martyrs whose blood he has had upon his sword. It is important not to forget the other side – the communists who remained true to their convictions during the German occupation of France and gave a lead to the resistance,

---

[8] Original German edition, *Theologie der Hoffnung* (1964); Eng. trans. London (1967). The original German quickly ran through five printings. In view of the strongly this-worldly character of Moltmann's thought, it is ironic that in the catalogue of the London Library, which I gratefully use, his book appears under the heading 'Religion: Future State'!

[9] But the Christian cannot but ask why it is that the Marxist system has so far failed to produce equality among human beings, or a more humane political and economic system. Marxist faith is not recognisably effective in its works.

and the many in other countries who have endured oppression, imprisonment, and sometimes death for the sake of what they believed to be the truth.

These are the aspects of Marxism that have made possible the development of a Marxist-Christian dialogue of a type and on a scale that would hardly have been thought possible a generation ago. The first international meeting of Christians with Marxists, at which Professor Moltmann was one of the speakers, was held in June 1967. The movement for closer encounter has spread to France, to Czechoslovakia and to other countries on the continent of Europe. A number of the leaders in the movement for 'liberation theology' in Latin America have gone farther than most of their colleagues elsewhere in frankly accepting the Marxist analysis of society, and in holding that revolution is the only method by which the necessary changes can be brought about.[10]

The pathway to understanding is not free from obstacles. Some of the Marxists who have taken part in a dialogue with Christians have fallen into disfavour with their fellow-Marxists; some of the Marxist-Christian theologians are deeply suspected by others of the tribe. But a beginning has been made, and on the part of those most deeply concerned there is no thought of turning back.

Christians have often looked at Marxism with more or less favourable eyes. But this is a two-way process. Marxists have also begun to look at Christianity, and to take it seriously; the most impressive work known to me is *A Marxist Looks at Jesus*.[11] The Czech writer, while remaining a convinced Marxist, holds firmly that Jesus is a historical figure with whom his fellow-Marxists ought greatly to concern themselves. Two quotations may make clear the deep seriousness of this work, and of the promise that it holds out for a real dialogue between Christians and Marxists:

Even though ... men with the words of Jesus on their lips have made

---

[10] On the question whether revolution must always be violent these Marxist-Christian thinkers are divided.

[11] Milan Machoveč (London, 1976), This work passes in German (Stuggart, 1972) under the better title *Jesus for Atheists*.

and make the harshest demands on others while absolving themselves, though the principle of the 'speck in the eye of the brother' was one of the reasons which led Marx to accuse Jesus' followers of hypocrisy, double-dealing and Pharisaism, one must nevertheless acknowledge that something immensely great and important entered human history through the message of Jesus... That is why Jesus' demand for change, his conception of the eschatological call to conversion could for centuries be the basis for the intellectual history of the West from St Augustine to Luther and Hegel (pp. 111–12).

In Christianity the dogmatised image of Jesus Christ has never been able thoroughly to banish the image of the man Jesus of Nazareth. This has often been driven underground, preserved by saints or heretics who often were brought to the very limit of their human strength and possibilities because they asserted the meaning of Jesus' words against the authoritarian guardians of dead conventions (p. 203).

This is not Christian faith. But has a Christian any right to sweep it away as though it had no value?

A second form of no-faith, or of qualified faith, is that which calls itself scientific humanism, or simply humanism for short. This is associated especially with the name of Sir Julian Huxley, the learned biologist, who was at one time president of the United Nations Educational, Scientific and Cultural Organisation, and whose aim is neatly summed up in the title of his book *Religion without Revelation*.[12]

It is the idea of revelation to which Sir Julian especially takes objection. In the world of science man is left on his own. He has to observe, to classify, to form theories, reject or modify them, and thus laboriously to understand and to master his world. No outside power will come to his aid and supply him with information which would otherwise be inaccessible to him. It would be very nice if, as in *Alice in Wonderland*, plants and liquids were neatly labelled 'Eat me. Drink me.' In our real world the

---

12 London, 1927; new edn. 1979. The same ideas are set out by a large variety of writers in the work, *The Humanist Frame* (London, 1961), of which Sir Julian Huxley was the editor.

human race has had to discover, by often painful experiment, which are the poisonous and which the harmless substances. The idea of special divine aid to man belongs to the childhood of the race and should now be discarded. To believe that such aid is possible, still more to regard ourselves as in any way dependent on it, would be to condemn ourselves to perpetual infancy. We must stand upon the dignity of our manhood, and accept the responsibility and the risks without either timidity or rashness. The responsibility, as Sir Julian sees it, has become specially heavy in our time. Until now the progress of evolution has been haphazard and uncontrollable by man. Now science has put into our hands the means by which we can discern the direction in which evolution is going or ought to go, and we ourselves can take a hand in determining, to some extent at least, the direction.

The evolutionary process, as now embodied in man, has for the first time become aware of itself, is studying the laws of its own unfolding, and has a dawning realization of the possibilities of its own future guidance or control. In other words, evolution is on the verge of becoming internalised, conscious and self-directing.[13]

A somewhat similar view had been reached, though not along exactly the same route, by the Jesuit palaeontologist Pierre Teilhard de Chardin. It was this that led Sir Julian to interest himself in Teilhard de Chardin's views: in consequence the world was presented with the edifying spectacle of the sceptical English biologist writing the preface to the most celebrated work of the pious and basically orthodox French Jesuit, *The Phenomenon of Man*.[14]

Certainly there have been times at which Christians have understood revelation in the sense to which Sir Julian takes exception – as the communication of information to which men would not otherwise have access. Such a view belongs rather to the past than to the present. Once this little misunderstanding has been cleared up, there is much in the attitude of the humanists which Christians can only welcome and approve.

---

[13] J. Huxley (ed.): *Evolution as a Process* (London, 1954) p. 13.
[14] *Le Phénomène Humain* (Paris, 1955); Eng. trans. *The Phenomenon of Man* (London, 1959).

There has been a great tradition of Christian humanists, who have delighted in all the manifestations of human creativity, and have made their own contributions to man's investigation of his world.[15] Moreover, it is to be noted that a number of professed humanists desire to find a place for many things to which Christians attach particular value. They appreciate art. They recognise that, if human life is to be safe and orderly, there must be a place for morals and ethical principles. Some would even find a place for religion, provided that this is purely immanent – it must be no more than man's reverence for the highest ideals that he himself has been able to discover.

The weakness of the humanists is a widespread failure to recognise the power of evil in the world. If all human beings were as nice and as virtuous as the best of the humanists (unaware as many of them are of their debt to the Christian tradition), the world would be a better place than it is. But most of us have had experience in ourselves of the truth of William Temple's remark: 'The trouble is that I can be good if I want to, but I don't want to.' It is the problem of the rebel will that scars the past of the human race and haunts its present. Drug addicts are not in general wicked; they are weak, and need to be cared for and helped. It is hard, however, not to feel that those who make themselves rich by engaging in the drug-traffic have wilfully, deliberately and defiantly sold themselves to that which they know perfectly well to be evil. No Christian would deny that such people can be saved; but neither they, nor the victims of their malpractices, are likely to be saved by good advice.

So we can applaud what can only be called the faith of the humanists as far as it goes, and can indulge the hope that they may come to be aware of a number of things that they have overlooked, and so be led to see that they must go farther, if they are to be consistent in following to its final conclusion the argument that has led them to their present position.

*

---

[15] As one outstanding study of such a contributor one may mention C.E. Raven: *John Ray: Naturalist* (Cambridge, 1950[2]).

There is a third use of the term secularisation, to which some attention should be paid, since it has become current in certain circles, and is liable to lead to a good deal of confusion. To put it bluntly: is secularisation a friend or an enemy of Christian life and Christian civilisation?

When, in 1928, Christians from all over the world (but not from the Roman Catholic section of the Christian church) met at Jerusalem for the second World Missionary Conference, the attention of the members was drawn to the great increase of secularism, a negative outlook which many regarded as the antithesis of the Christian faith and as the greatest danger to it. Some were prepared to go so far as to suggest that the adherents of all the theistic religions should form an alliance to defend the religious outlook on the world against the secular menace.

A quite different approach was adopted by a number of Christian theologians, who posed the question whether the secularisation of thought must necessarily be regarded as such an evil thing; should not Christians perhaps regard it as part of God's providential ordering of the world, as something that they ought to welcome rather than to reject? The principal champion of this view was Professor Friedrich Gogarten, who in 1953 published a book with the title: *Peril and Hope of the New Age: Secularisation as a Theological Problem.*[16] Gogarten distinguishes between two views of nature – the mythical, in which nature is understood as possessing mysterious powers, before which man must bow in insignificance; and the rational or secular, in which man sees nature objectively as something which it is his right to investigate and to master. This is what is meant by the secularisation of the world. It was in ancient Israel that the protest was first raised against the 'sacralising' of all being, against the supremacy of fate, against the divinising of kings and kingdoms.[17]

With the emergence of the idea of God as the creator of the world,

man did not face a world full of ambiguous and capricious gods who

---

16 *Verhängnis und Hoffnung der Neuzeit: Die Säkularisierung als theologisches Problem* (Stuttgart, 1953).

17 A. van Leeuwen: *Christianity in World History* (London, 1965), p. 331.

were alive in the objects of the natural world. He had to do with one supreme creator God whose will was steadfast. Nature was thus abruptly desacralised, stripped of many of its arbitrary, unpredictable, and doubtless terrifying aspects.[18]

These ideas have become familiar to English readers, not directly from Gogarten, few of whose works have been translated into English, but through Dr A. van Leeuwen's book, *Christianity in World History*, the popularity of which is vouched for by the fact that a second printing was called for only a year after the first appearance of the book. Van Leeuwen develops the ideas of Gogarten extensively and persuasively. This secular view of the world derives from Christian ideas, and in particular from the idea of God as creator. It is this secular approach that has made possible the development of science in the modern world. Hence, although science has often detached itself from its Christian roots, this is a development of which Christians ought not to be afraid, and which they ought rather to welcome. In any case, this tendency is now irreversible. Western culture is an offspring of the Christianisation of the west. Wherever western culture has spread, it carries with it the destruction of the mythical view of the world, which is still that of the non-Christian religions. It may seem that the western world is growing less religious than it was; but this does not seriously matter, since 'Christianity is now operating in the shape of a technological culture, which may be said to be its secularised form.'[19]

Van Leeuwen's book is based on wide though uneven learning. But it is confusing, and often the exact direction of the argument is difficult to grasp. This is partly due to a fundamental defect of terminology. At one point in the quotation given above, reference is made to the sacralisation of everything. The correct term for the opposite process is desacralisation, and to this word van Leeuwen, and his translator, should have confined themselves. Instead, he tries to make a distinction between secularisation, in the sense indicated above, which he regards as a good thing, and secularism, which he regards as a bad thing. But

---

[18] T.S. Derr: *Ecology and Human Need* (Philadelphia, 1975), p. 11.
[19] J. Macquarrie: *God and Secularity* (London, 1968), p. 58.

the distinction is not clear to the ordinary reader, and endless confusion has been the result.

In English, the contrast between the secular view of the world and the religious is that between a world from which God has been once and for all excluded and which therefore is to be understood only in three-dimensional terms, and a world in regard to which the possibility will be at least entertained that there is another aspect which can never be reduced to the three-dimensional, and which therefore holds out as arguable the hypothesis that God exists and that he matters. The danger is that, under the influence of western science and technology, the heirs of ancient cultures in India and elsewhere may not merely carry out the necessary task of desacralisation, but may move onward to the point of secularism, that is, to the total abandonment of anything that goes beyond what men can touch and see and handle.

Experience shows that this is no mere theoretical danger. When the British government, from 1855 onwards, undertook the task of introducing western education into India, out of consideration for the feelings of the non-Christian peoples of that country a guarantee was given that there should be no religious or moral teaching in the schools controlled by the government, though there would be freedom for such instruction in schools set up by religious bodies. Even a century ago the daily and periodical press in India was flooded with bitter protests from writers of all classes against the 'godless' education that was being provided – old religious traditions and ways of looking at things were being destroyed, a vacuum created which evil spirits of every kind were rushing in to fill.

Moreover, it is not the case that the entry of the scientific and technological understanding of the world will immediately be followed by the disappearance of the mythical or magical view. Oil and water can co-exist without commingling; so can the scientific and the magical understanding of the world. Advertisements in the Indian papers reveal the regularity with which students about to take an honours examination in physics will purchase an amulet 'guaranteed to supply the wearer with the ability to pass every examination', to help them in the examination room.

Enough has been written to show that the controversy, if controversy it really was, arose only from inaccuracy in the use of words and imprecision in thought.

Few today would deny the benefits to be derived from scientific research, and from the diffusion of scientific knowledge and thinking through the world. Christians, who are committed by their belief in God as creator to the view that all knowledge of the truth is from God, and that every scientific discovery is in its degree a revelation of the wisdom and purpose of God, would not wish to withhold a tribute to all that scientific progress has done for the welfare of the human race.

Equally, however, few of those who have pondered the history of the human race in the twentieth century would be likely to hold that the knowledge of science and the application of the refinements of technology alone will be of benefit to mankind. The Germans were among the most advanced nations; in some fields of technology they led the world; yet this did not save them from an almost passive submission to the demands of totalitarianism and a tame acceptance of the horrors of Nazi rule. How this could come about appears to be a riddle which it passes the wit of man to solve. If there is any truth at all in Christianity, the church must continue to protest against the Promethean arrogance of man in supposing that he can do it all himself, that he can master nature and the world without looking beyond the narrow confines of space, time and matter to some as yet undisclosed forces which may save him from disaster.

The stage has now been cleared for the consideration of secularism, in the exact and proper sense of the term, as a point of view or understanding of the universe, and of secularisation, as a process through which man can impose his will on the universe without reference to any real or imagined powers outside himself.

Historians and others have debated the question, perhaps unanswerable, of the date or period at which we may regard the modern world as having been born. The eminent French academician Paul Hazard[20] has argued persuasively, on the basis

---

[20] In his book *La Crise de la conscience européenne 1680-1715* (Paris, 1961[2]; Eng. trans. *The European Mind*, London, 1963).

of immense learning, that we should look not to the Renaissance or the Reformation, terms which it is difficult to define with the necessary precision, but to that last quarter of the seventeenth century in which Newton produced his *Principia Mathematica* (1687), and John Locke published his *Essay Concerning Human Understanding* (1690). Newton brought order into a chaotic universe, and scattered for good many haunting mythologies; Locke taught us, in Greek phrase, to think human thoughts, to abandon speculation and to recognise the limits of what is possible for the human intellect. Newton was a devout, though unorthodox, Christian believer; Locke paid at least lip service to Christian faith, though the exact nature of his belief may be open to question. Neither had the intention of expelling God from his world. And yet, perhaps unknowing, they did start the process through which God was excluded from the world as no more than an exploded myth or a distant and non-operative deity, and man was left in confrontation with a world from which transcendence had been banished.

Perhaps the first scientist to proclaim the total autonomy of science, its emancipation from religious considerations, was the French mathematician and astronomer Pierre Simon de Laplace (1749-1827). What Laplace wrote, in his *Essai philosophique sur la probabilité* (1814),[21] has so often been quoted and misquoted that it may be well to note exactly what he said:

> We should then regard the present state of the universe as the consequence of its previous state, and as the cause of that which will follow it. Consider the case of an intelligence which in any given instant was able to comprehend all the forces by which nature is animated, and the situation, respectively, of all the entities of which nature is made up. If that intelligence was sufficiently vast to submit all these data to analysis, it could embrace under the same formula the movement of the largest bodies in the universe and those of the lightest atoms; nothing for such an intelligence would be uncertain, and the future no less than the past would be present to its eyes.

Tradition records the equally famous story of the conversation between Laplace and the emperor Napoleon. 'Monsieur Laplace,'

---

[21] Paris, 1825[5], pp. 3–4.

said the emperor, 'they tell me that you have written this big book on the System of the Universe[22] and have never even mentioned the Creator.' 'Sire,' replied Laplace, 'I had no need of that hypothesis.' Laplace was too prudent to deny outright the existence of a Creator; he was simply asserting the mutual independence of science and religion; these deal with wholly different spheres, neither of which overlaps with the other. But if God is reduced to the Deist concept of a creator, who after one act of creation left his universe to follow the course laid down by unalterable laws, he might seem to be no longer very interesting.

There have always been scientists who were also devoutly religious men. The incomparable Michael Faraday (1791–1867), who by his experiments in the fields of electricity and magnetism has perhaps done more than any other human being to alter the face of the earth, saw no contradiction between these achievements and devout membership of the small Christian body of the Sandemanians, in which he was an elder. The friends of Sir Joseph John Thomson, whose famous lecture delivered at the Royal Institution on 30 April 1897 may be taken as the starting point of nuclear research, knew that he was a believing Christian as well as an outstanding scientist. We now know, on the authority of Lady Thomson, that he knelt humbly in prayer every day of his life. A.S. Eddington, whose delightful book *The Nature of the Physical World* (Cambridge, 1928) can still be recommended as an introduction to the modern understanding of the world, found his spiritual home in the Society of Friends. But a large number, perhaps the majority, of scientists in the nineteenth century, were quite content to say goodbye to God, and to devote their attention to a universe 'unmysterious, mechanically determined... basically simple in structure at the atomic level, and, statistically at least, unchanging in form'.[23]

So the scientist, and his disciples, may well echo the words of Laplace, if the question of God and religion is raised: 'I have no need of that hypothesis; I have plenty to occupy me in the world which I know and can observe; I do not feel tempted to explore what cannot be more than a hypothetical world, and to exchange

[22] Napoleon was probably referring to the work of 1790, *Exposition du système du monde*.

[23] A.P. Peacocke: *Creation and the World of Science* (Oxford, 1979) p. 54.

my certainties for the improbabilities which are all that the Christian faith can offer.'

Some of the scientists, then, have dismissed the idea of God as unnecessary if not actually harmful. Not to be outdone, the philosophers have weighed in, and declared the case against God, if not proven, so nearly proven as to make him irrelevant.

In the nineteenth century the attacks launched against the Christian faith by Thomas Henry Huxley (1825-95) and W.K. Clifford (1845-79) were so petulant as to seem almost vindictive. The attacks of later philosophers are less histrionic and more sophisticated, but perhaps all the more deadly for that. If their arguments proved to be sound and convincing, there would be nothing left to argue about; any form of theistic faith, and not only faith in Jesus Christ, would be as dead as a doornail.

Some years ago Professor J.N. Findlay believed that he had succeeded in proving the existence of God impossible. He claimed that, since theism is committed to asserting the necessary existence of God, 'the Divine existence is either senseless or impossible'.[24]

Professor Anthony Flew, in *God and Philosophy* (1966), has expounded in 194 pages what he believes to be a conclusive demonstration that the Christian idea of God in untenable. Fortified by his Methodist upbringing and by a considerable acquaintance with Christian theology, he has built up, on the basis of what he calls the Stratonician presumption, what he regards as an unanswerable case against Christian belief. Strato was the successor next but one to Aristotle as head of the Lyceum in Athens. His principle, as defined by Flew (p. 69), is that 'whatever characteristics we think ourselves able to discern in the universe as a whole are the underivative characteristics of the universe itself. This is for us atheism.' He repeats the claim on the last page of the book:

We therefore conclude... that the universe itself is ultimate: and, hence, that whatever science may from time to time hold to be the most fundamental laws of nature must, equally provisionally, be

---

[24] *New Essays in Philosophical Theology* (Oxford, 1967), pp. 54-5. Professor Findlay later changed his mind. See further D.Z. Phillips (ed.): *Religion and Understanding* (Oxford, 1967).

taken as the last words in any series of answers to questions as to why things are as they are. The principles of the world lie themselves 'inside' the world.

Both from the side of the natural sciences, and from that of philosophy, the scales seem to be heavily weighted against any form of religious belief. It is certainly difficult to be a Christian believer. Yet the possibility has to be faced whether it is not really more difficult to be an honest atheist. The point has been put somewhat trenchantly by John Macquarrie, whom no one could accuse of being unaware of the problems involved:

> From some of the books being put out nowadays, one might conclude that atheism had proved its case and is the only possible belief for any educated and up to date person... This is an utterly ridiculous and arrogant claim. I should say myself that theism is a much more *reasonable* belief than atheism, and always has been... The very fact that there is a world rather than just nothing, that this is an ordered and structured world rather than just chaos, and that this world has brought forth spiritual and personal beings, makes atheism a most improbable thesis.[25]

Macquarrie may have given us a useful hint. It is difficult to be both intelligent and an atheist. What is possible within the limits of this chapter is, perhaps, to look at the views of some who would rule out the religious aspect of human life, and to consider whether the views that they hold do not contain within themselves, perhaps without the knowledge of those who hold them, indications which reach out beyond the limits of atheism.

Macquarrie speaks of an ordered and structured world. But can it be *proved* that this is an ordered and structured world? I do not think that it can be proved. But this need not unduly disturb us. A number of affirmations are almost universally taken to be true, though absolutely convincing proof of their truth has never been satisfactorily carried out. The best known is perhaps Goldbach's conjecture that every even number greater than two is the sum of two prime numbers. This has never been proved, though it has been shown to hold good in every case to which it

---

25 *God and Secularity* (London, 1968), p. 108.

has been applied, even to millions of numbers.[26] Similarly, Avogadro's law, relating to the volumes of gases at the same temperature and pressure, has been shown experimentally to work, though definitive proof is still lacking. So, though the structural consistency of the universe cannot be proved, and though its structure may be more flexible than was at one time supposed, scientific work would be impossible unless the scientist felt able to take for granted what he cannot prove, that he has a generally orderly and reliable universe to work with. If this were not so, astrology would have as good a chance of being true as astronomy.[27]

If, then, there is at least a probability that the world is ordered and structured, how did it get so? Some atheists seem to believe in the eternity of the physical universe, and so avoid the question as to how anything came to be. Others, knowing well that many questions may be asked to which no answer can be found, still feel themselves impelled to ask whether all things had a beginning and, if so, of what nature that beginning might be. It seems that a number of responsible scientists are tending towards the view of the 'big bang'.[28] In a brilliant book, which has no religious stance, for or against, *The First Three Minutes*, Steve Weinberg has calculated that the original state of this universe requires a 1,000/1 ratio of protons to nuclear particles, and that everything that follows from that initial burst of incandescent energy can be traced through to the universe as we now know it. Weinberg, as an honest scientist, recognises that at this point scientific explanation halts. But this just moves the ultimate question one stage further back; what caused the initial and immense explosion of energy? The Christian thinks that he knows. He has learned to think of God as illimitable energy; why should not that energy disclose itself in something other than itself? Clearly this cannot be proved; at least it takes seriously the

---

[26] Goldbach formulated his principle in 1742. Every mathematician I think, takes it for granted that it is true, even in the absence of irrefragable proof.

[27] This is the point laboured almost to excess by Professor Stanley L. Jaki, in such works as *Cosmos and Creation* (1981), and in his Gifford Lectures *The Road of Science and the Ways to God* (Edinburgh, 1978).

[28] This is not the only view. It has to compete with the theories of a steady-state universe, and an oscillating universe. On these see A.R. Peacocke: *Creation and the World of Science*, pp. 97-9.

fact of order in the world, and recognises the possibility that this universe has its origin in something other than itself. The universe may be very old, but it is neither eternal nor self-explanatory.

Mention has been made of the possibility that the universe is not quite so calculable and predictable as Laplace imagined it to be. In 1927 Werner Heisenberg put forward his 'uncertainty principle', involving an element of 'randomness' in the universe. This has given rise to some rather fantastic views and theories; not long after Heisenberg announced his discovery, a scientist well qualified to pass a judgment suggested disapprovingly that the time would come when the Christian believer would make use of the principle to support his doctrine of the freedom of the will, whereas the atheist would use it as justification for his view that chance and chance alone rules in the universe.[29] Heisenberg's work was that of a physicist, and relates only to physical phenomena; it deals only with the fact that, in the micro-world of sub-atomic existents, the laws which hold in a larger world do not obtain, and that we have to deal with averages rather than precise calculations. This does introduce an element of flexibility into the universe, of which account must be taken. The important change is that the theory has put paid to the idea of the purely objective observer – 'the scientist now finds that he in fact has a role in the creation of the world that he is describing... even in so traditional a model of an objective science as physics, the completely uninvolved spectator has been shown to be an impossibility'.[30]

The idea of randomness has been introduced, though in a very different connection, in a work by Jacques Monod, which has been very widely read, *Chance and Necessity* (London, 1972): 'The ancient covenant is in pieces; man at last knows that he is alone in the unfeeling immensity of the universe out of which he emerged only by chance' (p. 167). Monod's point is that, on the molecular level, genetic mutations are unpredictable, and that the existence and development of life, including the life of human

[29] See P.W. Bridgman in *Harper's Magazine* (1929), pp. 443–51, quoted in *Encycl. Brit.* (11th edn.) s.v. 'Uncertainty Principle', vol. 22, p. 680.

[30] R. Schlegel: 'The Impossible Spectator' (1975), quoted in A.R. Peacocke: *Creation and the World of Science*, p. 56.

beings, are due to chance only. Man has been accustomed to read his own consciousness into inanimate nature, and this is now seen to be illegitimate. Monod draws from his argument the conclusion that human life is meaningless. It may seem paradoxical that he does not draw from his theories the pessimistic conclusion that nothing is worth while; human existence may be absurd; but the autonomy and validity of human values, especially as these are authenticated by the results of scientific study, are to be maintained. In terms a little like those used by Rādhākrishnan in refuting a deterministic interpretation of the law of *karma*, Monod is convinced that, even in a world marked by randomness, man has a high vocation: 'Neither his destiny not his duty have been written down. The Kingdom above or the darkness below; it is for him to choose.'[31] The voice of the unbeliever seems to be strangely akin to the voice of the Christian believer.

Christians, as against Leibniz ('On the ultimate origin of things', 1697), have long been familiar with the idea that God's creative activity need not have been exhausted by the production of one universe, that with which we are familiar, but that he may have, or intend to have, under his control an unlimited number of universes so different from ours that we cannot even conceive what they may be like.[32] This, however, is the only universe which we know. As knowledge advances, scientists become increasingly aware of the limitations, and as it appears the inescapable limitations, of our knowledge – 'an island in the infinite ocean of the unknown', as one of them has picturesquely expressed it. On the other hand, scientists have been prepared to recognise, as they perhaps did not in the days when the influence of Laplace was still strong, that one of the most remarkable facts about this universe is that it has been able to produce sentient beings, which are able to stand back from the universe, to subject it to investigation, in part at least to understand it, to manipulate it, and in part to change its character. It is clear that if what the physicists call the fundamental constants (the velocity of light, etc.) had been only slightly different, none of this could have

---

[31] J. Monod: *Chance and Necessity*, (1972), p. 167.
[32] On the creativity of God, Keith Ward has written well in *Rational Theology and the Creativity of God* (1982), especially ch. 4, 'Creation', pp. 67–89.

come about – 'no galaxies, no stars, no life would have emerged' (Sir Bernard Lovell). In the light of what has come to be called 'the anthropic principle', the physicist J. Wheeler has written:

> No theory of physics that deals only with physics will ever explain physics. I believe that as we go on trying to understand the universe, we are at the same time trying to understand man . . . Man, the start of the analysis, man the end of the analysis – because the physical world is in some deep sense tied to the human being.[33]

To the Christian student this sounds like an echo of something important heard long ago. One of the principal arguments of Professor Pringle-Pattison's noble work *The Idea Of God*[34] is precisely that man is organic to the universe. One page (211) bears the title 'Man Organic to Nature'; this is explained in the words:

> From the side of the higher Naturalism, I sought to emphasize man's rootedness in nature, so that the rational intelligence which characterises him appears as the culmination of a continuous process of immanent development . . . the existence of such living centres capable of feeling the grandeur and beauty of the universe and tasting its manifold qualities is what is alone really significant in the universe.

The philosopher and the natural scientist seem in their thoughts to be converging towards a meeting point on the significance of human beings in the universe. Is it possible that the meeting point is to be identified as something that the Christian student had heard even longer ago, and that is the basis of his faith – God created man in his own image, in the image of God created he him?

Science had perhaps a rather hard time of it, emancipating itself from the thrall of theology and from the tendency of theology to attempt to set a limit to the questions that science might ask and

---

[33] Quoted by A.R. Peacocke: *Creation and the World of Science*, p. 66.
[34] Oxford, 1920².

to the solutions that it might propound. Once the emancipation had been achieved, the sciences were launched on a glorious career, of which those who have engaged in such studies may justly be proud. The rate of progress is now so rapid that most of the books and papers written ten years ago are already out of date. The time-lag between theoretical achievement and the application of the theoretical to practical ends is steadily diminishing. It is not surprising that to countless men and women, not least in the undeveloped countries, science appears as the new god who has arisen above the horizon, with almost unlimited power to unlock all mysteries and with endless benefits which it can disclose and use to the good of mankind.

Those who are occupied with the practical application of scientific discovery to the needs of man are in many cases characterised by a generous and serious optimism. Problems are there to be solved, but there is no reason to doubt that solutions can be found. One disease after another has been found to be curable. There is little doubt that our world could support in comfort a considerably larger population than at present it has to deal with. With the advent of the computer the multiplication table no longer troubles us; even the least gifted can parade as mathematical geniuses. It seems likely that the time will come at which this planet will no longer be able to support life of the kind that we know. The more confident of our planners suggest that, in that case, it may be possible for the human race to migrate to worlds as yet unknown and start all over again.

These are dazzling prospects. Yet anxiety will not be stayed. W.H. Auden was perhaps right to give to one of his most ambitious projects the title The Age of Anxiety. Man can control his environment as never before; is he so successful in controlling himself and his desires? The physicists and the astronomers are perhaps more ready than their predecessors of a century ago to recognise a certain flexibility in the universe, and so to hold out a measure of freedom to the human being. But is man really free? The biochemist and the geneticist seem to descend upon us with the idea of unalterable genes by which our nature and our destiny are prescribed. Psychologists of some schools see man as controlled by ungovernable impulses that are so deeply hidden in the unconscious that they are unlikely ever to come completely under rational control. What we are is to a large extent determined by our actions and emotions in the past. The freedom that we imagine ourselves to enjoy is little more than an illusion; this is the situation in which we have to be content to live. But the desire for freedom does seem to be one of the deepest impulses by which the human psyche is swayed – to know that I am myself, to some extent at least self-determining, that my choices are real choices, and that as a responsible being I must stand by the choices that I have made. Without freedom, no responsibility; without responsibility, is there any such thing as genuinely human life?

As far as we can trace the course of evolution, it does seem to tend in the direction of greater freedom. The animate creature seems to have greater freedom than the inanimate. What we call the higher mammals seem to have a more highly developed consciousness than what we call the lower forms of life. The self-conscious human being seems to have greater freedom than even the elephant to react to his environment, to modify and control it. He can stand back from the universe, assess and criticise it; he asks strange questions about himself and about others and about reality. He is aware that he has the capacity for saying 'Yes' and 'No', for acting responsibly in situations that call for moral decision.

This is not to say that we always say 'Yes' when we ought to say 'Yes', and 'No' when we ought to say 'No'. We may be misled by passion or prejudice, we may overlook important evidence. What matters is that we do know the difference between Yes and No.

We do eventually assent to one of the alternatives. We come off the fence on one side ... if we are reasonable, we accept the one which is supported on balance by the evidence we have been considering and reject that which is not ... It is important to emphasize that we do have the power of waking ourselves up and deciding consciously and autonomously whether to assent or not, even though we are not capable of maintaining ourselves in that state all the time.[35]

If it were not so, there would be no place in life for either philosophy or religion.

★

---

[35] H.H. Price: *Beliefs* (London, 1969), pp. 206, 238. The whole discussion of Assent, and Freedom of Assent, seems to me acute and very well argued.

It is not the business of the physical scientist as such to indulge in moral judgments of the kind that are expressed in such phrases as 'this is better than that' or 'this is right and that is wrong'. But Price is surely right when he writes that:

[ethical words are] so deeply rooted in our discourse that it is very difficult to get rid of them, and therefore very difficult to describe human actions in completely non-ethical terms. We do happen to be moral beings, after all. Or rather, we do not just happen to be. For if we were not, we should not be persons, though we might still be intelligent creatures with a human shape.[36]

Price is far from being alone in making the discovery that, if we deal with human beings as persons, and still more if we deal with them as persons in society, the ethical dimension, much as we might wish to elude it, confronts us as something more than a convenient general term for the infinite flexibility of human responses to circumstances and environment.

One recent writer, uncommitted to any particular religious affiliation, who has dealt sincerely with this dilemma, is P.F. Strawson. He writes:

It is certainly possible, in a coolly analytical frame of mind, to mock at the whole notion of the profound truth; but we are guilty of mildly bad faith if we do so. For in most of us the ethical imagination succumbs again and again to *these* pictures of man, and it is precisely as truths that we wish to characterise them while they hold us captive.[37]

Utterances of this kind suggest that contemporary thinkers, while not dependent on any religious inspiration, are reaching out beyond the ethical in isolation to the idea of a total structure of reality in which the ethical and moral institutions of humanity have a place. Without the cement of moral responsibility, can any human society exist? Human beings are certainly capable of fashioning ideals. But, unless there is some kind of order outside

---

[36] *Beliefs*, p. 388.
[37] 'Social Morality and Individual Ideals' in I.T. Ramsey (ed.): *Christian Ethics and Contemporary Philosophy* (London, 1966), pp. 282–3. More fully on thinkers of this type in B. Mitchell: *Morality: Religious and Secular* (Oxford, 1980).

themselves towards which these ideals reach out, is there any hope of their ever emerging from the world of mere imagination? Unless there is some kind of stable order in the world, is there any hope that human purposes may step forward from projection in the direction of fulfilment?

Thinkers who deal with ethical questions are rightly cautious in the affirmations which they make. But there are indications that some among them are moving towards a convergence with the point of view of those to whom it seems natural to include religion as one of the factors that may be included in the consideration of ethical and moral questions. They recognise the importance of the study of man in society, and not only of man as an individual. They affirm the significance of the exercise of purpose in the formation of human personality and in the activity of human persons. This leads on, almost inevitably, to the fundamental question as to the nature of a universe in which purposes can be formed by human creatures, with a reasonable possibility that some at least of these purposes may be carried forward into the realm of fulfilment.

There are, as we have seen, philosophies which hold that the universe is basically chaotic, and that, if we seem to find a measure of order in it, this is just because we have imposed that order on it from within our own inner consciousness. If this view of the universe is correct, it would seem right to conclude that no human purpose could be formed within it with any reasonable hope of success in carrying out what was planned. There is, however, another view. It appears to be part of the experience of every one of us that purposes are daily formed by human beings, and that given favourable circumstances a surprising number of these purposes can reach the expected and desired fulfilment.

If this is true, if we have found the universe to be at least so far reliable and amenable to the use that we desire to make of it, is it possible to take one step farther, and to hazard the guess that the whole universe might make sense in terms of purpose? Is it possible to conceive of one single purpose so vast that all the myriad phenomena of the world as we know it, and far beyond the limits of our knowledge, can be related to it?

The statement that the universe is the stage on which is being enacted one all-embracing purpose, in which all things are included, and since every purpose is directed to some goal which is as yet unachieved, the universe is moving towards some consummation the nature of which can as yet be only dimly imagined, does not contain any logical self-contradiction. In the nature of the case, the truth of the statement cannot be conclusively proved. It belongs to that realm of fundamental assumptions on which we all act, although we know that they are beyond proof, and the validity of which can be worked out only by their ability to 'save the phenomena' in Platonic phrase, to account for all that is or all that can be. The fundamental assumption of the Christian is that spirit is prior to matter, and that this accounts for the nisus, the upward tendency, of nature towards spiritual reality, and for the desire which is present in some human beings at least to realise their spiritual being in fellowship with the one original Spirit.

Some materialists would affirm the contrary – that it is not necessary to look beyond matter, that three-dimensional existent of which we are aware, though we cannot very easily define it. Matter, the materialist would maintain, contains within it all potentialities, so that by some mysterious process it produces from within itself order and beauty, life and consciousness, and all those qualities which we value as being especially human. If this definition is accepted, it is clear that what the materialist calls 'matter' hardly differs at all from what the Christian calls 'spirit' – except that the Christian takes seriously the possibility of personal confrontation and fellowship with that mysterious reality which lies beyond all phenomena. The Christian is prepared to hazard the guess that Spirit, in letting loose that energy through which our world came into being, had in mind one central purpose – the aim of enjoying for ever the fellowship of intelligent and free spirits which had freely chosen to live in fellowship with him. If this really was the aim, it would explain many things. If the purpose had been to make all men as comfortable as possible all the time, the world would have to be very different from what it is. There may be other worlds in which the aims of Spirit are carried out without friction, without strain or frustration. But, if freedom is a condition for the fulfilment of the purpose, the element of risk, of suffering, of disaster, of apparent failure, cannot be excluded.

★

We have tried to indicate the questions which we would like our secularist friend to ask, believing that these are implicit in the various disciplines with which he and his colleagues are concerned, if he will pursue them to the very end, and holding that, though the answer for these can no more be guaranteed than for the thousand other questions which he asks in his professional capacity, it is not necessary to despair at the outset of at least a tentative, and therefore provisionally satisfying, answer. He is deeply concerned about his own rationality, and will not be fed on dreams and vague desires. We can assure him that our concern also is with the right use of reason, but that it is also our concern not to exclude any of the questions that can be asked, and not to evade the possibility that the answer might come by way of dialogue with an unseen power and not through the exercise of our own powers of ratiocination alone. To hold that, this being so, the death and resurrection of Jesus mark the central point in the history of the world is neither illogical nor irrational.

★

We are left with the most difficult problem of all: how are we going to persuade the secularist to ask the questions which, for his own good, we are convinced that he should be asking? It is certain that, if you never ask a religious question, you will never get a religious answer.

This problem, however, cannot be dealt with simply as a problem of religious or Christian apologetic. It is basically a question of the fullness and adequacy of the human response to all the aspects of reality by which we are confronted here on earth. To Wordsworth's Peter Bell, 'a primrose by a river's brim/ a yellow primrose was to him,/and it was nothing more.' Education, in all its forms is concerned with that 'something more' which was lacking to Peter Bell.

The point can be illustrated from the spectrum, into which clear light is refracted by the prism. Most of us can see clearly the seven colours, made up of the primary colours and their combinations. We are well aware that what our eyes can see is not the entire spectrum, but only a part. There are other rays, of which we can observe the effects but which we shall never see. At one end are the ultra-violet rays, the power of which will not be doubted by anyone who has stayed out too long unprotected under bright sunlight, and at the other end the infra-red rays, the use of which in photography and other ways is steadily being extended. But those who are partially colour-blind can see fewer colours than those who are more fortunate; and those who are completely colour-blind see everything as a monochrome in which there is no distinction of colours at all.

If there are seven colours of the rainbow, there are at least seven aspects of the wonderful world by which we are surrounded to which we ought to be able to respond. There is the aspect of the existent (natural science); of the event (history); of the beautiful (aesthetics); of mental process (psychology); of the better and the worse (ethics); of the transitory and the permanent (metaphysics); of ultimate obligation (religion). An ideal education, such as is hardly to be hoped for, would help to make every pupil sensitive to every one of these aspects of reality, awareness of which is indispensable to the fullness of human life.

'Religion' as the seventh of our aspects, is not to be identified solely with Christianity or any other form of specifically 'religious' faith. The most admirable thing about the secularist is his unconditional devotion to the truth, and this may be said to be his religion, just as for the Marxist the cause of Marxism, for which he is prepared to die, has many of the characteristics of a religion. But conversely Christianity is not to be identified with religion in any narrow sense. Christian faith is concerned with the universe as a whole, and with every aspect of it, including the life of man as a spiritual being and the life of man in society. It is for this reason that the Christian must protest against such emphasis on one aspect as would paralyse the potential response of the developing individual to each of the others.

In many countries today, including the United States, state education is required by statute to be entirely secular; the inculcation of any religious dogma is excluded. Christians in France say that this is in itself no bad thing. If the great story of French culture is honestly and adequately taught, the pupil cannot fail to be introduced to the great seventeenth century, with Racine and Pascal and Bossuet; even if he does not become a Christian believer, he will be aware of what faith and greatness are. The same is true of English culture if it includes, as it should, Milton and Treherne and Blake and the hymns of Charles Wesley. The danger is that, with the increasing emphasis on technological efficiency and contemporary relevance, some of these other aspects may be underplayed or excluded. Shakespeare's Cleopatra remarks 'and then what's high, what's noble/We'll do it after the high Roman fashion/And make death proud to take us.' Young people who, in the course of their education, have never been introduced to 'what's high, what's noble' have been defrauded of an essential part of their inheritance.

For centuries the Bible was the staple and the foundation of education in the west. The teaching was often mechanical and even obscurantist. But, even so, the Bible corresponded better than many modern systems and theories to the real concern of education. It is indirectly concerned with each of the seven aspects of reality to which allusion has been made. The doctrine of creation demands that serious attention should be paid to the terrestrial realities. History in the Bible is not made up of bare annals, but is concerned with the relationship between God and the nations of the world. The Bible contains considerable sections of the greatest literature in the world; should any pupil in a secondary school in Britain be allowed to complete the educational process without having read the Book of Job? Jesus and Paul are unrivalled in the art of understanding human nature in its depths and in its heights. The Bible is a book of choice, unsparing in its delineation of those who consciously choose the worse rather than the better. It is a book of values, and those who study it are trained in the discrimination of that which is of permanent from that which is of temporary value. It is a book of decision; Luther expressed the biblical attitude, succinctly and courageously, when he said 'Here I stand; I can no other.'

It may well be that, until our educational systems are reformed, dialogue between the Christian and the uncompromising secularist will be difficult. It is no use talking to a colour-blind man about the use of colour in the French post-impressionists, nor to a tone-deaf man about the beauties of polyphonic music. In so far as a rigidly secular education has conditioned the minds of young people, it is hard for them to see and hear, when the subject of discussion is faith, especially the Christian faith. For a period, perhaps a long period, this may make the task of the Christian apologist extremely difficult.

Yet to bring the argument to a pessimistic conclusion would be premature. It is fortunate that human beings are rarely logical.

The Christian may find the situation far more favourable to him than he has any right logically to expect. Young people refuse, as they always have done, to become just what their elders wish them to be. They will pay far more than they can afford to hear a first-rate rendering of Bach's *Mass in B Minor* or Handel's *Messiah*, perhaps with only the dimmest idea of the spiritual dimension of what they are going to hear. The secularist himself can sometimes be heard indulging in a reckless use of the words 'good' and 'bad', which ought not to be in his vocabulary, and be found engaging, at great personal cost, in causes which can far more logically be defended by a Christian than by a secularist. The first task of the Christian may be no more than to sit still and listen sympathetically. He may hear far more than he expects to hear. 'The still, sad music of humanity' continues to sound. The Christian and the non-Christian may find that they have many more concerns in common than they had imagined, and that dialogue may be honestly entered into on a far deeper level than either had supposed to be possible.

CHAPTER VIII

A Search for Light

The period through which the world lived after the end of the Second World War was for a great many people a time of disillusionment, disruption and despair. Paul Tillich, who was for a number of years the most influential Christian thinker in the United States of America, summed up the character and the needs of that time as follows:

> It is not an exaggeration to say that today man experiences his present situation in terms of disruption, conflict, self-destruction, meaninglessness and despair in all realms of life. This experience is expressed in the arts and in literature, conceptualized in existential philosophy, actualized in political cleavages of all kinds, and analysed in the psychology of the unconscious. The question arising out of this experience ... is the question of a reality in which the self-estrangement of our existence is overcome, a reality of reconciliation and reunion, of creativity, meaning and hope.[1]

It may be objected that in generalisation of this kind there is as much falsehood as truth. The vast majority of people lead their lives singularly unperturbed even by the clash of armies, and hardly touched by what seem to others to be revolutionary changes in society and in the climate of opinion. But Tillich's many contacts in the world of art and psychology meant that his voice was heard far beyond the limits of the theological world; he had his ear to the ground on many levels of society in America, in Europe and in Asia.

More than a generation later similar utterances come from the pen of considerably more recent writers. In the publication blurb

---

[1] Paul Tillich: *Systematic Theology*, I (1951), p. 49.

on the cover of a book by the Cambridge scholar Don Cupitt, we
are told of the contemporary crisis of meaninglessness, moral
breakdown and impending catastrophe. Cupitt notes the point
that awareness of change and the threat of change penetrate far
more deeply into society than in past days; we used to live, he
wrote:

> with an objective sacred order, but when that order breaks down it
> appears to bring everything, but *everything*, else down with it. Up to
> a century ago only a few intellectuals knew the bad news... Today,
> word has gone round... We all know that the old foundations of the
> moral order are gone... Confined to a small élite, moral scepticism
> may not be too serious a matter, but when it becomes widely diffused
> many individuals find it too hard to bear and social life begins to
> disintegrate.[2]

Neither Tillich nor Cupitt wrote from the background of a
wide acquaintance with what we now call the third world,
though Tillich fairly late in life had spent some time in Japan, and
Cupitt gives utterance from time to time to a rather euphoric
understanding of Buddhism (e.g. *ibid.*, p. xii). Each writes from a
western standpoint. Had both enjoyed a wider range of
experience, they might have felt that their generalisations about
the modern discovery had relevance to countries far outside the
western ambience. Marxism had bred in Asia scepticism as to all
the old ways of thought; now it seems that Chinese scepticism is
directed against Marxism itself, at least in the form in which it
was delivered by Mao Tse-tung. India is a vast country. One
visitor is impressed by a revival of Hinduism, another may find
himself confronted by a development of materialistic thinking so
vast that it raises the question of whether India can still be called
a religious country.

So Tillich's analysis, with some necessary reservations, may be
allowed to stand as an introduction to this chapter.

★

The year in which Tillich published the first volume of his

---

[2] Don Cupitt: *The World to Come* (London, 1982), pp. xii-xiii.

Systematic Theology (1951), was marked also by the death of Ludwig Wittgenstein (1889–1951), the acute philosopher of language, whose work in its earlier phases seemed to be destructive of every possibility of ethical or religious thought. Working along the same lines as Bertrand Russell (though the two later diverged radically from each another), Wittgenstein reached the conclusion that the only propositions which are meaningful and convey information are those which belong to the area of the natural sciences. All other propositions are either tautological or nonsensical. The affirmations of logic and mathematics are tautological; others, and particularly those of metaphysics and theology, are nonsensical. He sums up his conclusions in the formidable words: 'What we cannot speak about, we must consign to silence.'[3] The problem of meaning and meaninglessness has rarely been so clearly and radically stated.

Fifteen years later than Tillich, a distinguished historian Geoffrey Barraclough, in a book appropriately called *An Introduction to Contemporary History* (1964), dealt with the problem in detail in a world-wide setting. This has been a revolutionary period in literature and in the arts. The aim of the revolutionaries in all these different fields has been essentially the same – to break up the bourgeois synthesis and to become free from it. The bourgeois synthesis reflected a static society, which believed itself to have solved the main problems of humanity, and was therefore complacent and self-satisfied; what seemed all-important was to match content with appropriate form. This repudiation of the bourgeois age was pungently expressed by the Spanish writer J. Ortega y Gasset.

We feel that we actual men have suddenly been left alone on the earth... Any remains of the traditional spirit have evaporated. Models, norms, standards are no use to us. We have to solve our problems without any active collaboration of the past.[4]

So the author ceases to be concerned with either representation or communication – his task is simply to set down, apparently at random, whatever his inner sense brings to the

---

[3] *Tractatus Logico-Philosophicus* (1922), p. 189.
[4] *The Revolt of the Masses*, pp. 27–8, quoted by Barraclough (1967 edn.), p. 244.

surface at any particular moment. Gertrude Stein brings together words at haphazard, not to convey but to suggest, with the result that in the end, as one not unfriendly critic put it, she has 'gone so far that she no longer even suggests'.[5] The artist Kandinsky, looking at one of his pictures upside-down, asked himself 'Why should my pictures have forms and figures?', decided that for the future they should not, and led the way to a completely abstract art. In the field of music it was said of Schönberg, with his theory of atonality, that 'his music had become so abstract, so individual and so divorced from all relation to humanity as to be almost unintelligible'.[6]

Barraclough is right in seeing that, though these phenomena, this sense of meaninglessness manifested themselves first in the western world, they began at a rather later date to show themselves in what we now call the third world. During the brief and rapid period of decolonisation, African countries were alight with the sense of liberation, expectancy and hope. As in country after country coup followed military coup, the ugly face of dictatorship and injustice prevailed, all too soon hope was changed into disillusionment, cynicism and even despair. There was sorrow over the loss of a largely imaginary African identity, and over the frustration of finding neither a way back into the African past, nor a way into a future and unrevealed identity more adaptable to the new exigencies of the present.

If this was the whole story of the twentieth century, and especially of the second half of it, to write a book about faith would clearly be a futile enterprise. There is, however, enough on the other side, enough evidence that the darkness of doubt may be followed by a new dawn of faith, that to give some account of both sides of the story, though difficult, may seem to be worth while.

Tillich, though more aware than many, through his experience as a German chaplain in the Second World War, of the avalanche of doubt by which faith was threatened, believed that it was possible to lay again the foundation of faith, and wrote his three memorable volumes of *Systematic Theology*, with their skilful

---

[5]Edmund Wilson: *Axel's Castle; a Study in the Imaginative Literature of 1870–1930* (London, 1961), p. 195.

[6]Alfred Einstein: *A Short History of Music* (1959 edn.; London, 1961), p. 201.

counterpoint of the basic needs of human thought and the answers indicated in the Christian revelation. The later, and final, Wittgenstein saw many things which had been hidden from the young Wittgenstein, and almost sang a funeral dirge over the author of the *Tractatus Logico-Philosophicus*. It is, according to his later utterances, important to understand the rules of the language game which people play; but it is a mistake to suppose that there is only one kind of language. In an earlier chapter we have noted the seven aspects of the universe of which we have to take account; each of these aspects has its own appropriate language, and even this does not exhaust the possibilities.[7] This is what Wittgenstein came to realise and to express in his posthumous work *Philosophical Investigations*.[8] We must take seriously the aspects of command, story-telling, riddles and the guessing of answers, thanking, cursing, greeting, praying. The last of these does not guarantee any relationship of religion to reality, but it does make clear its significance to human beings. It is perhaps not without significance that one of the most distinguished of the pupils of Wittgenstein, who is also one of the most lucid expositors of his thought, Norman Malcolm, in middle life startled his philosophical colleagues by deciding to be confirmed in the Episcopal Church in America.

Barraclough ends his survey of disintegration with the hope that a new adjustment to reality, to the new reality of the post-revolutionary world, may come not from the weary west of Europe and North America but from Asia and Latin America. He draws attention to the 'new youth' in China, a movement which some hold to be of even greater significance than the Marxist revolution under Mao Tse-tung, and quotes from Chen Tu-Hsiu the principles of new and creative writing:

(i) To overthrow the painted, powdered and obsequious literature of the aristocratic few, and to create the plain, simple, and expressive literature of the people.

(ii) To overthrow the stereotyped and over-ornamental literature of classicism and to create the fresh and sincere literature of realism.

(iii) To overthrow the pedantic, unintelligible and obscurantist

[7] See p. 217
[8] Trans. G.E.M. Anscombe (Oxford, 1958).

literature of the hermit and recluse, and to create the plain-speaking and popular literature of society in general.[9]

Of a number of these contemporary movements it is possible to write only tentatively, since their forms of expression are still in process of development. It seems already clear that faith, in one form or another, is beginning to take the place of the purely negative approach of anxiety and despair. If this is true, Christian faith may have to face the challenge of presenting itself in quite new forms to a world in which faith no longer appears to be merely nonsensical. This will be a subject for a book of the future.[10]

★

In the meantime, it is possible to identify a movement of the last fifty years, which has perhaps now passed its zenith but for a time was highly influential, especially on the minds of younger people – the movement called Existentialism. The term stands not for one single coherent doctrine, but for a certain attitude to life which is recognisable in a number of thinkers of very different backgrounds and tendencies. In the history of the movement it is possible to see three stages – the repudiation of all belief; the slow emergence out of the darkness of unbelief into the twilight of an as yet hesitant and uncertain faith; and then the attainment of clarity in a faith which holds all things together in a new and contemporary synthesis.

All existentialists, of whatever stripe, look back to the Dane, Søren Kierkegaard (1813-55) who, little regarded in his lifetime, has come a century after his death to be regarded as one of the great creative thinkers of the nineteenth century.[11] Behind Kierkegaard stands the pyrotechnic thinker Johann Georg Hamann (1730-88), in praise of whom writers as different as

9 Barraclough, pp. 262-3.

10 But already gallant beginnings are being made by apologists and philosophers, who are prepared to take seriously the possibility that God may exist.

11 See the striking contemporary tribute by Don Cupitt: 'He is by far the most important and highly gifted modern Christian writer.' *J. of Theol. Studies* (Apr. 1982), p. 324.

Goethe and Hegel wrote and to whom Kierkegaard constantly admits himself to be indebted.[12]

The best starting-point for the study of Kierkegaard is his dislike for the philosophy of Hegel, which in his student days exercised immense influence in thinking circles in Germany. Hegel (1770-1831) had made a really great attempt to create a world-system of thought in which everything would find its place and nothing would be left unaccounted for. 'The System' was the particular object of Kierkegaard's wrath, for he was convinced that there were many things that could not be reduced to system, and the chief of those was man himself in the richness and variety of his individual and personal *existence*. So his principles were:

A: A logical system is possible;
B: An existential system is impossible.

   An existential system cannot be formulated. Does this mean that no such system exists? By no means; nor is this implied in our assertion. Reality itself is a system - for God; but it cannot be a system for any existing spirit ... It may be seen, from a purely abstract point of view, that system and existence are incapable of being thought together; because in order to think existence at all systematic thought must think it as abrogated, and hence as not existing. Existence separates, and holds the various moments of existence discretely apart; the systematic thought consists of the finality which brings them together.[13]

Kierkegaard is often hard to understand, and in consequence has often been misunderstood. The gravest misunderstanding is that Kierkegaard was an apostle of the 'flight from reason', which has been a sorry feature of our times. He was at all times prepared to pay the utmost deference to reason, provided that the limitations of reason were borne in mind. What he was implacably opposed to was that kind of systematising reason,

---

[12] There has been a great awakening of interest in Hamann in Germany, but not as yet in England, perhaps because he is so difficult. The first full-scale study of Hamann in English is R. Gregor Smith: *J.G. Hamann: A Study in Christian Existence* (1960). For a recent but rather inadequate study see T.S. German SJ: *Hamann on Religion and Language* (Oxford, 1982).

[13] *Concluding Unscientific Postscript* (Eng. trans., 1941), p. 107.

which works out a neat and simple solution for a complicated problem – only by disregarding all those factors in the situation which make any such simple solution impossible. His frequent use of the term 'the absurd' has misled many of his readers. 'Christianity is the absurd, held fast in the passion of the infinite.'[14] In English this can easily be taken to mean the nonsensical, the totally irrational. This is not what Kierkegaard meant. In mathematics absurd is 'that which cannot be fitted into a pattern', the remainder that is left over, when we have done our best to find a neat and tidy solution. The absurd for Kierkegaard is that which can never be fitted into any kind of rule. It is the exceptional, the individual, the irreducible, which can be apprehended but cannot be classified in terms of anything else. All human experience is of this kind. Of this kind also is Christianity – the absurd in the sense that it cannot be reduced to a set of rules; it shines, if at all, by its own light. If it is to be apprehended, this cannot be by the way of intellectual analysis but only by way of surrender.

We are now in a position to consider three great principles of Existentialism as Kierkegaard understood it.

In the first place, the ethical is the realm of generalisation, of common rule and order. Ethical rules will serve as a useful general guide for conduct, but no ethical rule will ever be exactly applicable to the particular situation of an individual man. Any man is likely to find himself in a situation where the ordinary rules of ethics simply do not apply. Convention and human formulations no longer help, and he finds himself driven to act in a way for which the only appropriate term is paradox.

This was the agonising dilemma with which Dietrich Bonhoeffer was faced in the days of Nazi rule:

Reality lays itself bare. Shakespeare's characters walk in our midst. But the villain and the saint have little to do with systematic ethical studies. They emerge from primeval depths and by their appearance they tear open the infernal or the divine abyss from which they come and enable us to see for a moment into mysteries of which we had never dreamed.[15]

---

[14] *Concluding Unscientific Postcript*, p. 192.
[15] D. Bonhoeffer: *Ethics* (Eng. trans., 1955), p. 3.

The individual cannot truly rise to the point of being an individual, unless he is prepared, at whatever cost, to raise himself above the level of the universal, the general rules of the ethical, and to act as he, that particular man, is called upon to act at that particular point of time. Conventional rules will guide us up to a certain point but at any moment we may reach a situation which is not covered by any conventional rules.

Secondly, we are led to the question as to where the fullness of man's personal reality can be experienced. Kierkegaard's answer is that this can come about only in the direct confrontation of man with God. This is an experience unlike anything else in the world. It can neither be taught nor learned. The increase of knowledge and the lengthening down of Christian history do not make it any easier to believe than it was in the beginning. No man can live another man's Christian experience. Each is, in the nature of the case, unique and different from any other, and no direct communication of such experience from one to another is possible. One may guide another some distance on the way; but each in the end must make for himself the leap of faith.

But, thirdly, faith must not be understood, or rather misunderstood, as intellectual assent to a particular form of doctrine. It means total self-commitment. It means willingness to bear witness to what is believed, and in the modern world this will necessarily involve suffering:

> To *suffer* for the doctrine. It is this which changes everything endlessly with respect to becoming a Christian, this which imposes endless weight... To *suffer* for the doctrine. But there can be no question of that in these times when Christianity has fully triumphed and all are Christians! I could be tempted to say, 'Woe, woe unto thee, thou hypocrite!' But that I will not do... No, the requirement of suffering for the doctrine is at this instant just as much in force and just as applicable as it was at the beginning.[16]

It is at this point that the thought of Kierkegaard approaches that of Karl Marx. I have often wondered whether Karl Marx and Søren Kierkegaard had ever heard of each other. All probability is against it. But, if they had, I think they would have understood

---

[16] S. Kierkegaard: *Judge for Yourselves* (Eng. trans., 1941), pp. 211, 213.

each other remarkably well. Many philosophers, and many ordinary men as well, have held that, when we have understood something, we have done our duty by it. Kierkegaard and Marx take the view that understanding is true understanding only when it is conceived as a preparation for action; he who has understood is thereby committed to presenting a challenge to that which is. The business of the philosopher is not simply to understand the world but to change it.

> The Existential thinker is the interested or passionate thinker... Feuerbach and Kierkegaard prefer the term 'passion' for the attitude of the Existential thinker. In his beautifully written *Grundsätze der Philosophie der Zukunft*, Feuerbach says, 'Do not wish to be a philosopher in contrast to being a man... do not think as a thinker... think as a living, real being... think in Existence.' 'Love is passion, and only passion is the mark of Existence.' In order to unite this attitude with the demand for objectivity, he says: 'Only what is an object of passion – really is.' The passionately living man knows the true nature of man and life.[17]

Before turning to those who would claim the title existentialists in any exact sense, it is desirable to pay brief attention to two German philosophers, neither of whom would have claimed any specific religious allegiance, but whose words have exercised great influence on the continent of Europe, and rather more ir America than in England.

Edmund Husserl (1859–1938) stands about as far as it is possible to imagine from the empirical tradition which has been powerful in British philosophy from the time of Locke. To his philosophy he gave the name of phenomenology, a descriptive science. But the last thing that he desired was to study phenomena in their setting in the three-dimensional world. His aim is to penetrate behind the phenomena to universal essence, of which alone it is possible to attain that certain and precise knowledge which always escapes us in relation to mere empirical facts. The student of philosophy is reminded of Plato's world of ideas, of which alone real knowledge can be obtained in contrast to the 'right opinion', which is the best that can be made of the

---

17 Paul Tillich: *Theology of Culture* (1959), pp. 89–90.

external and observable world. So Husserl is concerned with the basic structures of consciousness, with that which underlies any true experience of reality.

It may be noted that Paul Tillich commends the phenomenological approach to theology: 'the meaning of a notion must be clarified and circumscribed before it can be approved or rejected ... thus avoiding the danger of trying to fill in logical gaps with devotional material.'[18]

More than in any other thinker of the twentieth century dependence on Kierkegaard is evident in the writings of Martin Heidegger (1889-1976). Heidegger's thought is not easy to grasp, and the language in which it is expressed is constantly obscure, whether in the German original or in English translation, but he is so important as a link between the nineteenth century and the twentieth, and so much of his terminology is passing into common speech, that the attempt must be made to understand what it is that he is talking about.[19]

Heidegger calls his philosophy the philosophy of being. It has generally been assumed by thinkers that we know fairly well what we mean when we say 'I am'. But is this really the case? If we are to think at all, must we not start with a careful analysis of the nature of man's existence? If we attempt to do so, we may find that the problem is far more complex than we had supposed at the outset.

The first point to note is that for Heidegger existence is always existence in this world. He has made a radical break with the rationalist tradition of western thought, and with the idea, familiar to all who have made any study of scholastic thought, that Essence precedes Existence, and that Existence can in some way be derived from Essence. We must never think of man in terms of substance or nature, generalised concepts that have no relatedness to this particular man in his situation of today. Nor must we suppose that we can think of man as a pure 'ego', a detached individual, as though he could be separated from the history that has made him what he is, and from the world, which includes the world of other selves, that surrounds him and in

---

[18] *Systematic Theology*, I, p. 106.
[19] A.J. Ayer has written perceptively, but not altogether sympathetically, about the thought of Heidegger, in *Philosophy in the Twentieth Century* (1982), pp. 226-30.

which he has to move.

Secondly, Heidegger insists passionately that existence is always individual and cannot be reduced to any form of classification. This runs counter to the methods and approach of a good deal of modern science. The tendency there is to treat human beings like any other object of observation. The social sciences spend their time in working out new formulae for the classification of men and women. It is not to be denied that such studies have a value for purely pragmatic ends; but, if we imagine that they can bring us any nearer to understanding the reality of man as man, we must be prepared to find ourselves mistaken.

For, to take up the third capital point in Heidegger's argument, there are two possible forms of being in the world. *Things* exist in one way. *Human beings* exist, or can exist, in another. For the existence of things Heidegger uses the term *Vorhandenheit*, which really means 'just being there' – they have significance for man only in so far as he can make use of them, in so far as they can serve as instruments for his purpose. *Existenz* is the being of man as a conscious subject, with awareness – awareness of himself, of the world and of other existences.

The two possibilities are characterised by Heidegger as authentic and unauthentic existence. Unauthentic existence is that of the crowd, where everything is ruled by conventions as to what one does and does not do, where a man hardly needs to make any deliberate personal choice but can drift along in the almost perfect anonymity of the crowd. But by accepting this kind of life man rejects his own true existence, and falls down almost to the level of an object, a thing. 'Man-in-being' can lose himself to the being that meets him in the world, and be taken over by it.[20]

The reality of existence is to be found only in choice, in decision, in the deliberate acceptance of the authentic and rejection of the unauthentic existence. A man must become independent of others, of their judgment of him, of what they expect of him, and take his stand just upon what he authentically is, in the expectation of what he can become. There are no outward norms, no rules by which he can be guided (Heidegger

---

[20] M. Heidegger: *Sein und Zeit* (8th edn. 1957; Eng. trans., *Time and Being*, paperback edn. 1977), p. 36.

has excluded God from his scheme of things).
This is freedom. Yet freedom is always accompanied by
anxiety. Heidegger makes a distinction between fear and anxiety.
Fear is always related to something which is in the world, which
is conceived as terrible – or rather the empirical world itself is
regarded as a sphere out of which something terrible might
emerge. But this belongs to the realm of unauthentic existence. It
is an unauthentic mood, and from this one who has chosen
authentic being is by definition free. And yet such a one is a prey
to 'anxiety',[21] that most characteristic of all the moods of the
contemporary world.

To what is anxiety related? Heidegger's answer is 'to
Nothingness'. The mood of nothingness, of total meaninglessness, is not unfamiliar – it is closely related to that accidie of the
medieval monks, which might be a fleeting anguish, but could
become a serious and dangerous mental illness. Boredom is one
of its contemporary signs.

Not boredom with a particular book or play or form of work, but
finding oneself drifting in the abyss of existence as in a mute fog
which draws everything into a queer kind of indifference. The sense
of wholeness here comes out in the fact that *everything* is meaningless,
pointless, tasteless, colourless.[22]

When this mood is on us, it is impossible to say 'Yes' to life,
since life has become unbearable. What we do to the totality of
being in this mood cannot be termed 'annihilation' (*Vernichtung*),
since after all it goes on existing. Heidegger invents for this
attitude the new word *Nichtung*, nihilation, the total personal
rejection of that which is.[23]

It is only a courageous man who can look straight in the face of
nothingness and accept it, accept his own existence as 'thrown
forward to its own end'. Outward help there is none. Man has
nothing to rely on except his own inner resources. Yet it is just at

[21] Note that *Angst* is a phenomenon which Kierkegaard has also dealt with at
length.

[22] David E. Roberts: *Existentialism and Religious Belief* (Oxford, 1959²), p. 176.

[23] It is this word and concept that Sartre represents by the extraordinarily
clumsy and unnatural word *néantisation*, reducing that which is to the state of the
néant, nothingness.

this point that, in the opinion of Dr Macquarrie,[24] the Existentialist system is open to the approach of the reality of God. Heidegger has rightly seen that the truth of man's life lies in relatedness. The man who has chosen authentic existence is related to his own self in a new way, he has a new understanding of his own being. He can find relationships with other authentic selves at a level far deeper than the superficial encounter which passes as such in the unauthentic world. But, if he has not entered into relationship with God, the source and ground of all Being, is he not bound to be pursued by such an anxiety as Heidegger has so penetratingly analysed?

> For in this fundamental malaise, which springs from man's very being, there is disclosed not only the self and the world, but also God. The disclosure does not indeed yield the explicit knowledge of God, but directs man to God as the ground of his being ... For what is this anxiety or dread, this basic malaise, this uneasy restlessness, this feeling of not being at home in the world, this disclosure which shatters the illusory contentment and security of everyday existence, but the *cor inquietum* of Christian experience? ... Confronted with the disclosure of that anxiety which relates to nothing in the world but arises from his own being, man has an alternative to that flight into an inauthentic existence of surrender to the world – namely, recourse to God, Who is the ground of being, Creator of both man and the world.[25]

★

The type of thought that we now commonly call existentialist was slowly maturing in Germany between the wars. After the end of the Second World War in 1945, it burst upon the world almost with the force of a revelation through the genius of a group of French writers and thinkers. Three of these writers may serve as examples of the very various directions in which Existentialism can develop, and of the possibilities that exist

---

[24] John Macquarrie: *An Existentialist Theology* (1955). Though this book deals mainly with Rudolf Bultmann, it contains the most lucid account known to me in English, of the thought of Heidegger.

[25] J. Macquarrie: *ibid.*, p. 71.

within it of a new discovery of the reality of God.
Each of them had been marked by the scars of the tragedies
through which France had lived – the surrender of 1940, the
German occupation, the glories and squalor of the resistance, the
deep disillusionment that resulted from the failure of so many to
take advantage of the new possibilities that the liberation opened
out before them. The mood is perfectly expressed by a character
in one of Gabriel Marcel's plays:

> Do you not sometimes get the impression that we are living – if it can
> be called living – in a broken world? Yes, I mean broken, just in the
> sense in which a watch can be broken. The spring is no longer
> working. As far as outward appearances go, nothing is changed.
> Everything is in its right place. But, if you put the watch to your ear,
> there is nothing to be heard. You understand; this world – what we
> call this world, the world of men – at one time or another it must have
> had a heart – but now you get the impression that this heart is no
> longer beating.[26]

As a consequence of this mood of brokenness, a great deal of
French Existentialism has found expression in novels and plays
rather than in the form of systematic exposition. Yet there have
been a number of more or less systematic attempts to
communicate the nature of this strange broken world in which
these writers feel themselves to be living.

Jean-Paul Sartre (1905-80) in his autobiography Les Mots (1964;
Eng. trans., Words, 1964) has given us a scathing picture of the
bourgeois Protestant society into which he was born. This
society, as Sartre has depicted it, seems to have come as near as is
possible to Karl Marx's picture of the bourgeois world. There
imagination is at a discount. In that world of getting and
spending, everything is ruled by convention, and all the moves in
the game can be foreseen and calculated in advance. This means
that there is no possibility of authentic existence; the only course
for one who would truly live is to escape, to be free whatever the
acquisition of freedom may cost.

For Sartre, with his determination to live, the renunciation of
that world had to be total. With the repudiation of the

----

[26] Le Monde Cassé (1935).

conventional relationships of the society that he had known he seems to have cut himself off from human relationships, and never to have found another world in which he could be happily at home.

Freedom for Sartre is the breath of life; it is, therefore, in no way surprising that for him the central problem is that of freedom. But whereas for most people freedom is a treasure, something to be arrived at and striven for, for Sartre it is a heavy and intolerable burden. 'I am condemned to be free.'[27] Man is on his own; there is nothing to help him. If Heidegger is uninterested in the idea of God, Sartre has positively and almost vindictively rejected it. The norms and standards accepted by the majority of men, merely because they come from the past, are irrelevant and can give no guidance. Man is alone, and it is his business to create himself:

> Freedom coincides at its roots with the non-being which is at the heart of man. For a human being to *be* is to choose himself; nothing comes to him either from without or within himself that he can receive or accept. He is wholly and helplessly at the mercy of the unendurable necessity to make himself, even in the smallest details of his existence. Thus freedom is not *a* being, it is *the* being of man, that is to say his non-being ... Man cannot be at times free and at other times a slave; either he is always and entirely free, or he is not free at all.[28]

Sartre is keenly aware of the difference between the existence of objects and the existence of persons. One of his besetting fears is that of being reduced to the level of an object. Therefore 'the other' is to him always a menace, and not a means of liberation into fellowship. How is this to be understood? Another looks at me. As he fixes me with his eye, I become the *object* of his thought – he thinks of me as this or that – Frenchman, writer, merchant, or whatever it may be. By doing so he reduces me from the level of a personal subject to that of an object, a thing. So he menaces my freedom, he appropriates me and enslaves me to himself. This is the theme of the best known of all Sartre's works, *La Nausée* (*Nausea*).[29]

---

27 *Words*, p. 515.
28 *Ibid.*, p. 156
29 1948; Eng. trans., Penguin Books, 1949, 1962.

Sartre seems never to have conceived the possibility of a genuinely 'I – Thou' relationship.[30] He is familiar with the cool appraising stare of the destructive other. He seems never to have encountered that unmistakable look in the eye of someone we have never seen before, which sends out an immediately apprehensible message as from an 'I' to a 'Thou', and asks for an answering message in return. Once this personal relationship has been established, there can be no question of the one self destroying the other or desiring the destruction of the other. Each enjoys the other in freedom, and maintains the freedom of the other. Each is to the other a cause of the enrichment of life. All this Sartre seems unable to understand. According to him, I can seek to possess the other – in that case I reduce the other to the status of an object, of a thing; or I can allow myself to be possessed – and in that case I permit myself to be reduced to the level of an object, a thing. In neither case is love or community possible.

The point to which Sartre is prepared to carry this perverse understanding of human relationships comes out well in the astonishing passage in which he deals with generosity.[31]

Giving is a primitive form of destruction ... So generosity is above all else a destructive function. The passion to give, which at certain moments seizes certain people, is above all else a passion for destruction ... But this passion for destruction, which underlies generosity, is nothing else than a passion to possess. Everything that I abandon, everything that I give, I enjoy in a superior manner by means of the gift that I make of it ... But at the same time the gift casts a spell on the one to whom I give it ... To give is to impose servitude on another ... Generosity is thus a feeling structured by the existence of the other, and which manifests a preference for appropriation by way of destruction.[32]

---

[30] The phrase has become familiar through the thought of another thinker – Martin Buber (1878-1965) – who probably would not have called himself an existentialist, though he is often classed with them (as by Will Herberg in his book *Four Existentialist Theologians*). The whole basis of Buber's thought is precisely that distinction between persons and things with which we are so much concerned in this chapter.

[31] I note that Gabriel Marcel also deals with this passage in *The Philosophy of Existence*, p. 60, calling it 'his astonishingly distorted analysis of generosity'.

[32] *L'Être et le Néant*, pp. 684-5.

It is not surprising that the final word in Sartre's philosophy is one of rather acid pessimism and frustration. On man is laid the heavy burden of perpetually creating man. Yet this is an aim that can never be achieved; and if it could be achieved, what would be the value of the achievement?

All human reality is a passion, in that it forms the plan of losing itself in order to lay a foundation for being, and at the same time to constitute that Consciousness (*En-soi*) which escapes contingency by being its own foundation, the *Ens causa sui*, which the religious call God. So the passion of man is the opposite of the passion of Christ; for man loses himself, in so far as he is man, in order that God may be born. But the idea of God is self-contradictory, and we lose ourselves in vain. Man is a futile passion.[33]

Albert Camus (1913–60), whose tragic death was a grave loss to European literature, had many points of contact with Sartre, and for a time worked closely with him in Paris. But whereas Sartre represents a gospel of meaninglessness, of which the logical conclusion would seem to be despair, Camus seems to represent Existentialism feeling its way towards the belief that there may after all be meanings and values, and that out of despair a new hope may be born.

If it were necessary to select one book as representative of existentialist thinking and striving, I should be inclined to choose Camus's *L'Homme Révolté* (*The Rebel*).[34] In this extraordinarily able book Camus traces the principles and the imperfections of the European revolution. He is himself committed to the principles of revolution. Yet he is deeply disturbed by the evident fact that revolution leads to killing, and to the justification of much that is evidently unjustifiable. 'We have arrived at the period of premeditation and of the perfect crime ... it is philosophy which can serve for every purpose, even for that of transforming murderers into judges.'[35] How has this come about?

The text of the book may be said to be the famous phrase of

[33]*Ibid.*, p. 708.
[34]Paris, 1951; Eng. trans., 1953, 1971[2].
[35]*Ibid.*, p. 13.

Nietzsche, 'God is dead'. To understand this, it is necessary to look back to the context in which Nietzsche (1844–1900) used the phrase. He does not regard himself as the violent iconoclast, dethroning a God who is still sitting in authority on his throne; he is the cool observer, remarking the fact, which others do not yet seem to have noticed, that Dagon has fallen from his throne, and asking what is to be done about it.

Nietzsche set out his idea in the form of a parable. A madman ran into the market-place calling out 'I seek God'. The bystanders, who did not really believe in God, were amused and said, 'Why? Is he lost? Has he taken a sea-voyage? Has he emigrated?' But the madman cried out again, 'Where is God gone? I mean to tell you. We have killed him, you and I! We are all his murderers!... Is not the magnitude of this deed too great for us? Shall we not ourselves have to become God merely to seem worthy of it? There never was a greater event – and on account of it, all who are born after us belong to a higher history than any... hitherto.' But the madman was before his time. The meaning of his message could not reach his hearers. And so he went into one church after another, and intoned his Requiem aeternam deo. When asked what he was doing, he replied, 'What are these churches now, if they are not the tombs and monuments of God?'[36]

Nietzsche died, insane, in 1900. But, unlike the God in whom he so passionately disbelieved, he has refused to lie down and die. There are still those who find in him a tonic such as they find in the words of no other writer. There are Christians who are aware that their faith will not suffice them, unless it has been subjected to the rigorous testing of Nietzsche's vigorous and astringent mind. He seems to appear again at crises in human thinking such as we are considering in this chapter. The idea that God is dead rises again, as we shall see in the sequel, under various transformations, from its own ashes.

We recognise in Camus the familiar existentialist pattern of 'man for himself'. But is it really the case that man can exist without any form of transcendence? Is it possible that the nihilism, the despair, the self-destruction, the mutual destruction, by which the progress of the revolution has been marked,

---

[36] F. Nietzsche: Die fröhliche Wissenschaft (1882; Eng. trans., Joyful Wisdom, 1909).

are due just to the disappearance of the transcendent dimension? Is the affirmation that 'God is dead' quite such good news as it appeared to be to those who first affirmed it?

Camus does not come to the point of openly accepting this conclusion. Yet towards the end of his book there is a rather striking change of mood.

This comes out first in what Camus has to say about art. The strict revolutionary, if he is an orthodox Marxist, should not be able to admit the possibility of art at all. There is no room in his world for imagination or creativity. Science excludes both. Nothing new can ever really happen, because history is merely the explication of that which in principle was there from the beginning. Equally, the fully consistent existentialist should not be able to admit the existence of art. For all things exist in the fugitiveness of a perpetual becoming in which there can be no meaning or order. But traditionally the artist is the man who fixes reality in a moment, who expresses that unity of the universal and the particular after which Hegel aspired. 'The great creators are those who, like Piero della Francesca, give the impression that the fixation has just taken place, that at that precise moment the projector stopped dead.'[37]

Is the artist merely imposing an order and a beauty that are not there at all? Or is he right when he says that his creativity is of the nature of response, a discovery of a deeper reality than that which lies merely on the surface of things?

Nietzsche could refuse to admit the existence of any transcendence, moral or divine, maintaining that to admit any such transcendence would lead men to take a low view of this world and this life. But it may be that there is a living transcendence of which beauty is the promise, which could lead us to prefer this mortal and limited world to any other possible world.[38]

The revolution is based on the conviction that this world can be made better than it is. The artist lives in the same tension between 'that which is' and 'the better world'. Is he entirely wrong? Every man craves for some principle of unity within his

---

37 L'Homme Révolté, p. 317.
38 L'Homme Révolté, p. 319.

existence, some hint at least of meaning. The artist is expressing for us that which is within us all:

> It is not enough to live. Man needs a destiny, and that without waiting for the arrival of death. It is therefore correct to say that man has the idea of a better world than that which now exists. But 'better' in this sense does not mean *different*; it does mean unified.[39]

Camus himself never admitted explicitly that he was moving in the direction of what a Christian would call faith. He affirmed that his famous novel *La Peste* (1947; Eng. trans., *The Plague*, 1948; 2nd edn., 1967), was in fact one of the most anti-Christian of all his works. This strange book is the story of the city of Oran under an imaginary visitation of the plague, and of the actions and reactions of the men who have to live with this terror. Once again, man cannot turn to any transcendent reality, to any God, to help him out of his misery; his only resources are in himself. Yet out of the terror emerges beauty, and a picture of what can only be called a kind of secularised and non-religious saintliness. At the end the doctor Rieux, who has endured the suffering of the whole period of tragedy, leaves on record his judgment that 'in times of disaster one learns that there is more in men to admire than to despise'. He is the type of those who, for all the torments of their own inner self-contradictions, knowing that they cannot be saints do not admit that disaster should tyrannise over mankind, and take upon themselves the responsibility of being doctors.[40]

Is this so very far from Christian faith? This Christian progression is continued in the last, and in the opinion of many critics the finest, of all the writings of Camus, *La Chute* (1956; Eng. trans., *The Fall*, 1957), the confessions of 'the penitent judge' who unsparingly reveals and analyses the mixture of altruism and baseness of which he is made up. A particularly percipient critic has written of this work:

> Nor can the specifically Christian or pre-Christian elements in *La Chute* – so clearly signalled both in the title and in the name of the

[39] *L'Homme Révolté*, p. 324.
[40] *La Peste*, p. 331.

narrator-protagonist [Jean-Baptiste Clamence] – be glossed over. Under its surface of irony, and occasional blasphemy, La Chute is profoundly Christian in its confessional form, in its imagery and above all in its pervasive message that it is only through the full recognition of our sinful nature that we can hope for grace.[41]

There were those among the admirers of Camus who felt that sooner or later he would be compelled by his own honesty to recognise all that was implied in the admissions that he had made. Death came too soon, and interrupted the pilgrimage. But perhaps it is not unfair to describe the thought of Camus as 'Existentialism in search of a faith'.[42]

★

In the third of our trio of thinkers, Gabriel Marcel, Existentialism has found a faith.

Born in 1889, Marcel was rather older than the other French existentialists. And throughout his career he followed a highly individual way. Interested from a very early age in philosophy, Marcel found himself increasingly dissatisfied with what he read. The only true starting-point for a philosopher must be the incredible richness of the actual data of everyday life; this being so, the more we reduce things to a system the further we shall move from reality. Science can build up assured results; it is not so with philosophy:

> The stage always remains to be set; in a sense everything always starts from Zero, and a philosopher is not worthy of the name unless he not only accepts but wills this harsh necessity ... This perpetual beginning again, which may seem scandalous to the scientist or the technician, is an inevitable part of all genuinely philosophical work;

---

[41] Conor Cruise O'Brien: Camus (1970), p. 81. O'Brien adds the extraordinarily interesting note (p. 91 n. 27): 'When in a review in The Spectator of the English version of The Fall, I stressed its Christian tendency, Camus wrote to his English publishers, Messrs Hamish Hamilton, confirming that this approach to the novel was sound.'

[42] In the Journal de Genève for 26 February 1960 I found quoted this very striking word of Camus: 'The certainty of a God who would lend significance to life is far more attractive than that of the power to do evil with impunity.' I do not know the source of the quotation.

and perhaps it reflects in its own order the fresh start of every new
awakening and of every birth ... The conviction that reality cannot be
'summed up' ... came to me very early ... It seemed to me from then
on that there was a danger of making an illicit use of the idea of
integration, and that the more one relied on the richest and most
concrete data of experience, the less this idea appeared to be applicable
to reality.[43]

Clearly the attitude to which Marcel had been led was a
profoundly religious one; it is not altogether surprising that in
1928 he felt himself led to ask for baptism in the Roman Catholic
Church.

How, then, as a Christian did Marcel remain in the ranks of the
existentialists, and can he point the way for us towards a
Christian understanding of Existentialism? What we have to say
on this subject may be summed up under the three heads of
Incarnation, Mystery and Sensitiveness.

The plain fact is that man is not simply a thinking instrument.
We must take account of him in the totality of his existence; and
that means, to start with, that we must recognise the elementary
fact that man is a body, and that it is in the first place through the
body alone that all experience comes to him. This is the basic
affirmation of Existentialism, as against the rationalism which
would tend to identify the reality of man with his thought, and
which since the time of Descartes has dominated the greater part
of western philosophical thinking.

This amounts to saying that it is impossible to make any real
distinction between
   Existence
   Consciousness of oneself as existent
   Consciousness of oneself as linked to a body, as incarnate ...
In the first place, an existential view of reality cannot be other, as it
seems, than that of an incarnate personality.[44]

A little farther on Marcel speaks of incarnation as 'the central
datum of metaphysics ... the situation of a being who is revealed

---

[43] G. Marcel: The Philosophy of Existence (1949), pp. 93–4.
[44] G. Marcel: Etre et Avoir (1938; Eng. trans., 1951), pp. 9–10.

to himself as linked to a body'.[45] Marcel is, of course, not using the term 'incarnation' in any technical or theological sense. He is simply recognising that 'I am I', tied to a particular point in time and space. This determines my point of view. No two people can see the universe in exactly the same way. This diversity need not be damaging; it should be the starting-point for any serious, and that means existential, thinking about the great problems of man, the world, and reality. But it can hardly be doubted that this apprehension is related to Marcel's Christian faith. When his concepts were enlarged to include the idea of revelation, it seemed to him natural and appropriate that revelation should come by way of incarnation, through the actual entry of the divine into the conditions of earthly life as we experience it.

As a Christian Marcel has entered into the world of faith. What place does he now accord to philosophy? Does he attribute to it any particular usefulness? Like other existentialists Marcel has given expression to a great many of his ideas through drama and autobiography. Even in his Gifford Lectures he can hardly be said to have reduced his thinking to systematic order – he would perhaps say that, if he had done so, he would have killed it. Yet it is clear that he does regard philosophic thinking as a genuinely human activity, and one which can have a special value of its own:

The immense service which philosophy could perform for us... would be to awaken us increasingly, even before our death, to that reality which unquestionably surrounds us on every side, but to which, as a result of our situation as free beings, we have the terrible power of presenting a systematic refusal. Everything shows more and more clearly that it is possible for us, in some fashion, to seal hermetically the prison in which we choose to live... On the other hand, in proportion as we learn to pay attention to the invitations, often faint but innumerable, which stream out from the invisible world, all perspectives are transformed. I mean that they are transformed *here* in this lower world; for in the same breath life itself is transformed and clothed with a dignity to which it could not possibly aspire, if regarded as no more than an excrescence produced in some strange fashion in a universe which of its own nature is alien to spirit and to all the demands of spirit.[46]

---

[45] *ibid.*, p. 11.
[46] G. Marcel: *Le Mystère de l'Être*, ii, 187.

These three writers, whose works were extremely popular and widely read in many languages, have been taken as a kind of paradigm of adventurous and courageous thinking over a period of about a quarter of a century. It must not be supposed that all seekers during that period can be fitted into one or other of the slots represented by Sartre, Camus and Marcel. Still less should it be supposed, because the picture drawn here reaches its climax in the composure and acceptance of reality manifest in Gabriel Marcel, that the dispute is at an end, and that all serious thinkers have reached a quiet haven of belief. The debate between belief and non-belief goes on.

It is difficult to spot trends and changes of opinion, and to be certain in what direction movements of thought are taking place. Perhaps the one thing more than another that is observable is the extent to which those who find themselves in deep disagreement with one another are prepared to take one another seriously. Some argumentation is still marked by triviality. Some are content to score rather cheaply off opponents. But ridicule is felt to be unworthy of the cause. There appears to have been real progress in the recognition of the right of every human being to think prudently, to believe sincerely, and to give vigorous but courteous expression to everything of the truth of which he is convinced.

It was noted earlier that Nietzsche shows a tendency to emerge from his grave, and that his doctrine of the Death of God finds echoes in the thought of writers who were born many years after his death. For some years the 'Death of God' movement had considerable vogue in America, though less in England. A popular statement of what is involved is to be found in a book by T. J. J. Altizer and William Hamilton, *Radical Theology and the Death of God*.[47]

Altizer held the view that, in the death of Jesus, God actually died, and that there is therefore no point or purpose in turning to him as he no longer exists. This view has not found wide acceptance. The belief most generally held by theists is that, if God exists at all, he must be eternal. 'Great Pan is dead' was

---

[47] Penguin Books, 1968.

spoken of one of the nature gods in whom polytheists have believed; a god who is involved in the natural world or identical with it could naturally be subject to decay and death; but such gods are totally different from the God in whom monotheists believe and to whom they attribute the quality of immortality. Altizer seems to be using the word 'God' in a sense very different from that which in general it is held to convey.[48]

William Hamilton is representative of a number of theologians who are in revolt against the static idea of God to which they were brought up. It is true that Christian scholastic theology has been far too subservient to Greek philosophy, to the One of Aristotle who seems to have no function other than the eternal contemplation of his own unity, to the god of Parmenides who could not possibly enter into relationship with anything outside himself, who could not by any stroke of the imagination become incarnate in a world of time and space. If that is the god whom Hamilton and his colleagues represent as dying, it is quite clear that that is a god who ought to die. These rational theologians are almost at one in their devotion to Jesus of Nazareth, in whom they see dynamism, power, the one who has it in him to release the best that is in man. But they have not seen the way to relate this Jesus to the god in whom they had been brought up to believe.

But, in order to believe in God, is it necessary to believe in a static God, remote, impassible, so far above his creatures that it seems impossible for them to know him or for him to care for them? A number of theologians have found release in what has come to be called 'process theology', based on the work of the distinguished mathematician and philosopher A. N. Whitehead, whose masterpiece is called *Process and Reality, an Essay in Cosmology.*[49] One of the ardent supporters of the view, Stuart Ogden, makes what is perhaps an excessive claim for these new ideas:

---

[48] T. J. J. Altizer's thought is perhaps best expressed in his book *The Gospel of Christian Atheism* (London, 1967). It is clear that he uses the word 'Gospel' also in a sense very different from that which it has ordinarily borne.

[49] New York (1929; corrected edn. 1978). The chief philosophical exponent of similar views in America was Charles Hartshorne, whose teaching is summed up in his book *Reality as Social Progress: Studies in Metaphysics and Religion* (1953).

Protestant theology now has at its disposal just the conceptual resources which make a relatively more adequate Christian theism a possibility... Especially through the work of Alfred North Whitehead the ancient problems of philosophy have received a new and modern treatment, which in its scope and depth easily rivals the so-called *philosophia perennis*.[50]

Not everyone would be inclined to place the work of Whitehead quite on this towering level.[51] But all, I think, would subscribe to the admirable quotation from Henri de Lubac, which Ogden prints as an introduction to his book:

Whenever it abandons a system of thought, humanity imagines it has lost God. The God of 'classical mythology' is dead you say? It may be so; but it does not worry me over much... And if 'classical mythology' disappeared, it was surely because it did not correspond adequately with being. Nor was its idea of God adequate for God. The mind is alive, and so is the God who makes himself known to it. 'God is dead' or so at least it seems to us... until, round the next bend in the road, 'we find him alive again'.[52]

The 'death of God' idea has again taken shape in recent times in the work of the Cambridge theologian, Don Cupitt, in a book entitled *Taking Leave of God*.[53] From the fact that a third impression was called for in the year following the first publication, it is clear that the book has aroused considerable interest and attention. What is the new truth that Cupitt is trying to impress upon a world that, in his opinion, is far too closely tied to what he calls 'traditional, realistic, mythological Christianity?'[54]

---

[50] *The Reality of God* (1963; London 1967), p. 56.
[51] William Temple, in *Nature, Man and God*, Gifford lectures (1934), X, 'Transcendence', points out a number of aspects of the thought of Whitehead which other philosophers have not found convincing.
[52] Henri de Lubac: *The Discovery of God*, p. 167.
[53] London 1980. The title page includes a quotation from the medieval mystic Meister Eckhart: 'Man's last and highest parting occurs when, for God's sake, he takes leave of God.' A second book by Don Cupitt, *The World to Come* appeared in 1982.
[54] p. xii.

The writer had been at pains to make his intention clear. He tells us in his preface (p. xii) that:

> Traditional Christianity is now our 'Old Testament', by which I mean that we now stand towards traditional, realistic, mythological Christianity in the same sort of relationship as Christians have always stood in towards the Old Testament ... there has taken place a great meaning-shift, a change of dispensation.

Some readers may be inclined to think that it is the writer who has remained in the Old Testament dispensation, that he has not yet discovered the New Testament, and the immense change that took place in human life and thinking through the coming of Jesus Christ. When Christians use the term 'God', they mean the Father of our Lord Jesus Christ and nothing else, though they have often been stupid and slow in making explicit the nature of the illumination that has come to them. Anything that helps to make that illumination clearer they are certain to welcome; anything that goes beyond its limits they may be inclined to regard with suspicion.[55]

On the last two pages of the book its purpose is once again made clear: 'God is needed – but as a myth. We need myth because we are persons ... God is a myth we have to have ... It is not an altogether easy admission to make, but it is forced upon us and once we have made it there is no going back' (pp. 166–7). So the course of revelation has been neatly inverted. Genesis tells us that 'God made man in his own image, in the image of God created he him.' Now we are told that autonomy demands that we create God, our own individual and personal myth. Some readers may be inclined to think that the myth which they create in their own image may not be very worthy of worship, indeed may be less than respectable; they may prefer to cling to the reality of God as made known in the face of Jesus Christ.

It is true that in the western world the observance of religious

---

[55] Keith Ward, in *Holding Fast to God; A Reply to Don Cupitt* (London, October 1982), has set out clearly, and to my mind devastatingly, the weaknesses in Cupitt's arguments.

customs and practices is much on the decline, though much on the increase in many parts of Asia and Africa. It would be premature to conclude from this that the search for God is at an end, or that it is other than a major concern for a great many people who would hesitate to apply to themselves the term 'religious' in any ordinary sense of the term.[56] The decline in religious practice is observable, and can be easily verified from the kind of information supplied by opinion polls. To take a specimen almost at random, David Hay[57] records that in the Church of England, between 1960 and 1970, baptisms approximately halved, and confirmations per thousand of the population aged ten to twenty years dropped by more than half.[58] The Methodists in England, happily united since 1931, had in 1933 a membership of nearly 770,000; by 1960 it had declined by almost 100,000, and in the next ten years by another 100,000. For the United States similarly exact figures are not available, but it is a reasonable estimate that, although 80 per cent of the population regard themselves as having some relationship to the church, about 70 per cent are effectively unchurched.

This is undoubtedly one aspect of the situation. Believers whistle to keep up their courage by asserting that what the churches have lost in numbers they have gained in sincerity. That may be true, but, if true, clearly it is known only to God 'who trieth the hearts'. But is this the whole picture? Dr Judith Brown, a highly qualified observer, has included in a recent book[59] a chapter with the engaging title 'How Dead are the Gods? The Christian Experience' (pp. 57–88). It is generally assumed that the intellectual areas of the population have been most extensively alienated from the Christian faith, indeed from any recognition of the spiritual element in human life. Dr Brown's researches, though limited in extent, suggest that this is

---

[56] The work of scientists, such as Stanley C. Jaki (*Cosmos and Creation*, 1981) and philosophical theologians, such as Keith Ward (*Rational Theology and the Creativity of God*, 1982; also *The Concept of God*, 1974), may be mentioned by way of illustration.
[57] *Exploring Inner Space* (Penguin, 1982), pp. 64 ff.
[58] These figures are available because of the honesty of the Church of England in publishing facts and figures unfavourable to itself, as well as those which are more favourable – an excellent practice which for the time being seems to have been abandoned.
[59] *Men and Gods in a Changing World* (1980).

a hasty estimate. She found, in her investigations in Manchester University, that among students 33 per cent admitted to attending places of worship often, and 31.1 per cent to being present at worship 'sometimes'. Among members of the teaching staff the percentages were 30.9 and 24.7 respectively. Of the students questioned, 60.4 per cent professed belief in God; only 19.8 per cent claimed to be atheists; among lecturers the percentages were 45.7 and 18.5 per cent respectively; but whereas only 19.8 per cent of students classed themselves as agnostics, among lecturers the percentage had risen to 35.8 per cent.

'Prayer patterns' added further interesting information. Naturally atheists, both among students and teachers, stated that they never prayed. But among students 38.6 per cent claimed a fairly regular habit of prayer; among lecturers the percentage was 29.6 per cent.

Too much emphasis should not be laid on so limited a survey. But the exceptional capacity of the investigator, and the touching honesty shown in the answers given, lend to these results a greater significance than can be attached to the ordinary opinion poll.[60] Almost more valuable are Dr Brown's comments that 'although church-going has slumped in the last hundred years there has not been any equivalent decline in belief' (p. 69); and that:

> manifestations of hankering after and exploration of the mysterious and numinous occur outside the Christian tradition as well as beyond the boundaries of its structures. At a high level of insight and intellectual sophistication people from a variety of disciplines brood and write on the spiritual deprivation of contemporary society, the dangers of this for the individual, the community and the natural environment, and the need for an experience of the transcendent (p. 84).

---

[60] Dr Brown mentions (p. 64) the fact, which I had also observed, that in the mid-1970s only 29 per cent of those polled for the *Anno Domini* programme said that they believed in a personal God. But the sharp difference of this figure from those given in other almost contemporary polls suggest that the question was put in such a way as to suggest that belief in a personal God involved accepting the idea of an old bearded man in the sky, which 71 per cent of those questioned, if they understood the question in that sense, rightly repudiated.

This sense of the modern malaise, and of the hidden search for that reality which has traditionally passed under the name of God has been well expressed by a young academic who combines the functions of a Christian priest with those of a teacher of English literature:

We must distinguish carefully between an atheistic denial of the existence of God and... a sense of the 'disappearance of God'.[61] I believe that for many who would call themselves humanists, God exists, but he has vanished and is now out of reach, and it behoves the Christian apologist to be aware of the tragedy – rather than the crime – of this annihilation... when the gods 'came to nothing', we 'shared likewise this experience of annihilation'.[62]

If this is true, the defender of the Christian faith must find out where the humanist is, and learn to approach him with a language not of easy dogma and platitudes, but of mystery, awe, ambiguity and tension.

The reality of an awareness in many people – though they themselves may be scarcely aware of it – of what for convenience may be called the fourth dimension of beauty, value, mystery and awe, has recently received confirmation from two sources, on assumptions and methods which are not specifically Christian, and may be different from those which the Christian may generally be inclined to make, but which are no less for that reason deserving of his attention.

A number of years ago the attention of an American psychologist, Abraham Maslow, was directed to the capacity of quite ordinary people for having what he was, I think, the first to describe as 'peak experiences'.[63] These were recognised by those who had undergone them as being exceptional, and of exceptional value in their effect on attitudes to life. Such experiences need not be in the narrow sense religious.[64] But Maslow notes religious experiences as a major element among

---

[61] Quoted from J. Hollis Miller: *The Disappearance of God: Five Nineteenth Century Writers* (Harvard, 1963).
[62] David Jasper, in *New Fire* (No. 51, Summer 1982), p. 103.
[63] A. Maslow: *Religions, Values and Peak Experiences* (1964).
[64] Of four 'peak experiences' of my own which I can recall, three were associated with music, art and natural scenery, and only indirectly with religion.

the ecstatic experiences. If some refuse to admit that they have had any such experiences, the psychologist tends to regard this not as an inability to have such experiences, but as a profound fear of being overcome by emotion, which 'is enough for him to mobilize all his stamping-out and defensive activities against the peak experience'.

In England the initiative in the scientific and rigidly objective study of religious experience was due not to a priest or to a psychologist but to a zoologist. Sir Alister Hardy, formerly professor of zoology in the university of Oxford, had become deeply interested in the religious experiences to which quite ordinary people lay claim as having happened in their own lives. In 1969 he set up in Oxford the Religious Experience Research Unit.[65] A surprising number of ordinary people have responded to the request for an account of experiences; by 1979, 4,000 of these had been received, classified and analysed. The results have been conveniently set forth in popular form by another zoologist David Hay, in a book entitled *Exploring Inner Space.*[66] If one record is to be selected from many as typical, the following may serve as an example:

At certain times I was acutely aware of a presence or power ... I was very aware of being on the verge of the possibility of understanding profound things, which were life-giving in so far as they released me from rather negative emotions and created a feeling of ease, well-being, confidence, and led me very quickly back into normal contact with people, rather than isolation.[67]

By no means all who reported experiences associated them with religion, though a great many did, and, as the research was carried out in the main in Great Britain, 'religion' in the majority of cases meant 'the Church of England as by law established', or some other variety of the Christian faith. But the connection with religion was in some cases established in very curious ways – as in the case of the researcher, engaged in a study of heart disease in Maryland, who discovered that those who went to

---

[65] As recorded in three books – *The Divine Flame* (1966, 1978²); *The Biology of God* (1975); *The Spiritual Nature of Man* (1979).
[66] Penguin Books, 1982.
[67] *Ibid.*, p. 196.

church once a week were only half as likely to die of heart disease as those who did not engage in worship, and found on further study that the same correlation existed in relation to pulmonary emphysema and cirrhosis of the liver.[68]

It is important not to attach more importance to these investigations than they will bear. Such studies, even if extended to the limit of possibility, would not prove the existence of God. They cannot demonstrate that those who claim such experiences have been in touch with anything that actually exists outside the limits of their own imagination. It is still possible for the sceptic to state that all such experiences belong only to the realm of illusion; that they are the product of an over-heated imagination, though many of those reporting the experiences could not readily be described as imaginative; that they are the expression of an infantile desire for support from outside in the face of the discouraging situations of which life in the modern world is full.

What they do show is that, in the secularised atmosphere of society in the west today, many are unsatisfied with the harsh realities of a purely three-dimensional existence, and that the search for what, in the broadest sense of the term, can be called a spiritual reality is so wide-spread as to be almost universal. This being so, it can hardly be maintained that the belief in a spiritual dimension of the universe can be dismissed as purely irrational, though it may belong to the realm of those many things that can be known but cannot be proved. The exploration of the possibilities of such a dimension should not be dismissed as simply a waste of time.

The Christian believes that the impulse which underlies this enquiry and this restlessness have been expressed with magisterial precision by Augustine of Hippo: 'O God, thou hast made us for thyself, and our souls are restless, until they find rest in thee.'

The search for truth, of which an attempt has been made in this chapter to give an outline, has been carried on in a number of differing ways, starting from various presuppositions and arriving at a variety of results – or abandonment of any result. If it is desired that some common denominator be found, it could perhaps be stated in the two terms 'integrity' and 'autonomy', on

---

[68] *Ibid.*, pp. 163-4.

which all who may be classed as existentialists, whether they would call themselves by that name or not, would insist. Nothing may be allowed to interfere with the right of the individual to independent self-hood. No one may prescribe the line of research to be followed. No limit may be set to the questions that may be asked and, if consent is given to any conclusion, it can be only on the basis of an awareness of truth. No compulsion can be respected other than the sheer compulsion of truth.

To these affirmations the enquiring Christian is likely to be able to give unqualified assent. There are, of course, human beings, perhaps the great majority among them, who want only answers, and are prepared to accept answers dictated by any authority which commends itself as reliable or at least as worthy of veneration. Such an attitude may be regretted, but it should not be condemned out of hand. The Christian is committed to reverence for the past, for its great achievements, and for those notable figures who have fought valiantly for the truth as they have understood it. At the same time the Christian is compelled to recognise that faith which depends on anything other than overwhelming conviction of the truth of what is offered, has lost a large part of its proper quality of faith.[69] The Christian also is committed to freedom of enquiry; conviction is recognised not as subservience but as emancipation into new regions of freedom, previously overlooked or only dimly apprehended.

This being so, there is a great deal in the stand of the existentialist which the Christian is able cordially to approve, though he may wish to add some corollaries relating to aspects of the truth which the existentialist may be in danger of overlooking.

Ethical standards and norms and the traditions of society cannot be relied on to give us the guidance that we need. Every moment is different from every other moment; each may make its own special and individual demand which cannot be reduced to any rule.

Thought which does not lead to action is barren. It is the

---

[69] There are many factors in true and genuine faith. Too much emphasis must not be placed on the power of purely intellectual argument. If the believer expresses his belief in the words 'I see', this is not to be taken necessarily as blind and unthinking submission.

business of the thinker not merely to understand the world but also to change it.

Truth is not something that can be done up in a package and learned in a formula. Communication of any truth that matters can only be indirect, and it can be apprehended only by a process which is more than merely intellectual.

Life can be lived only in the atmosphere of decision; what is meant is a readiness for constantly renewed decision, and not a decision that can be taken once for all. Every decision involves a risk – a risk of losing oneself; but this risk has to be accepted as a part of human living.

A human self can live only in freedom. But this freedom implies freedom to be in revolt, to rebel against convention that time has made unreal, against everything that is insincere and hypocritical, against the partial idea that would set itself up as absolute truth.

None of this need be strange for Christians, since it is all contained, though not in such terms as these, in the doctrine of the Holy Spirit. If those who search could understand what is meant by the doctrine of the Holy Spirit, they might find that many of their objections to the Christian faith, and even to the Christian church, would fall to the ground. Christian life must be a continuous process of self-criticism, even of self-creation. It is the task of the Holy Spirit to lead the church into all truth. But there is no reason to suppose that this task has yet been accomplished.

In the light of this doctrine there are certain questions, the existentialist answer to which the Christian may rightly ask the existentialist to reconsider.

The existentialists, especially those of the type of Heidegger and Sartre, tend to assume that the reality of human existence is most clearly seen and experienced in loneliness. But is this true? Is man in his loneliness, the wolf-child, genuinely human? Is not the richest life that which is most fully related to other selves, in marriage, parenthood, friendship and the rest, and which has learned to find in the other not the enemy but the fulfilment of the self? 'The fellowship of the Holy Spirit' is no meaningless Christian phrase.

We can fully accept the existentialist dictum that a large part of a man's business is to make himself. The self is not given ready-made; it has to be acquired by disciplined and devoted effort.

Much of this can be accomplished only by trial and error, and there is no certain and infallible guidance. Yet we may venture to suggest to the existentialist that man is not left without any clue as he attempts to find his way in the maze of existence. The pattern of human existence is already there, not in a code or a manual of ethics but in the life and person of Jesus Christ. One life cannot give immediate guidance or direction to another life. But it can be inexhaustible in significance. This is the meaning of the Christian claim that free persons are being recreated by the Holy Spirit after the likeness of him who made them, namely Jesus Christ.

The existentialist tends to rule out the possibility of grace. But this is hardly a matter that can be settled on *a priori* grounds. The existentialist first encloses himself in the loneliness of his own personal existence, in which he is shut off from any help that any hand, human or divine, could offer. Then, by a process of extrapolation, he concludes that there is no help anywhere in the universe. But this is circular reasoning. The reality of grace cannot be demonstrated in the same way as a proposition in geometry. In the last resort it can only be experienced. But those who have experienced life as full of kindness, who are themselves prepared to be the servants of other selves and are willing to ask the ultimate question as to the nature of a universe in which such things are present realities, may find it not unreasonable to think that human kindness exists because there is an ultimate kindness hidden at the heart of the universe. If this hidden kindness is not passive but active, the most appropriate term for the expression of its nature is 'grace'.

It is quite true that at the end of every man's life stands death. It is foolish to forget this. Human beings should have the courage to face their end, to recognise the limits that death will impose on all that we can do here, and so learn like the Greeks to think only mortal thoughts. We must be prepared also to face the *possibility* that death may mean total extinction – the end of everything. But the existentialist must not be surprised if some of his interlocutors are not prepared to accept in this connection mere dogmatic assertion offered without proof. In a matter where demonstration is impossible, we do well to keep a mind open in either direction. The Christian has no right to ask for more than this. If he feels within himself a joyful certainty that death is a beginning rather than an end, this must come from his assurance that a living Spirit is at work within him. For himself he can confidently believe that 'if the Spirit of him who raised Jesus from the dead dwells in you, he who raised Christ Jesus from the dead will give life to your mortal bodies also through his Spirit which dwells in you' (Rom. 8: 11). He cannot convey this faith to the existentialist by any form of direct communication; he has the right to affirm that that alone is a true Existentialism which takes account of all the possibilities of human existence, without excluding any.

CHAPTER IX

Christendom

What does it mean to be a Jew in the 1980s? What does it mean to be a Buddhist in the 1980s? These are some of the questions with which we have been dealing throughout these studies. The book would be incomplete, unless we could come to the point at which we ask, 'What does it mean to be a Christian in the 1980s? What are the problems faced by the Christian churches in the modern world, and how do they attempt to deal with them?' Christians are encouraged to expose themselves to the various challenges presented to them by the other forms of religious faith that exist in the world. When all these challenges have been taken seriously, can Christians put forward any solid reasons for continuing to be Christians, for holding that the Christian answers to the various problems of life are more satisfactory than the others that have been offered to them, for committing themselves, in the words of the famous Barmen declaration of 1934, to the conviction that 'Jesus Christ... is the sole Word of God, to which we must hearken, and which we must trust and obey, whether in life or in death'?

In our exposition of many faiths we have tended to by-pass one solid and inescapable fact – the existence of Christendom. The Christian faith is not an ideal or a memory; it is not a theory or a set of convictions. It is a faith that for good and evil has become incorporate in a body, a church, which has had a long and complex history, which is mainly situated in the west and is inextricably linked with the history of the nations of the west, and which manifests many of the strengths and weaknesses of other human societies and corporations.

Many Christians resent these painfully material associations of their faith, and in one way or another refuse to recognise them.

Some would fall back on the old distinction between the visible and the invisible church. The visible church may be poor and wretched and naked and blind; the invisible church is without spot or wrinkle or any such thing. For Christians this is a useful, indeed almost a necessary, distinction. It is of no interest whatever to non-Christians. For them the Gospel cannot be separated from its integument; it presents itself to them in terms of that which they can see and hear and experience in relation to the visible church.

Other Christians feel that the empirical church is involved in so grave a betrayal of true Christian faith that the only way to live Christianly is to go out from the church and start again. Certain individuals may have experienced a real vocation to make such a radical break with the past. But, when we are face to face with the non-Christian world, the attempt to make such a break will avail us nothing. We cannot deny our own past; we are what the history of centuries has made us. Whatever we try to make of ourselves, the Gospel will always take the shape of that vessel in which it is carried. This has always been the experience of those who have gone out to preach the Gospel of salvation without particular forms or attachments; they have ended by reproducing with singular exactness the form of Christian life to which they have been themselves accustomed, even when they believe themselves to have given their converts the fullest scope to develop in liberty.

Theologically, we have been discovering anew that the church is not an appendage to the Gospel; it is itself a part of the Gospel. The Gospel cannot be separated from that new people of God, in which its nature is to be made manifest. Practically, this has always been known to everyone who has ever attempted to talk with the adherents of faiths other than his own. Even where it is only two individuals who meet to talk, each brings with him the whole of what he is and of what his faith has made of him. The community is implicit in the individual, the church in the believer. We may feel that the Gospel towers over us, judging us; yet, as far as the world is concerned, we are ourselves the Gospel; there is none other.

Christian faith, then, always presents itself as a strange amalgam of the divine and the human; it nowhere exists in its purity, but always in conjunction with very human and imperfect Christians. If we are prepared to recognise this, it behoves us to take a sternly realistic view of the perils to which the Christian

society, just like every other religious society, is exposed by the
mere fact of living in the world.

1. In the first place, there is an inevitable tendency for the living
experience of faith to seek after a satisfactory intellectual
expression as a legitimate medium of communication. The
Gospel starts from the tremendous Person and the glowing
poetry of Jesus of Nazareth. It passes through the imaginative
and still mainly poetical interpretations of Paul and John. But
even before the end of the New Testament period, the original
inspiration is beginning to die away; faith, which had once been
existential, a matter of total commitment to the One who is
believed, is undergoing a transformation into 'the faith',
something that can be communicated in doctrinal formulations
such as demand intellectual assent rather than the obedience of
faith.

2. Secondly, experience becomes frozen in an institution. We
start with the glad freedom of voluntary service, in which
greatness and authority are measured only by devotion to the
cause and by willingness to take the place of a servant. Already in
the second generation permanent officials are beginning to
appear. The charismatic is being replaced by the institutional. A
hierarchy develops. The whole-time servants of the church
expect to be paid for their service and the ecclesiastical career
begins to attract. The church acquires property and even wealth.
As early as the fourth century a pagan historian, Ammianus
Marcellinus, remarks that the larger bishoprics, especially that of
Rome, are natural objects of ambition to those who hope to
acquire them. By this time the church is beginning to take on an
appearance not very different from that of any other property-
owning society. It may claim protection from the law, and enter
into litigation if its rights are threatened. There is one further
stage of possible degradation – if the church, not content with
equality, begins to claim privilege as against other societies. The
whole of Christian history shows that this is a temptation to
which the church has always been peculiarly vulnerable; it
acquires privileges in time of prosperity, and will then move
heaven and earth to see that these privileges are in no way
diminished.

3. The life of the church tends, within a limited span of time, to be determined by convention and conformity. It is taken for granted that those born within the Christian society will be Christians. Provided that they show a minimum of conformity to the rules and practices of the community, they may expect to enjoy its privileges. The ordinances of the faith – baptism, confirmation and the rest – take on a social rather than a religious character, and are observed with little regard to their Christian significance.

4. Finally, the faith comes to be identified with a certain culture. Christianity, dominant so long in the west, is one of the ingredients in western culture. The church tends to identify itself with that culture and with the nations in the life of which it finds expression. Then to be a Christian means primarily to be a western man, and has little to do with personal relationship to the Gospel of Jesus Christ.

It is at this point that demonic powers can take hold of a religion, and use it for purposes very different from those to which it ought to be consecrated. For four centuries western culture has been explosive, dynamic and expansive. It has spread itself abroad through the world. This has been also the period of the great expansion of the Christian church. However honestly western Christians may attempt to dissociate themselves from the cultural association of religion, there is always the danger that they may unconsciously desire the propagation both of this faith and of this culture. This danger is particularly great when a supposed cultural superiority is associated with economic, or still worse military, power. One who interests himself in the spread of the faith on such terms as these has made himself the master of the Gospel instead of its servant; he is using it to further his own ends. The extent to which Christian missionaries have been imbued with imperialistic aims has doubtless been greatly exaggerated by their critics. Yet there is enough substance in the criticism to make the thoughtful Christian acutely uncomfortable.

★

Having said all this, we must go on to recognise that each of these four developments – dogma, institution, convention, culture – is inevitable, and that similar phenomena are to be traced in every religion.

1. Religion, we may say, is an experience and should not attempt to be more. But man is by nature a reflective animal, and nothing can prevent him from reflecting on that which he has experienced and from attempting to understand it. Everyone has in some degree or other the analytical gift; it is through question and analysis that understanding is reached. The moment that this process is applied to religion, the formulation of doctrine has begun. Once the questioning spirit has been aroused, it is no use saying that this or that question must not be asked; sooner or later it will be asked, and some attempt at least to provide an answer must be made.

Islam starts with the tumultuous experience of the Prophet on the mountain. Its technical creed is the shortest and simplest in the world. Yet Islam too in course of time developed more elaborate creeds,[1] and had its period of scholasticism, when subtle question and interpretation grew into a mountain of erudition. The Jew produced the Talmud. In India the *Bhagavadgītā* is 'revelation'. But questions of interpretation arise; the commentators get to work. Saṁkara and Rāmānuja have both left their classic commentaries, and have shown the diversity of meaning that one text can be made to yield.

The believer is inclined to sigh over the immense outpouring of human labour that has gone into these books, and to wonder whether the scholars have done anything but crush living faith under their mountainous productions. But this is a narrow and unjust view. The importance of doctrine must not be exaggerated; but rightly understood it can serve two useful purposes. It can save later generations from having to do the whole work of question and answer for themselves and from the start. And against certain possible roads it can place a warning that these have been explored and found to lead nowhere. And even doctrine, if it takes such a form as the *Te Deum*, can be turned into an instrument of praise.

---

[1] One of the best expositions of this process is a book which in the course of time has become a classic – A. J. Wensinck: *The Muslim Creed: its Genesis and Historical Development* (Cambridge, 1932).

2. Almost every new Christian group starts with the idea that it will not become an institution; it will return to the simplicity of the primitive days and will refuse to be weighed down by the worldly considerations that come with wealth and property. Some groups have been more successful than others in avoiding the steps by which a society is turned into an institution; but the beginnings of the process are observable in almost all of them. At the start there is no ordained ministry. But ere long one or two begin to stand out as specially gifted, and responsibility comes more and more to fall into their hands. As numbers grow, the work of the ministry becomes more exacting, and can hardly be carried out in the spare time of those who are already earning their daily bread in the world. A demand for a better-educated ministry begins to make itself felt and the servants of the church must be trained. Most groups find it necessary to own some kind of place of meeting, and at once are launched on all the problems involved in the possession of property. It is possible to watch with interest the development of all these phenomena in the Pentecostal groups, some of which have already taken many steps away from the 'sect-type' to the 'church-type' of organisation.[2]

Religions, such as Christianity and Islam, which have regular services of worship and expect the faithful to attend them, are specially faced by the problems of institution and property. The mosque and the church are among the most familiar buildings in the world. Hinduism and Buddhism have much more flexible organisations. Yet every Hindu village has its shrines, probably communally owned by the villagers and maintained by their joint efforts. Every shrine must have its ministrant, though his duties may be few and occasional, and for the fulfilment of those duties he will expect some remuneration.

3. Conformity to established tradition is the mark of institutions, not only of religious bodies, which have existed through a series of generations. There is bound to be a difference between one who has been born into the Christian fellowship and one who has joined it from without of his own volition. Those who

---

[2] The early history of the Pentecostal groups is brilliantly set out by Nils Bloch-Hoell: *The Pentecostal Movement* (1964), pp. 1-94.

have long worked in a rapidly growing Christian community, like the late Bishop Azariah in the villages of Dornakal in South India, are wont to lament the decline in the second and third generation. Where is the enthusiasm of the first converts? Why have acquiesence, and even apathy, taken so quickly the place of personal conviction and the willingness to suffer? It must not be supposed that all is loss, when the day of first beginnings is over and a new Christian group has moved forward into the life of a settled community. In the first generation everything is discovery and conflict – a situation which lends itself both to high achievement, and also to certain traumatic divisions within the human personality. There is something to be said for the calmer period in which a number of things can be taken for granted, moral standards are accepted in principle though not always observed in practice, and a deeper process of spiritual development can begin.

As soon as a Christian community is formed it is faced by the problem of the coming generation. In Russia this is settled for the church by the government – no religious instruction of any kind may be given to a young person under eighteen years of age. In certain families in the west, in which the parents are of different religion or confession, for the sake of peace and quiet in the home agreement has been reached to keep religion out of it, and 'to let the children make up their own minds, when they are old enough to think for themselves'. But most people would not regard this as a satisfactory solution. Even those Christian bodies which practise only adult baptism do not regard the children of Christian parents as entirely outside the covenant; in fact in many cases infants are solemnly dedicated to God though not baptised. In almost all religious bodies some provision is made for the instruction of the young in the tenets of their religion; it is notable that at the present time even Hinduism, which has relied so much on practice and the externals of devotion, is beginning to feel the need of more formal religious teaching.[3]

It has to be recognised that there is an immense difference between teaching, which can be directly apprehended and even

---

[3] The dilemmas of contemporary Hinduism have been brilliantly delineated by Judith M. Brown in *Men and Gods in a Changing World* (London, 1980), especially ch. 2 'How dead are the gods? The Hindu Experience' and ch. 4 'Gurus and Gospels'.

memorised, and real religious communication which, as Kierkegaard so clearly saw, can be made only indirectly. But to say
that one is not the same as the other is not to say that either is
unimportant. And, even if no such regular teaching is given, it is
impossible to keep religion away from the children. They will ask
questions about it, even in Russia. Impressions are being formed
in them, far below the level of conscious response. Memory may
recall only such marginal things as hot-cross buns on Good
Friday. Yet probably there are few Jews who are not stirred by
some recollection of Passover meals in the old home; and, even in
secularised America, there are not a few who recall that
Thanksgiving is intended to be a thanksgiving to Almighty God,
and is declared to be so every year by the President. Tradition and
traditional observance may become the chief obstacles to true
religion. They can also form the channels in which the streams of
true religion will flow, if the windows of heaven should again be
opened.

4. It is vain to imagine that religion can be kept uncontaminated
by the process of cultural development. It cannot be kept
separate from culture, and it ought not to be kept separate from
culture.

Religion is so many-sided a thing that it is bound to affect the
life of man at every point. All western law is in its origin most
deeply indebted to the Romans; yet no one concerned with the
common law in England can fail to observe the effect on it of the
Judaeo-Christian tradition, with its insistence on moral, as
distinct from merely legal, responsibility. We take it for granted
that Sunday will be a day of rest, but this is a Judaeo-Christian
cultural assumption, and not a universally accepted principle.[4]
The cultural significance of the weekly day of rest, quite apart
from its religious value, cannot be exaggerated;[5] it is interesting
to note, in a mainly Hindu and Muslim city such as Madras, how
many of the shops are closed on Sunday mornings. The
difference is immediately felt in a Hindu village, where leisure is

---

[4] Islam, of course, has its one day of rest in seven, in this following the Judaeo-
Christian tradition.

[5] G. von Rad rightly points out that the Jewish sabbath is primarily the day of
rest for man and beast, and that it is only much later that we hear of religious
services being held in connection with it. *Moses* (Eng. trans., 1960), p. 52.

still regulated in the main by the recurrent Hindu festivals, and where the would-be Christian may find himself ironically greeted by his neighbours with the words, 'Go and become a Christian, and take a rest on Sunday.'

Religion and culture *ought* not to be separated. This is the point on which Christopher Dawson has so admirably insisted.[6] If religion tries to live in a world of its own, unrelated to the other aspects of the life of man in society, it becomes anaemic, precious and uninteresting, the plaything of those who have a special penchant for that kind of thing. If culture tries to exist without religious sanctions, it becomes demonic; it is then the expression of the titanic in man, of his unbridled lust for self-expression and self-development, unchecked by any higher norms in the light of which man is held to be answerable. In the past religion and culture have always dwelt together as sometimes somewhat uneasy bedfellows. The tragedy of our own day is that for the first time in history they seem irremediably to have fallen apart. Christopher Dawson ends his book with two penetrating and pregnant observations:

> We are faced with a spiritual conflict of the most acute kind, a sort of social schizophrenia which divides the soul of society between a non-moral will to power served by inhuman techniques and a religious faith and moral idealism which have no power to influence human life. There must be a return to unity – a spiritual integration of culture – if mankind is to survive... This does not mean a new religion or a new culture but a movement of piritual reintegration which would restore that vital relation between religion and culture which has existed at every age and on ev·r evel of human developm·nt.[7]

If we set out to look for true religion and undefiled, we are not likely to find it. Wherever we encounter it, the gold of pure religion is likely to be mixed with a certain measure of alloy. But this means that every religious faith must live in a state of perpetual self-criticism. The alloy may serve to make religion

---

[6] Notably in *Religion and Culture* (1948), ch. I and III.
[7] *Ibid.*, pp. 217-18.

workable. Carried beyond a certain measure it will assuredly make it unworkable.

Critics of Christendom have an easy task ready to hand. The principles of the Gospel are so lofty that it is not difficult to represent the churches as in a state of permanent treason against their Lord. It would be unfair, however, not to look at the other side, and not to recognise the immense travail of self-criticism which has been going on within the Christian churches, and precisely along the line of the four developments or dangers which we have been analysing.

1. The church has inherited a vast system of doctrine, mainly derived from the contact between Greek and biblical thought, in two stages; first directly, in the days of the great Greek Fathers and the Christological controversies of the fourth and fifth centuries; secondly, in the Middle Ages, when Aristotle came back to the west via Arabia and Spain, and the consequent refertilisation of the western mind found its most perfectly proportioned expression in the *Summa* of Thomas Aquinas (1225-74). Almost till our own day Christian doctrinal thinking has moved within the limits of the traditional questions and the categories derived from the enquiring mind of the Greeks. We live in a period of reaction. Those questions and answers were right and necessary at a certain stage of Christian development. Must we not now get behind them, and learn again to think *biblically*, in categories more directly derived from the Christian revelation itself?

In this connection it is natural to think of the work of Karl Barth (1886-1968). Barth deliberately set himself to eliminate Greek ideas and metaphysical concepts, and to express the Christian faith in the framework of the dominating idea of the Word of God as revelation. Even those who least agree with Karl Barth have been compelled to take him seriously; even Roman Catholics have admitted that he, by his writings, has awoken in them a new enthusiasm for dogmatic theology.

But it would be a grave error to limit the movement of contemporary theology to the Barthian school. Everywhere there is a sense of freedom and discovery. Part of this is due to the new schools of interpretation of the Old Testament, and to a recognition of the special Hebrew genius in its relatedness to the Christian revelation. The Greek mind does not work in the same way as the Hebrew.[8] The answers to our questions to some extent depend on the way in which the questions are framed, and this in turn depends on certain linguistic and psychological structures. Is it not likely that, if we go back to the less abstract, more pictorial, way of thinking of the Hebrew, we shall ask of revelation different questions from those propounded by the Greeks? This point will come before us again in connection with the right of peoples with an entirely different background, such as the Chinese, to ask of the biblical revelation such questions as would never occur to a western thinker.[9]

2. In the churches, radical questions are being asked as to the relevance and adequacy of old forms of organisation and ministry to contemporary situations.

One of the oldest structures of the Christian society is the parish, a geographical area within which every soul is the pastoral responsibility of a single shepherd, or of a group of shepherds. This worked admirably in a rural society, when the vast mass of the people lived in small villages and could be personally cared for by the resident parson. Is such a structure relevant in the days of industrial civilisation and of the concentration of human beings in the enormous cities of the modern world? I do not think myself that the parish will ever be superseded. Yet it is reasonable to ask whether the church should not relate itself to some of the other structures of human life – to the place in which men work as well as to the place in which they sleep. The system of industrial chaplaincies is now well established in Great Britain and elsewhere. The effectiveness of such specialised ministries may be questioned; those who practise and support them can at least claim to have drawn attention to needs that should be met, and to possibilities that

---

[8] An interesting study of the contrast is T. Boman's *Das Hebräische Denken im Vergleich mit dem Griechischen* (1954; Eng. trans., *Hebrew Thought Compared with Greek*, London, 1960). This book, valuable as it is, needs to be read in the light of the criticisms directed against it by Professor James Barr in his work *The Semantics of Biblical Language* (1961). There is a difference, but it is less absolute than Boman supposes.

[9] As an example of the new liberty acquired by Christian thinking, we may point to the volume *Believing in the Church: The Corporate Nature of Faith* (A Report by the Doctrine Commission of the Church of England, London, 1981).

have not as yet been fully worked out. Traditional ministries are not adequately meeting the needs of Christian witness in the world today. In this field radical thinking is going on in many places.

Even those who through prejudice or conviction are opposed to the ordination of women to the ministry of the church are fain to recognise that the church has failed to make adequate use of the gifts of one half of its membership. What ought to be the special contribution of women to the life of the church? It may be that we do not yet know the answer to this question: it is something that the question is being seriously asked.

No church is satisfied with the use that it is making of its laymen. In such days as these, do we not need a revival of the prophetic as against the more institutional forms of ministry? And is it not likely that, as in the Old Testament, the majority of those called to exercise this ministry will be laymen? Many of the existing lay movements tend towards an increasing clericalisation of the faithful layman, and this is exactly the opposite of what is needed. It is the merit of the Department on the Laity of the World Council of Churches that it has passed beyond this narrow viewpoint, and tried to view the problem of lay ministry as a function of the total life of the *Laos*, the people of God.[10]

3. The church of God can never completely separate itself from its traditions. But in many areas the simple fact of opposition is making plain to the churches the truth that they cannot live on their past.

This is most plain in communist countries, and, in this field as in others, our best evidence seems to come from East Germany. There the traditional structure has been that of the *Volkskirche*, in which everyone is baptised and confirmed and pays church taxes. Now the communists, with their secular alternative to confirmation, have rudely broken through all that, and have made it plain that the characteristic dimension of Christian faith is not consent but decision. Co-existence between a communist government and Christian faith is never easy. But the attitude of

---

[10] It is significant that when the World Council of Churches commissioned a book, *The Layman in Christian History* (eds. S. C. Neill and H. R. Weber, 1963), this proved to be a pioneer book – no such survey had ever before been undertaken.

the authorities is not in every case one of total hostility to the churches, and many Christians in East Germany hold that their situation is spiritually much healthier than that of the prosperous and well-established churches in the Federal Republic in the west.[11]

Communist totalitarianism naturally presents to the churches the sharpest challenge to rethink their nature and their status. But in many other traditionally Christian countries the church has been reminded that it is now in a minority. It cannot rely on the general stream of public opinion to carry it forward; it can rely, humanly speaking, only on the wills and the determination of those who have made a definite and personal commitment of themselves to Christ. The traditional is yielding to the existential. This is all to the good, provided that in recognising the difference between committed Christians and those who, while not uninfluenced by the Christian tradition, do not commit the direction of their lives wholly to that tradition, the churches do not develop the faults of a minority which feels itself to be on the defensive. At all times deeply committed Christians have been a minority; in times when that minority has felt itself to be a dynamic minority with the future in its hands, its achievements have been sensational, and quite out of proportion to the numbers of those directly engaged in the Christian enterprise.

4. The western world is almost morbidly obsessed by a guilt complex over its identification of Christian faith with its own culture. This is so strongly felt by the younger generation as to make difficult any presentation of the call to missionary service overseas. 'When we have made such a mess of things in the west, have we any right to export our culture overseas, and to offer it to these others?' If the question is put in this form, clearly the answer can only be 'No'. But the course of the argument that we have so far followed excludes the simple defence often put forward by the supporters of the Christian missionary enterprise – that we do not go abroad to spread our culture but only to preach the pure Gospel of Jesus Christ our Lord. As we have

---

[11] It is interesting that in 1981 the World Council of Churches found it possible to hold a session of its Central Committee in Dresden, the great city of Saxony, well within the communist-controlled zone.

seen, this is precisely the thing that we can never do – we can go only as ourselves, and that means as specimens of western man.[12]

The western churches are at the present time making almost frenzied efforts to disentangle the Gospel from the western habiliments in which it has been clothed.[13] It is not clear that these churches are as yet fully aware of the complexity of the problem that they have taken in hand. We may note four points which must be kept separate and distinct:

On the whole the western churches are now penitent churches. They have come to recognise that 'empirical Christianity', the churches as they now are, with their all too human elements and their involvement in the things of this world, stand under the judgment of God, no less than other human structures and organisations, religious or secular. In this sense at least Christianity is 'one of the religions', and must accept the fact that judgment is to begin at the house of God.

The immediate task is to discover how the Gospel can again become the vivifying force in western culture, how the gap of which Mr Dawson has so poignantly spoken can be bridged. This is a different task from that of winning back the individual to the faith. It demands the penetration of whole populations by the Christian idea on the emotional and subconscious level, so that ordinary people come again to think and to feel in a Christian way even when they are not making any conscious profession of Christian faith. In a word, we have to reverse the process which Nietzsche alleged to have taken place without men's knowing it. Instead of 'God is dead' we must be able to affirm that 'God is alive again in the western consciousness' or at least that 'God is again striving to be born'.

But the western churches cannot hold over their offer of the Gospel to all the world until the process of recovery of the west

---

[12] Of course not by any means all Christian missionaries are western men and women; but, *mutatis mutandis* exactly the same will be true of an Indian Christian working for example among an African people.

[13] But note the paradox: 'It is amazing that while the Christian evangelist talks about the need for proclaiming the faith dissociated with the cultural forms which are part of the Western heritage, Hindu religious leaders advocate the dissemination of just these cultural forms as separated from their Christian foundations.' P. D. Devanandan: *The Gospel and Renascent Hinduism* (1959), p. 36.

has been completed. The dialogue between the religions has begun; it is essential that the Christian voice should be heard in it with ever-increasing clarity; in many parts of the world the Christian voice can only be a western voice. But, in their new humility, the western churches are prepared to learn from the mistakes of the past. They are better able than they were to distinguish between the essentials of the Gospel and the fortuitous accretions which are dear to the west, but have nothing to do with the central issues of faith in Christ. They go now to offer and not to impose.

In the past it was too readily assumed that out of the seed of the Gospel only one kind of tree can grow – sow the Word, and what you will see emerge is something like the culture of the western world. So it was natural for the early Portuguese missionaries to give their converts Portuguese names, some of which their descendants still proudly bear, and to expect them to conform as nearly as possible to the habits of their teachers and their rulers.

To a certain extent the analogy of the seed and the tree is correct. The possible forms of Christian living are not infinitely variable. For instance, the Christian society will always be, in principle, a strictly monogamous society. Such a society is different at its heart from one in which polygamy is permitted and encouraged. Monogamy is more than a western sociological ideal.[14]

Nor is it necessary to suppose that the west should withhold from others all the good things that have come to it from other than strictly Christian sources. A careful study of Plato and Aristotle might be for the Indian theological student an admirable intellectual discipline, preparatory, as it has been over many generations in the west, to thinking out independently the significance of biblical categories for the expression of Christian truth.

Yet, when these reservations have been made, we are now willing to recognise as never before that the creative powers of the Gospel are greater than we had supposed, and that its

---

[14] Many African Christians believe that an exception should be made in favour of polygamous males who have come into the Christian fellowship from the outside world; but very few would favour the extension of this exception beyond the limits of the first generation of believers.

working in the kingdoms of this world may be more flexible than we have allowed for. Vines are vines all over the world; but the vine has exceptional powers of drawing difference and variety from varying conditions of soil and sun and rain. What a Chinese Christian culture, with a genuinely Chinese and not a Graeco-Roman background, might become, we are as yet hardly able to imagine. Yet we have become convinced that such a development would be according to the will of God, and that, if widely differing patterns of Christian living were to develop in different parts of the world, that would tend to the enrichment and not to the impoverishment of the church, and to the glorification of Christ and not to his dishonour.

It has to be noticed that this Christian tendency towards self-criticism and consequent liberation from the past runs directly counter to what is happening in many other areas of the world. All great cultures in the past have been dependent on a religion. All great religions of the past have expressed themselves in a particular and recognisable pattern of culture. With the rise of nationalism in Asia and Africa and elsewhere, there has naturally been a tendency to think that national pride should find expression in one great religion, in the cultural tradition which has grown out of that religion in the past, and even in one great language in which that religion has traditionally found expression. There are groups in India which feel strongly that India should be Hindustan, and criticise the more tolerant affirmations of the Constitution as weakness. In Indonesia the *pesantren*, the traditional Islamic teaching institution, in which the study of Arabic and of the tenets of Islam is predominant, seems to be enjoying increasing popularity.[15] In Sri Lanka the Buddhists felt that their language, Sinhalese, should be the only official language. The attempt to impose this against the strong protests of a dissident minority threatened to break up the unity of the island, and still has in it disruptive possibilities.

In some at least of these 'non-aligned' countries, there seems to be a tendency towards a totalitarian outlook, in which nation, state, and religion are fused into a single complex unity.

If this is true, it may be that the Christian process of self-criticism and emancipation which we have been describing will

---

[15] V. S. Naipaul: *Among the Believers* (1981), pp. 308–26.

come to be seen in retrospect as one of the great spiritual happenings of our time, and one that can render immense service not only to the Christian faith but to all the other living faiths of the world.

If we are moving into a totalitarian era, as there is good reason to fear that we are, it is essential that there should be in every nation one body which recognises as the principle of its life that, beyond all claims that may be made by the state or any other human structure or society, there are supramundane values to which it is committed, and to which it must be loyal whether in life or in death. In the past, the church has often been content to be the handmaid or the servant or the ally of the state. If anything has been clearly learned in this century, it is that no such alliance can ever be more than conditional. The state, as one of the orders instituted or permitted by God, is entitled to the loyalty of men. But there is another loyalty which may not in any circumstances be circumscribed or compromised. Faith is coming to be recognised in a new way as the guardian of the freedom of the soul of man.

This may be felt on the national, or the local, or the individual level.

Throughout the whole of the Christian western tradition, from Constantine onward, the state has taken the church under its protection and in various ways made use of it for its own purposes. Gradually and painfully the battle for toleration has been won in most western countries; but still in most of them there is one dominant form of the Christian religion, which is in some kind of association with the state.

A radical departure from this tradition lends importance to the American experiment of the total separation of church and state – an importance not yet adequately realised by historians outside the United States.[16] Even in the United States this situation was reached only by a somewhat painful process of trial and error. Most of the colonies started with established churches, and were averse from the principle of toleration. But gradually the other

---

[16] One of the merits of Prof. Hermelink's great history of the nineteenth century: *Das Christentum in der Menschheitsgeschichte* (3 vols: 1951, 1953, 1955) is his clear recognition of the independent contribution that American Christianity has in this respect made to the progress of the Christian world as a whole.

view prevailed. What was granted to all forms of faith and of no-faith was not toleration but equality within the broad limits of the operation of the common law.

No solution of the relation of church and state is perfect. Even when there is no legal bond, churches can become subservient to public opinion, to social pressures and to the will of a majority. If the state is completely safeguarded against the influence of religion, it may become secularised, and government may come to be regarded as the field of operation of unbridled power politics without reference to any supposedly higher laws and powers. Churches, even though they have no legal status, can organise themselves to bring considerable pressure to bear on any democratically-elected government. Yet on the whole it must be recognised that the American experiment has worked well. The churches apparently flourish. Deeply secularised as it is, the nation seems yet to regard itself as in some sense 'a nation under God', a phrase which taken seriously helps to mitigate the light-hearted blasphemy of 'God's own country'.

It is significant that on the other side of the world another great nation has organised itself somewhat on the American pattern. India has declared itself to be a *secular* democratic republic. But the word 'secular' needs careful interpretation. Those who framed the Indian Constitution declared that they did not intend to disregard religion or to deny its significance in the life of society. But this state would not ally itself with any religion, would not claim for itself any authority in the name of religion or over the beliefs of its citizens. Not everyone in India is satisfied with this solution; but, in spite of some elements of resistance, it may be taken as reasonably certain that the present Constitution will be upheld.

This is the most favourable situation for the maintenance of the spiritual independence of the faith and of the church. It must not, however, be forgotten that the church is called to maintain that independence in all circumstances, however unfavourable, and that some of its greatest services to the freedom of the human spirit have been rendered precisely when its faithfulness has led it into conflict with the state, and on to the bitter road of persecution.

At the level of societies smaller than that of the nation, the local church should have the answer to the gnawing problem of the insignificance of the individual man. We cannot set the clock back. More and more our destinies are controlled by forces over which we have no control; we feel ourselves carried away like straws on a stream. But, in order to be human, human beings need a place in which their voice is listened to with respect, in which their votes count, in which they have a share in making the decisions by which they consent to live. If every other outlet is denied, the local church should survive the flood as that community in which precisely these necessities of the human spirit are offered to all the members without distinction.[17]

Here, perhaps, the churches of the Baptist and Congregationalist orders have the most to offer to our need. From the beginning they have professed and maintained the absolute equality of believers in the sight of God. They have taken it for granted that at any moment the right word might be given through the Holy Spirit to any member of the community, however insignificant. In the solemnity of the church meeting every member feels that momentous things are being decided, that the individual voice counts, and that the decisions all share in making will have significance for time and for eternity. Such things add space and dignity to human existence. And perhaps all this may prove of special value where many are passing out of the collective anonymity of the tribe into the collective anonymity of the great city.[18]

At a third point the church can safeguard the integrity of human beings. Kierkegaard held that an individual realises the true nature of his being only in immediate confrontation by the living God. There no one can help him. This is the moment of supreme loneliness in human life. Each comes to a point at which a decisive 'Yes' or 'No' has to be said. Certainly at the moment the individual cannot understand all that is implicit in the decision; he is of necessity entering into an uncharted future. His new life will be marked by that openness to the future, of which Rudolf

---

[17] For this principle to be effective, it is essential that the local church should not be too large. Ministers and lay leaders alike, especially in America, tend to be hypnotised by the bourgeois siren of *size*, and so to defeat their own excellent intentions.

[18] It should be noted that, in the creative period of the trade unions, the local trade union branch provided the members with just this sense of dignity, of being worthwhile. Research showed that, if the number of members grew beyond eighty, the effectiveness of the branch began to diminish.

Bultmann speaks. But the decision, if made, is his and no one else's. This is not individualism. On the contrary, it marks the advance from the mere individual, conditioned by the past, by tradition, and by the ceaseless levelling processes of modern society, into full personal existence, in which each takes full responsibility for his own decisions and is prepared to stand to them, come life come death.

No claim is here being made that the Christian churches are the only body in the world to concern themselves with the contemporary threat to personal existence. There are other groups, mainly humanistic in character, which share the same concern, and give roughly the same answer, though naturally translated into secular terms. The churches, however, may claim that in the last quarter of a century they have made considerable discoveries in all these fields, and, that though much is yet experimental and tentative, results have been sufficiently impressive to encourage further experiment in all these directions. They may maintain that in this period, in which all over the world there are evident such strong tendencies towards the totalitarian deformation of human existence in the political, the social, the economic and the intellectual fields, these are the kind of problems with which all the religions ought to be occupying themselves. They have, perhaps, the right to ask the representatives of the other religions how far they have concerned themselves with such problems, and what their experiences have been. This will not lead simply to a comparison of ideas and doctrines; it may fruitfully lead the dialogue on to the much deeper level of what may be called existential attitudes. What is our judgment on human life as a whole and on the value of the human person? It is on this level that discussion between the faiths may come to be truly creative.

★

At various points we have suggested that Christians may come with questions to their friends in the other faiths. Dialogue becomes dialogue only when question is met with question. We must, therefore, expect and welcome the questioning of others. It is for them, and not for us, to formulate their questions. But we may perhaps be allowed to identify five regions in which questions are almost certain to be presented, and in which Christians must be prepared to think out an answer.

1. The Christian faith has laid claim from the beginning to universality, as being a faith in which all human beings are entitled to share. How far is it today a genuinely international body?

On the purely superficial level, our answer lies ready to hand. There is no race and no religion in the world which has not yielded converts to the Christian faith.[19] But such an answer will not satisfy the questioner. He is concerned to know how far the western dominance in Christianity has receded, how far in fact, to put it bluntly, the Christian faith is still the faith of the white man.

The question is a fair one. The Christian can only reply that almost all the Christian churches in the world are now penitently aware of the pungency of the question, and are doing what they can to set right one of the gravest defects in the Christian pattern as it now presents itself. Racial pride and exclusiveness have played an undue part in the Christian consciousness, and they will not be exorcised overnight. But we really are making progress.

One line of advance is seen in the ecumenical movement. The progress made in sixty years is somewhat precisely measurable. At the great Edinburgh Missionary Conference of 1910, only seventeen out of more than twelve hundred people who took part were of non-white origin. At the fourth Assembly of the World Council of Churches held at Uppsala in 1968, and even more at the Conference on Church and Society held at Geneva in 1966, the voice of the third-world churches was plainly heard, and the representatives of those churches felt, perhaps for the first time, that they were being taken seriously by the leaders of the older churches. The majority of those present still come from the west and this is inevitable in view of the fact that by far the larger number of Christians in the world live in western countries. But the principle of complete spiritual equality has been established, and will never again be questioned.[20] At the first Lambeth

---

[19] This is a careful statement. As far as is known, there are no Christians in Tibet. But in Ladakh and elsewhere men of Tibetan race and speech have become Christians, and have even been ordained to the Christian ministry.

[20] The Roman Catholic parallel to this development has been the great development of the indigenous episcopate, and the appointment as cardinals of bishops from almost every major country in the world.

Conference of Anglican bishops held in 1867, out of about seventy bishops present there was one black bishop – from Haiti; at the eleventh, in 1978, out of 400 there were 118 bishops from the races of the third world.

There are, however, things in the Christian churches which are hard to defend, and which are rightly criticised by non-Christian friends. The reality of racial and colour prejudice spreads far beyond the limits of those areas in which it is specially a problem, is present in a great many people who have never been challenged by it as a practical issue, and has deep roots in human nature. It is good to be reminded of this; at the same time it is important not to forget the progress that has been made. If a complete list could be made of all the colleges in the United States which during the last twenty-five years have admitted black students for the first time, of all the areas in which segregation in the schools has been abolished, of all the positions of distinction to which blacks have been called, it would be possible to argue that a revolution in the Christian consciousness, comparable to that which marked the period of the Reformation, has come about in our time.

The situation is far more difficult when, as in South Africa, a method which the greater part of the Christian world holds to be wrong is defended as though it were itself a part of the Christian faith. Racial discrimination goes back as far as the beginning of history. The situation becomes serious when religious conviction is called in to hallow the forces of fear, of prejudice and of dislike. Yet even here it is possible to see the beginnings of a change. The younger theologians of the Dutch Reformed Church are not so sure as their fathers were that the doctrine of *apartheid* can be directly derived from the biblical revelation, and are no longer afraid to give formal expression to their opinions. When the religious foundations of a conviction give way, it is likely that the conviction itself is on the way to substantial modification.[21]

2. The Christian churches are challenged to show that they can really produce such fellowship, such community, as should be the

---

[21] The year 1982 has seen a notable expression, on the part of leaders in the Dutch Reformed community, of their dissent from the traditional Afrikaner understanding of *apartheid*.

natural fruit of the principles that they profess. Have we, in point
of fact, done as well as the trade union, the social club, the
regiment, the Antarctic expedition, and other forms of association in which individuals have come together for the promotion
of common aims?

Here we must honestly admit our gravest weakness. Yet we
can modestly claim that we have been more aware of the problem
than our critics, and have taken certain steps to meet the
criticism.

In the first place we may note the way in which the doctrine of
forgiveness has come back into the centre of Christian thinking –
we noted earlier that in Hinduism it seems to be almost
completely absent. There is no cement in society comparable in
strength to the willingness of men and women to forgive one
another. This is as true of the family as of any other society;
where a family has broken up, again and again the cause is found
to have been the denial of forgiveness where it ought to have
been granted. It is not easy to forgive. The one thing that more
than any other helps men to forgive is the knowledge that they
themselves have received forgiveness when they had done
nothing to deserve it. This is the message that has come to them
through Jesus Christ; the challenge of the apostle is that
Christians should live 'forgiving one another, even as God also
for Christ's sake hath forgiven you'.[22]

Secondly, there is the new emphasis on the whole worshipping
community as the instrument for evangelistic work. In the past
'evangelism' has been regarded as the special call or prerogative
of a limited number of people. Now the weight of the challenge
rests on the Christian people as a whole. And a people that is
divided within itself cannot hope to go forward to effective and
powerful witness.

Within the Christian world there has been over the last few
years a remarkable development of new experiments in various
forms of Christian life in community. These have sprung up
spontaneously and independently in many parts of the Christian
world. One of the best known is the Reformed Brotherhood of
Taizé in France. At the Reformation the reformed churches
vigorously repudiated the monastic life and everything con-

---

[22] Eph. 4: 32.

nected with it; one could hardly imagine a more unfavourable soil for the growth of what in many ways resembles a monastic order. Yet Taizé has survived the first forty years of its existence, has grown, has drawn in brothers from several countries, has manifested to the world what a living fellowship looks like, has created a movement among the young people of the world to which there are few parallels, and has exercised a profound influence on many who have not actually joined it.[23]

3. Our friends have the right to ask us whether we are absolutely honest in our self-criticism, and in our presentation of the faith that we claim to profess.

In this area it seems to me that we can stand up fairly well to criticism. The Christian churches have lived through two centuries of crisis, and though weather-beaten they seem on the whole to have survived remarkably well.

Two centuries ago, men began to ask new questions, and to devise new critical methods for the advancement of knowledge.[24] When once these methods had been evolved, it was certain that in course of time they would be applied to questions of religion and to the Christian faith in exactly the same way as to everything else. Some Christians naturally regarded such an approach as blasphemous. There were cries of alarm and despair. But neither alarm nor despair would stay the flood. And gradually the majority of thoughtful Christians have accepted the legitimacy of the critical approach. It is not a question of this or that solution to a particular problem. It is the new conviction that the Christian faith has nothing to fear from the humble and reverent use of those same methods that have proved so useful for the advancement of knowledge in other spheres.

A great gulf separates us from our fathers in the eighteenth century. We read the ancient classics of Christian theology for education and edification; it is not until we come to the works of Friedrich Schleiermacher (1768–1834) that we feel ourselves to

---

[23] From a very large literature, J. L. G. Belado: *The Story of Taizé* (1980; originally in Spanish, 1976) may be cited as giving a vivid picture of the origins and aim of the movement.

[24] The German movement commonly called the Enlightenment is generally held to have started with the great writings published between 1765 and 1780 by G. E. Lessing.

be listening to a man who might almost be our own contemporary.[25]

At every fresh alarm there have been further cries of anxiety and despair. There have been false formulations of problems and defences which really defended nothing. There has been the inveterate tendency to confuse outworks with the very citadel of the faith. Some Christians have made too many concessions in the name of progress to the supposedly progressive spirit; others ostrich-like have denied that there really was any problem. And yet the church of Christ is still there. Under the guidance of prophetic spirits, who have believed that God might have new truths to reveal through science or psychology and who have refused to be afraid of any challenge or any evidence, the churches seem to have settled down after the period of strain to a period of relative tranquillity.[26] We have learned not to mistake a skirmish for a battle, and not to suppose that, because some ancient formulation will not stand examination, the whole structure of the faith is in peril.

Yet it remains true that in 1983 we cannot present the Christian faith as our predecessors presented it in 1883, or theirs in 1783. Some things have been lost and others gained, and there will not be a unanimous judgment as to loss and gain. But what is certain is that all things have been changed. Part of the embarrassment of the modern missionary is that, having himself been exposed at least vicariously to these processes of change, he finds himself speaking to Christians and non-Christians to whom the questions are unintelligible, and the answers therefore necessarily irrelevant.

For the moment this seems to turn to our disadvantage. But this may be only a temporary drawback. For this tremendous effort of Christian honesty over two centuries puts us in a position from which we can demand of our partners in the dialogue that they should exercise equal honesty. Are they prepared, as we are, to submit the sources of their faith to the most minute critical examination, and to abide by the results?

---

[25] Schleiermacher's greatest work *The Christian Faith* was published in 1820/21 (Eng. trans., Edinburgh, 1928).

[26] But some distinguished teachers warn us that even relative tranquillity is extremely dangerous; books by Maurice Wiles, John Hick, Don Cupitt and other radical thinkers of their type effectively hold out the red flag.

It is not for the Christian to do the work of the Hindu or the Muslim or the Buddhist for him. But, if these friends come to be prepared to do such work, they may find that they can get help from the Christians who have been before them in the way, and that the dialogue into which they enter with Christian partners has entered into a new and perhaps unforeseen dimension.

4. The fourth question will relate to our willingness to accept new light, from whatever direction it may come, and to believe that other faiths may enshrine truths to which we ourselves have been blind.

Once again, the churches can point to their own record in support of the view that, slow as they may be to learn, they are not wholly unwilling to learn from others. They believe that all truth is present in Christ; but they are bound also to admit their blindness, and to recognise that they have sometimes owed to critics and enemies the discovery of vital truth that was all the time implicit in the life and teaching of Christ.

For centuries the Christian churches have poured adulation on womanhood in the person of the Virgin Mary, the mother of Jesus; they have been extraordinarily slow to draw the natural inferences as to the position of women in society. In the middle of the nineteenth century the married woman in England had no control over her property. No university was open to women students. In 1851 Culver-Stockton College in Canton, Missouri, received a charter from the state to educate men and women together.[27] But European universities were slow to recognise the possibility. Women were already making a great name for themselves as novelists; but the idea that they make for themselves a career as doctor or lawyer seemed to most people, even to Christians, ludicrous. There has been much in modern secular feminist movements that is disagreeable, and the secular champions of women's rights have not always recognised their debt to Christian fellow-workers. It has sometimes seemed to Christians that the aim of the feminists is to obliterate the difference between man and woman, which they themselves believe God to have implanted in the human race from the

---

[27] Women students had obtained admission to Oberlin College rather earlier, I think in 1836. But 1851 was the year of the first charter.

beginning. Yet few would be prepared to deny that things are far better today than they were a century ago, and that not all the good impulses have come from Christian sources.

The *Magnificat* is a great paean in favour of social righteousness.[28] But how much attention had the churches paid to it in the four centuries that followed the break-up of the medieval world? How much do we owe to Karl Marx and his friends for the quickened social consciousness in almost all the churches? To follow the declarations of Christian conferences, from the Birmingham Conference on Christian Politics, Economics and Citizenship of 1924, and the Stockholm Conference on Life and Work in 1925, down to the Assembly of the World Council of Churches at Vancouver in 1983 is to see how this sense of social responsibility has deepened and broadened in the churches. The violent accusation, constantly repeated by some conservatives, that the ecumenically-minded churches are no better than lackeys of Moscow both indicates the source of some of the lessons that they have learned, and suggests that they have learned their lessons well.

Now, this being the attitude of the modern churches, we may affirm that we are prepared to open ourselves in fullest measure to every challenge that the Hindu or the Muslim or the Buddhist can present, and to rejoice in anything that he can show us of truth or reality that we have not already seen. We may make in our minds the reservation that, if he convinces us of depths of mystical experience or ethical achievement of which we now know nothing, we may find in the end that this also was an aspect of the message of Christ that we had somehow overlooked. But we can honestly say that at every point he will find us open to conviction.

5. If this is a true and honest statement of the attitude of the Christian churches, his last question will be whether we are prepared for a recasting and restatement of Christian truth in the light of the new knowledge that may come to us. The answer to this question has already been given, when we were speaking of the possibility of new forms of Christian culture and of new Christian discoveries in the lands that are now non-Christian.

---

[28] But not, as is sometimes inferred, a programme of social action!

We must be, and are, prepared for such restatement.

But, here, too, it may be well to throw in a word of caution. It is possible to restate the Christian world-view in such general terms that it is reduced to a vague theosophy from which the particular challenge presented by Christian faith is eliminated. There are certain basic convictions which must be maintained, if Christianity is to be recognisably Christian. Of these I have listed seven:

(i) There is only one God and Creator, from whom all things take their origin.

(ii) This God is a self-revealing God, and he himself is active in the knowledge that we have of him as Father, Son and Holy Spirit.

(iii) In Jesus the full meaning of the life of man, and of the purpose of God for the universe, has been made known. Through the death of Christ God has reconciled the alienated world to himself, and through his resurrection brought into being a new creation.

(iv) In Jesus Christians see the way in which they ought to live; his life is the norm to which they are unconditionally bound and to which by his grace they are increasingly conformed.

(v) The Cross of Jesus shows that to follow his way will certainly result in suffering; this is neither to be resented nor to be evaded.

(vi) The Christian faith may learn much from other faiths; but it is universal in its claims; in the end Christ must be acknowledged as Lord of all.

(vii) The death of the body is not the end. Christ has revealed the eternal dimension as the true home of man's spirit.

To make these affirmations is not to deny the right of any of our interlocutors in the debate to challenge or to criticise any one of them. It is simply to state the limits of concession. If any one of these cardinal points came to be seriously modified, Christianity would become something unrecognisably different from what it is.

★

We now move back to the other leg of the dialectic. Throughout this chapter we have seen the Christian churches doing a great deal of house-cleaning, and preparing themselves, though still very inadequately, for their tasks in the modern world. Now it is time for the Christians to put a few questions to the other side. How does the Christian, after all this preparation, enter today into the dialogue with his friends of the other faiths? The answer is admirably given us by Dr Hendrik Kraemer:

> Therefore Christ's ambassadors in the world, in order to preach the Gospel, can and must stand in the world of non-Christian religions with downright intrepidity and radical humility. And the same applies to the Christian standing in the world of culture, wherever it may be.[29]

Kraemer spoke here, as he had spoken earlier, of an 'open congenial understanding' of the other faiths. This is the first and great requisite. But our problem, our razor's edge, is the combination of this openness with the conviction that the message of Jesus Christ is proclamation, challenge, and judgment. We shall come to the other faiths today not as dogmatists or critics, but in the spirit of humble questioning, entitled to ask our questions, because we have first submitted ourselves to theirs.

Our first question, perhaps, will be whether these other faiths have ever really heard of a God who acts. If the answer is 'No', is their thought about God in any way commensurable with ours? Where are we to find any common denominator of thought?

One of the battle-grounds is going to be the nature of history. It may well be that we do not ourselves yet fully understand what we mean when we speak of God as Lord of history. But we do know that, in contrast to the Greek idea of history as cyclic, in which all things come back to that which they were before, and to the Hindu-Buddhist concept in which ultimate significance cannot be attributed to history, we hold that history is significant. It is the sphere in which God is at work. This does not mean simply that he interferes cataclysmically at certain given moments; the whole of history is the loom of his weaving. All nations and events are related to his purpose, though they may

---

[29] *Religion and the Christian Faith* (1956), p. 338. The whole section pp. 335-9 needs to be read.

vary in their distance from the centre of that purpose. Now only one kind of God could be active in history in this kind of way; and no other kind of God could be the object of Christian faith.

This leads directly to our second question. Have our interlocutors ever really looked at Jesus Christ and tried to see him as he is? For, if we take the Gospels seriously (and at the same time as critically as you will), Jesus is not in the least like anyone else who has ever lived. The things that he says about God are not the same as the sayings of any other religious teacher. The claims that he makes for himself are not the same as those that have been made on behalf of any other religious teacher. His criticisms of human life and society are far more devastating than those that any other man has ever made. The demands he makes on his followers are more searching than those put forward by any other religious teacher.

To say all this does not necessarily mean that Jesus was right. It is simply a plea for plain honesty. The danger of the approach of 'congenial understanding' is that we may all get lost in a fog of geniality. The first period is that of approximation, in which we find out the similarities between the faiths. This must be followed by a period of reflection, in which we face with ruthless honesty the reality of the differences. Dr Kraemer is right in warning us of this:

> It is ... illegitimate to speak of a rectilinear transition from the world of religion (or philosophy or whatever you will) to the world of revelation. Becoming a disciple of Christ means always a radical break with the past. Christ is, as we have repeatedly said, the *crisis* of all Religion (and philosophy, good or bad); this is to say, as well the Judge as the great Transformer of all religion. It never means a gradual transition.[30]

So, when we invite our friends of other faiths to look at Jesus Christ, we should do so with a full sense of responsibility for what it may mean for them, if they should look on him and really see him. That might be for them the ending of an old world and the creation of a new; for, if any man be in Christ, there is a new creation.

---

[30] *Ibid.*, p. 338

Nor are we allowed, by the truth of Christ, to say 'Look at him, and do not look at us.' Dr Vicedom has written trenchantly of the way in which the messenger of the Gospel is identified by his hearers not merely with his message but with his God:

> God comes to the people through His messengers. It is by their behaviour that God is judged. If the missionaries succeed in entering into the life of the people, in adapting themselves to their way of living, if they learn the language and become in many ways the advisers, friends and helpers of the Papuans, gradually confidence in the missionaries is established. This confidence is at once transferred to God. God is always judged in the light of what the missionaries are. Unless this comes to pass, even in New Guinea we shall hear people say, 'Your God is a foreign God. He demands new ways of doing things. He speaks our language so badly that it makes us sick even to listen to you.'[31]

It is not only in New Guinea that such things are true. For the Christian, every study of his relationship to the other faiths and their adherents must end with the ancient words of the New Testament, 'What manner of persons ought you to be?'[32]

---

[31] G. F. Vicedom: *Church and People in New Guinea* (World Christian Books, 1961), pp. 16-17.
[32] 2 Peter 3: 11.

Select Bibliography

There is an immense and ever-growing literature on every aspect of the subject. This bibliography includes only a limited number of books, almost all in English. Many contain bibliographies which will serve as a guide to readers in search of more detailed information about the subjects treated. Some are out of print, and must be sought in libraries.

WORKS OF REFERENCE

Abingdon Dictionary of Living Religions, ed. K. Crim (Abingdon Press, Nashville, 1981).
Concise Encyclopaedia of Living Faiths, ed. R.C. Zaehner (Hutchinson, London, 3rd edn., 1977, pbk.).
Dictionary of Non-Christian Religions, ed. E.G. Parrinder (Hutton Educ. Publications, Amersham, 1971).
The World's Religions, ed. R. Pierce Beaver *et al* (Lion Publishing, Tring, 1982).
World Christian Encyclopaedia, ed. D.B. Barrett (OUP, Nairobi, 1982).

PERIODICALS

A great deal of relevant information can be found in periodicals. Especially to be recommended are:

International Review of Mission, with an extensive reviewing service, and regular bibliographies on many subjects. Published by World Council of Churches, Geneva.
Ecumenical Review: indispensable for progress in dialogue between the religions. Published by World Council of Churches, Geneva.

Also of value are:
Missiology, published by American Society of Missiology, Pasadena, California.
Missionalia, published in Pretoria, South Africa.

GENERAL

ANDERSON, J.N.D.: *Christianity and Comparative Religion* (Tyndale Press, London, 1970).
BOUQUET, A.C.: *Sacred Books of the World* (Cassell, London, Belle Sauvage Library, new edn. 1962).
BOUQUET, A.C.: *Comparative Religion* (Cassell, London, Belle Sauvage Library, new and rev. edn. 1961).
COLE, W.O.: *Five Religions in the Twentieth Century* (Hulton Educ. Publications, Amersham, 1981; new edn. 1982, pbk.).
CRAGG, K.: *The Christian and Other Religion: The Measure of Christ* (Mowbrays, Oxford, Library of Theology, 1977, pbk.).
HALLENCREUTZ, C.F.: *New Approaches to Men of Other Faiths* (World Council of Churches, Geneva, 1970).
KITAGAWA, J.M. (ed.): *Modern Trends in World Religions* (Open Court, La Salle, Illinois, 1959).
LEEUW, G. van der: *Religion in Essence and Manifestation* (Allen & Unwin, London, 2nd edn. 1964).
LING, T.O.: *A History of Religion, East and West* (Macmillan, London, 1968).
NEUNER, J. (ed.): *Christian Revelation and World Religions* (Burns, Oates, London, 1967).
PARRINDER, E.G.: *World's Living Religions* (Barker, London, 1967; Pan Books, new edn. 1974).
SAMARTHA, S.J.: *Courage for Dialogue* (WCC, Geneva, 1981).
SAMARTHA, S.J. (ed.): *Faith in the Midst of Faiths* (WCC, Geneva, 1977).
SHARPE, E.J.: *Comparative Religion; A History* (Duckworth, London, 1975; new edn. 1976, pbk).
SMART, R.N.: *The Religious Experience of Mankind* (Collins, London, Fontana Books, 1971).
SMART, N. and HECHT R.D. (eds.): *Sacred Texts of the World: A Universal Anthology* (Macmillan, London, 1982).
ZAEHNER, R.C.: *Concordant Discord: the Interdependence of Faiths* (Clarendon Press, Oxford, 1970).

JUDAISM

CRAGG, K.: *This Year in Jerusalem* (Darton, Longman & Todd, London, 1982, pbk.).

EPSTEIN, I.: *Judaism, A Historical Presentation* (Penguin Books, Harmondsworth, 1970).

HAMMERSTEIN, F. von (ed.): *Christian Jewish Relations in Ecumenical Perspective* (WCC, Geneva, 1978).

HESCHEL, A.: *God in Search of Man, A Philosophy of Judaism* (Calder, London, 1956).

KOENIG, J.: *Jews and Christians in Dialogue: New Testament Foundations* (Westminster Press, Philadelphia, 1979, pbk.).

OESTERREICHER, J.M. (ed.): *The Bridge: A Year Book of Judaeo–Christian Studies* (Pantheon Books, New York, 4 vols, 1955, 1956, 1958, 1962).

PARKES, J.: *Prelude to Dialogue: Jewish-Christian Relationships* (Vallentine Mitchell, London, 1969).

SANDMEL, S.: *We Jews and Jesus* (OUP, New York, 1973; Galaxy pbk.).

SANDMEL, S.: *Judaism and Christian Beginnings* (OUP, New York, 1978; Galaxy pbk.).

SCHNEIDER, P.: *Sweeter than Honey. Christian Presence amid Judaism* (SCM Press, London, 1966).

SCHOEPS, H.J.: *The Jewish Christian Argument* (Holt, New York, 1963).

TANNENBAUM, M.H. (ed.): *Evangelicals and Jews in Conversation on Scripture, Theology and History* (Baker Book House, Grand Rapids, MI, 1978).

VERMES, G.: *Jesus the Jew: a Historian's Reading of the Gospels* (Collins, London, 1973; SCM Press, London, new edtn. 1983, pbk.).

ISLAM

ANDERSON, J.N.D.: *Law Reform in the Muslim World* (Athlone Press, Univ. of London, 1976).

CRAGG, K.: *Sandals at the Mosque* (SCM Press, London, 1959).

CRAGG, K.: *The Dome and the Rock* (SPCK, London, 1964).

FYZEE, A.A.: *A Modern Approach to Islam* (OUP, Bombay, new edtn. 1982).

GIBB, H.A.R.: *Modern Trends in Islam* (Univ. Chicago Press, 1947; Octagon Books, 1971).

GOLDSMITH, M.: *Islam and Christian Witness* (Hodder & Stoughton, London, 1982).

GUILLAUME, A.: *Islam* (Penguin Books, Harmondsworth, 1954; Cassell, London, Belle Sauvage Library, 2nd rev. edn. 1973).

JANSEN, G.H.: *Militant Islam* (Pan Books, London, 1979).

NAIPAUL, V.S.: *Among the Believers: an Islamic Journey* (Deutsch, London, 1981).

NASR, S.H.: *Living Sufism* (Allen & Unwin, London, Mandala Books, 1980).

NAZIR-ALI, M.: *Islam: A Christian Perspective* (Paternoster Press, Exeter, 1983, pbk.).

PARRINDER, E.G.: *Jesus in the Qu'ran* (Sheldon Press, London, 1976, pbk.).

ROSENTHAL, E.I.J.: *Islam in the Modern National State* (Cambridge Univ. Press, 1965).

SCHIMMEL, Annemarie (ed.): *We Believe in One God: The Experience of God in Christianity and Islam* (Seabury Press, New York, 1980).

SHAH, I.: *The Way of the Sufi* (Penguin Books, Harmondsworth, 1974).

SMITH, W. Cantwell: *Islam in Modern History* (Princeton Univ. Press, 1957; new edn. 1977).

WELCH, A.T. & CACHIA, P. (eds.): *Islam: Past Influence and Present Challenge* (Edinburgh Univ. Press, 1979).

HINDUISM

BROWN, J.M.: *Men and Gods in a Changing World: Some themes in the religious experience of twentieth-century Hindus and Christians* (SCM Press, London, 1980).

CHETTIMATTAM, J.B.: *Patterns of Indian Thought: A Student's Introduction* (Geoffrey Chapman, London, 1971).

DEVANANDAN, P.D.: *The Gospel and Renascent Hinduism* (SCM Press, London, 1959).

DIEHL, C.G.: *Church and Shrine: Intermingling Patterns of Culture* (Uppsala, 1965).

HOGG, A.G.: *Karma and Redemption* (Christian Literature Society, Madras, 1908; reprinted 1970).

HOOKER, R.: *Journey into Varanasi* (CMS, London, 1978, pbk.).

HOOKER, R.: *Voices of Varanasi* (CMS, London, 1979, pbk.).

KLOSTERMAIER, K.: *Hindu and Christian in Vrindaban* (SCM Press, London, 1969).

PANIKKAR, R.: *The Unknown Christ of Hinduism* (Darton, Longman & Todd, London, rev. edn. 1981, pbk.).

PARRINDER, E.G.: *Upanishads, Gita and Bible: a comparative study* (Sheldon Press, London, 2nd edn. 1979).

RADHAKRISHNAN, S.: *Eastern Religions and Western Thought* (Clarendon Press, 2nd edn. Oxford, 1940).

SAMARTHA, S.J.: *Introduction to Radhakrishnan: the Man and his Thought* (YMCA, New Delhi, 1960).

SEN, K.M.: *Hinduism* (Penguin Books, Harmondsworth, 1961; new edn. 1970).

SPEAR, P.: *India, Pakistan and the West* (OUP, Oxford, Opus Books, 4th edn. 1967).

THAPAR, R. (ed.): *Change and Conflict in India* (Madras, 1978).

THOMAS, M.M.: *The Acknowledged Christ of the Indian Renaissance* (SCM Press, London, 1970).

TINKER, H.: *Ordeal of Love: C.F. Andrews and India* (OUP, Oxford, 1980).

ZAEHNER, R.C.: *Hinduism* (OUP, Oxford, Opus Books, new edn. 1966).

ZAEHNER, R.C.: *Hindu Scriptures* (Dent, London, 1966; Everyman Univ. Library, 1972).

BUDDHISM

COLLINS, S.: *Selfless Persons: Imagery and Thought in Theravada Buddhism* (Cambridge Univ. Press, 1982).

CONZE, E.: *Buddhist Scriptures* (Penguin Books, Harmondsworth, 1959).

DHARMASIRI, G.: *A Buddhist Critique of the Christian Concept of God* (Lake House Investments Ltd, Colombo, 1974).

HAMMER, R.: *Japan's Religious Ferment* (SCM Press, London, 1961).

HUMPHREYS, C.: *Buddhism* (Penguin Books, Harmondsworth, 1951; Cassell, London, Belle Sauvage Library, new and rev. edn. 1962).

HUMPHREYS, C.: *Exploring Buddhism* (Allen & Unwin, London, Mandala Books, 1974).

KADOWAKI, J.K.: *Zen and the Bible: A Priest's Experience*, Eng. trans., (Routledge, London, 1980, pbk.).

LING, T.O.: *Buddha, Marx and God, some aspects of religion in the modern world* (Macmillan, London, 2nd rev. edn. 1979).

MORGAN, K.W. (ed.): *The Path of the Buddha* (Ronald Press, New York, 1956).

OLDENBERG, H.: *Buddha: his Life, his Doctrine, his Order*, Eng. trans., (Indological Book House, Delhi, 1971).

SILVA, L.A. de: *The Problem of the Self in Buddhism and Christianity* (Macmillan, London, new edn. 1979).

SMITH, B.L. (ed.): *Religion and Conflict in South Asia* (Brill, Leiden, 1976).

SPAE, J.: *Buddhist Christian Empathy* (Chicago Institute of Theology & Culture, Chicago, 1980).

SUZUKI, D.T.: *An Introduction to Zen Buddhism* (Macleod, New York, 1949; Grove Press, London, 1964, pbk.).

Theology 'In Dialogue with Buddhism' Northeast Asia Journal of Theology (NE Asia Association of Theological Schools, Tokyo, 1978), Nos. 20/21 pp. 1–117; with a bibliography of books on Buddhism and Christianity.

THE PRIMAL WORLD

BARRETT, D.B.: *Schism and Renewal in Africa* (OUP, Nairobi, 1968).

EVANS-PRITCHARD, E.E.: *Theories of Primitive Religion* (OUP, Oxford, 1965).

GUNSON, N.: *Messengers of Grace: Evangelical Missionaries in the South Seas 1797–1860* (OUP, Melbourne, 1978).

HALIBURTON, G.M.: *The Prophet Harris: A Study of an African Prophet* (Longman, London, 1971).

HILLIARD, D.: *God's Gentlemen: A History of the Melanesian Mission 1849₁1942* (Univ. Queensland Press, Brisbane, 1978).

JENSEN, A.E.: *Myth and Cult among Primitive Peoples*, Eng. trans. (Univ. Chicago Press, 1963).

LAWRENCE, P.: *Road Belong Cargo: A Study of the Cargo Movement* (Manchester Univ. Press, 1964).

LESSA, W.A. and VOGT, E.Z. (eds.): *Reader in Comparative Religion: An Anthropological Approach* (Harper, New York, 4th edn. 1979, pbk.).

MARTIN, M.-L.: *Kimbangu: An African Prophet and his Church* (Blackwell, Oxford, 1975).

MBITI, J.S.: *African Religions and Philosophy* (Heinemann, London, 1969).

McVEIGH, M.J.: *God in Africa: Conceptions of God in African Traditional Religion and Christianity* (Claude Stark, Cape Cod, 1974).

PARRINDER, E.G.: *Africa's Three Religions* (Sheldon Press, London, 2nd rev. edn. 1976).

SHORTER, Aylward W.F. (ed.): *African Christian Spirituality* (Geoffrey Chapman, London, 1978, pbk.).

TAYLOR, J.V.: *The Primal Vision: Christian Presence amid African Religion* (SCM Press, London, 1963).

TEMPELS, P.: *Bantu Philosophy*, Eng. trans. (Paris, 1959); French trans. (Paris, 1949).

VICEDOM, G.F.: *Church and People in New Guinea* (Lutterworth Press, London, 1961).

NO FAITH AND FAITH IMPLICIT

CHADWICK, W.O.: *The Secularization of the European Mind in the Nineteenth Century* (Cambridge Univ. Press, 1976; new edtn. 1978, pbk.).

CROSSMAN, R.H.S. (ed.): *The God that Failed: Six Studies in Communism* (Hamish Hamilton, London, 1950).

GREGOR SMITH, R.: *Secular Christianity* (Collins, London, 1966).

HUXLEY, J.: *Religion without Revelation* (Greenwood Press, London, new edn. 1979).

HUXLEY, J. (ed.): *The Humanist Frame* (Allen & Unwin, London, 1961).

LASH, N.: *A Matter of Hope: A Theologian's Reflections on the Thought of Karl Marx* (Darton, Longman & Todd, London, 1981).

LEEUWEN, A.T. van: *Christianity in World History and the Meeting of the Faiths of East and West* (Edinburgh House Press, London, 1964).

LING, T.O.: *Karl Marx and Religion in Europe and India* (Macmillan, London, 1980).

MACHOVEČ, M.: *Jesus für Atheisten* (Kreuz Verlag, Stuttgart, 1973); Eng. trans.: *A Marxist Looks at Jesus* (Darton, Longman & Todd, London, 1972, pbk.).

MACQUARRIE, J.: *New Directions in Theology Today: Vol. 3: God and Secularity* (Lutterworth Press, London, 1968).
MARTIN, D.A.: *The Religious and the Secular* (Routledge, London, 1969).
MARTIN, D.A.: *A General Theory of Secularization* (Blackwell, Oxford, 1978; new edn. 1980, pbk.).
MIRANDA, J.P.: *Marx and the Bible* (SCM Press, London, 1977).
WEST, C.C.: *Communism and the Theologians: the Story of an Encounter* (SCM Press, London, 1958).
WILSON, B.R.: *Contemporary Transformations of Religion* (Clarendon Press, Oxford, new edn. 1979, pbk.).

EXISTENTIALISM AND AFTER

BARRACLOUGH, G.: *An Introduction to Contemporary History* (Penguin Books, Harmondsworth, 1967).
CAMUS, A.: *L'Homme Révolté* (Paris, 1952); Eng. trans.: *The Rebel* (Hamish Hamilton, London, 1953; Penguin Books, Harmondsworth, 1962).
CAMUS, A.: *La Chute* (Paris, 1956); Eng. trans.: *The Fall* (Hamish Hamilton, London, 1957; Penguin Books, Harmondsworth, 1963).
CAMUS, A.: *La Peste* (Paris, 1947); Eng. trans.: *The Plague* (Hamish Hamilton, London, 1948; Penguin Books, Harmondsworth, 1960).
HEIDEGGER, M.: *Sein und Zeit* (Tübingen, 1957); Eng. trans.: *Being and Time* (SCM Press, London, 1962).
MACQUARRIE, J.: *An Existentialist Theology* (SCM Press, London, 1955; Greenwood Press, London, new edn. 1979).
MARCEL, G.: *Being and Having,* Eng. trans. (Collins, London, and Harper, New York, 1965).
O'BRIEN, C.C.: *Camus* (Collins, London, Fontana Books, 1970).
ROBERTS, D.E.: *Existentialism and Religious Belief* (OUP, New York, 1957; Galaxy pbk., 1959).
SARTRE, J.P.: *L'Être et le Néant* (Paris, 1949). Eng. trans.: *Being and Nothingness* (Methuen, London, University pbk., 1969).
SARTRE, J.P.: *Les Mots* (autobiography) (Paris, 1964); Eng. trans.; *Words* (Hamish Hamilton, London, 1964; Penguin Books, Harmondsworth, 1969).

TILLICH, P.: *Theology of Culture* (OUP, New York, 1959; Galaxy pbk. 1964).

A SEARCH FOR LIGHT

CUPITT, D.: *Taking Leave of God* (SCM Press, London, 1980).
ELROD, J.W.: *Kierkegaard and Christendom* (Princeton Univ. Press, 1981).
HARDY, A.C.: *The Divine Flame* (Religious Experience Research Unit, Oxford, 1978, pbk.).
HAY, D.: *Exploring Inner Space: Is God still possible in the twentieth century?* (Penguin Books, Harmondsworth, 1982).
JAKI, S.C.: *Cosmos and Creator* (Scottish Academic Press, Edinburgh, 1981, pbk.).
JAKI, S.C.: *The Road of Science and The Ways to God* (Scottish Academic Press, Edinburgh, 1978; new edn. 1980, pbk.).
MASLOW, A.H.: *Religions, Values and Peak Experiences* (Ohio State Univ. Press, Columbus, 1964; Penguin Books, Harmondsworth, 1976).
PEACOCKE, A.R.: *Creation and the World of Science* (OUP, Oxford, 1979).
WARD, K.: *Rational Theology and the Creativity of God* (Blackwell, Oxford, 1982).
WARD, K.: *Holding Fast to God. A Reply to Don Cupitt* (SPCK, London, 1982, pbk.).

CHRISTENDOM

BAKER, J.A.: *The Foolishness of God* (Darton, Longman & Todd, London, 1970).
BARRACLOUGH, G. (ed.): *The Christian World: A Social and Cultural History of Christianity* (Thames & Hudson, London, 1981).
Believing in the Church: the Corporate Nature of Faith (Doctrine Commission of the Church of England, SPCK, London, 1981 pbk.).
CRAGG, K.: *Christianity in World Perspective* (Lutterworth Press, London, 1968).

DILLISTONE, F.W.: *Religious Experience and the Christian Faith* (SCM Press, London, 1982, pbk.).

EDWARDS, D.L.: *Religion and Change* (Hodder and Stoughton, London, 1969).

LUCAS, J.R.: *Freedom and Grace* (SPCK, London, 1976).

SMART, N.: *The Phenomenon of Religion* (Mowbrays, Oxford, 2nd rev. edn. 1978, pbk.).

Index

Africa, 59, 60, 61, 62, 64, 66-7, 70
Agapē, 153
Ahiṃsā, 146, 147
Ahmadiyya movement, 66, 68
Al Ghazzālī, 77
Ali, Sayyid Amir, 71
Alice movement, 186
Altizer, T.J.J., 244-5
Ambedkar, Dr B.L., 102
America, 273-4
Aquinas, Thomas, 266
Arabia, 70, 85
Arabic, 62, 63, 64, 69, 73
  language of Koran, 63
Aristotle, 205, 266, 271
Ārya Samāj, 95
Aryan truths, 145-7
Azariah, Bishop, 263

Balfour, A.J., 40
Bangladesh, 61, 65
Bantu, 168-9
Baptists, 275
Barr, James, 267
Barraclough, Geoffrey, 222-5
Barth, Karl, 266
Basham, A.L., 96, 104, 123
Ben-Chorin, Scholem, 49-50
Bhagavadgītā, 103, 113, 117, 118, 122, 261
bhakti, 117, 118
Bhave, Vinoba, 105
Bloch-Hoell, Nils, 262
bodhisattva, 154

Boman, T., 267
Bonhoeffer, Dietrich, 227
Bouquet, A.C., 133
Boxer riots, 11
Brahma Sūtra, 106, 111, 123
Brahmo Samāj, 97, 98
Brown, Dr Judith, 248-50
Browning, Robert, 56
Buber, Martin, 50-1, 236
Buddha, 125-8, 129, 130, 133, 138, 141, 145, 147, 149, 150, 156
Buddhism, 14, 15, 18, chap. V
  passim (125-58), 257, 282, 283, 285
  Zen form of, 131, 143-4, 151
Buddhist
  Societies, 134
  World Council, 134, 147
  World Fellowship of, 132
Bultmann, Rudolf, 275-6
Burma, 132, 148

Camus, Albert, 237-41, 244
Casalis (missionary), 162
Chadwick, W.O., 190
Chakravarty, Amiya, 98
Chardin, P. Teilhard de, 115, 197
Chen Tu-Hsiu, 224
China
  Muslims in, 60
Christian faith
  dialogue with Judaism, 44-5
  dialogue with Islam, 78-81, 89

dialogue with Hinduism, 123-4
dialogue with Buddhism, 132, 148-58
dialogue with Primal religion, 181-8
dialogue with Marxism, 191, 195
dialogue with Existentialism, 254-6
Cicero, 162
Clasper, Paul, 139
Clifford, W.K., 205
Codrington, F.H., 162
Communism, 268-9
Comparative religion, 13, 18
Comparative study of religions, 13, 19
Constantinople, 59
Conze, E., 131, 133
Cragg, Bishop Kenneth, 78, 80, 85, 88
Cranfield, C.E.B., 36
Crusades, 59, 60, 75-6
Cunningham, William, 192
Cupitt, Don, 221, 225, 246

Davids, T.W. Rhys, 130
Dawson, Christopher, 264, 270
'Death of God' movement, 244, 246
Dehqani-Taft; Bishop H., 43
Derr, T.S., 200
Devanandan, P.D., 98, 101, 109, 122, 270
dhamma, 129, 130, 143, 145
Dharmasiri, Gunapala, 148, 151
Dhavamony, M., 118
Diehl, C.G., 92
Dodds, E.R., 161

Donne, John, 28
Doughty, C.M., 12
Duff, Alexander, 97
Dutch Reformed Church, 278

Eddington, A.S., 204
Edersheim, Dr A., 43
Edinburgh Missionary Conference 1910, 277
Egypt, 59, 61, 65, 72
Einstein, A., 223
Existentialism, 225-47, 250, 254-5

Faith, chap. VII passim (189-219)
a search for, chap. VIII passim (220-56)
Faraday, Michael, 204
Farmer, H.H., 163
Farnell, L.L., 161
Feuerbach, 229
Findlay, J.N., 205
Flew, Antony, 205
Frazer, Sir J.G., 10
Fyzee, A.A., 72, 73

Gāndhi, Indira, 109
Gāndhi, Mahatma M.K., 99, 101-4, 105, 110, 117, 121
Gautama, see Buddha
Geneva Conference 1966, 277
Gibb, H.A.R., 63, 70, 71, 75, 87
Glover, T.R., 183
Gogarten, Friedrich, 199-200
Goldbach, 206-7
Gollancz, Victor, 49
Golwalkar, Shri, 96
Graham, Aelred, 151
Greece/Greeks, 60
Guillaume, Dr A., 84

hadīth, 69, 70, 74

Hamann, Johann G., 225
Hamilton, William, 244–5
Hardy, Sir Alister, 251
Hay, David, 248, 251
Hazard, Paul, 202
Hegel, 193, 196, 225, 239
Heidegger, Martin, 230–3, 235, 254
Heisenberg, Werner, 208
Hermelink, Professor, 273
Hijra, 82
Hindu/ism, chap. IV *passim* (91–124), 262, 264, 282, 283, 285
Holmes, Edmund, 146
Holsten, Walter, 135
Horner, I.B., 138, 140
Houtart, F., 160
Humanism, 196–8
Humphreys, Christmas, 134, 143, 146, 153
Hussain, Kamel, 80
Husserl, Edmund, 229
Huxley, Sir Julian, 196–7
Huxley, T.H., 189, 205

Ijmā', 70
Ijtihād, 70, 71
India, 59, 60, 61, 62, 65, 66, 71, 72, 261, 263, 272, 274
Indonesia, 60, 61, 62, 64–5, 68, 272
Iqbal, Muhammad, 58, 71
Iran, 61, 62, 64, 65, 68
Iraq, 60, 61, 65, 73
ishtadevatā, 107
Islam/Muslim, 10, 12, 13, 15, 16, 17, chap III *passim* (57–90), 179, 261, 262, 264, 282, 283
Israel, 37, 38, 41, 44, 45, 50, 51, 52, 53, 56

Jaki, L., 207
Jansen, G.H., 64, 65, 67
Japan, 133–4
Jasper, David, 250
Jātaka, 137, 150
Jews, chap. II *passim* (34–56), 257, 261
John of Damascus, 76
John XXIII, Pope, 10
Juadaism, chap. II *passim* (34–56)
Junod, H.A., 163

karma, 122–3, 137, 147, 151
Kenya, 67
Keysser, Christian, 168
Khandhas, 136–7, 141, 150
Kierkegaard, S., 225–30, 264, 275
Kimbangu, Simon, 187
Kivebulaya, A., 183
Koran, 63, 69–70, 71, 73, 74, 78, 81–2, 83, 85, 86, 90
Kraemer, H., 106, 285–6
Kraus, H.J., 54

Lambeth Conferences, 277–8
Lang, Andrew, 165
Laplace, P.S. de, 203–4, 208, 209
Latourette, K.S., 65
Leeuw, Professor G. van der, 15
Leeuwen, A. van, 200
Lenshina, Alice, 186
Levy, Rabbi Yom Tom, 34
Libya, 66
Ling, T., 133, 141
Liverpool conference, 10, 11
Locke, John, 203
Lovell, Sir Bernard, 210
Lubac, Henri de, 246
Luck, A., 183

Lull, Raymond, 77

Macdonald, D. Black, 77–8
Machoveč, Milan, 195
Macquarrie, John, 200, 206, 233
Mahāyāna, 128, 131, 154
Malalasekera, Dr G.P., 132
Malcolm, Norman, 224
Mao Tse-tung, 221–4
Marcel, Gabriel, 234, 236, 241–3
Marcellinus, Ammianus, 259
Martin, M.L., 187
Martineau, James, 98
Marx, Karl, 191–4, 228, 234, 283
Marxism, 14, 179, 191–6, 217 221, 224, 239
Maslow, Abraham, 250
Maurice, F.D., 194
mayā, 111
mayāvēda, 112
Mbiti, John, 179
Meiring, P.J., 68
mettā, 152–3
Michaud, Sister Jocelyne, 166
Miller, J. Hollis, 250
mission, 9, 11, 13
Mitchell, B., 213
Moltmann, Jürgen, 193–4, 195
Monod, Jacques, 208–9
Montefiore, C.J., 48–9
Montefiore, Bishop Hugh, 43, 48–9
Montezuma, 171
Muhammad, 10, 57, 58, 59, 69, 70, 82, 83, 85, 90
    'Life' of, 10
Muir, Sir William, 10
Müller, Max, 10,
Muslim, *see* Islam

Mutiny, 95

Nāgārjuna, 131
Naipaul, V.S., 68, 272
nāma, 137
Nānak, Guru, 15
Napoleon, 203–4
Neher, André, 53
Nehru, J., 104, 109, 124
New Guinea, 286
Newton, Isaac, 203
Nibbūta, 140–1
Nichiren sect, 133, 134
Nicholson, R.A., 74
Niebuhr, R., 42–3, 44
Nietzsche, 270
Nigeria, 61, 62, 67
Nirvāṇa, 127, 130, 139–41, 142, 143, 147, 154, 157
Nkrumah, Dr, 176
Nock, Arthur Darby, 164
Nygren, Bishop Anders, 36

Obote, Milton, 177
Ogden, Stuart, 246
Ogilvie, R.M., 162
Ogot, B.A., 185
Oldenberg, H., 125
Ortega y Gasset, J., 222

Pakistan, 61, 62, 64, 65, 66, 71
Pali canon, 125, 128, 131, 132, 141, 145
Paramahamsa, Rāmakrishna, 99, 100
Parkes, Dr James, 38–9
Parrinder, Geoffrey, 81, 86
Pascal, 22
Patteson, Bishop John C., 11
Paul, Saint, 36, 37, 38, 39, 55
Peacocke, A.P., 207, 210
Peck, E.J., 12

Pentecostal movement, 262
Philippines, 60, 62
Pinsker, Leo, 39–40
Pirouet, Louise, 183
Plato, 229, 271
Plotinus, 29, 73, 140
polygamy, 271
Porteus, S.D., 173
Price, H.H., 212–3
Primal religions, chap. VI passim (159–88)
Pringle-Pattison, Prof., 210

Radhakrishnan, S., 99, 105–8, 110, 111–12, 122
Ramaḍān, fast of, 72
Rāmānuja, 261
Ramsay, I.T., 213
Raven, C.E., 198
Reformation, 279
Reiniche, M.L., 92
Roberts, D.E., 232
Robinson, Bishop John, 152
Roman Catholic, 79, 266, 267
Roscoe, John, 163
Rosenzweig, Franz, 46–7, 55
Roszak, T., 190
Roy, Rammohun, 97–8
Rumi, Jalal al-Din, 73
Runciman, Sir Steven, 76
rūpa, 136
Russell, Bertrand, 222
Russia, 263, 264

Sadat, President of Egypt, 65
Saṁkara, 117, 261
saṃsāra, 94
Sankhara, 137
Sanna, 137
Śāntideva, 154
Sarasvati, Dayānand, 95
Sarma, D.S., 123

Sartre, Jean-Paul, 232, 234–7, 244, 254
Saudi Arabia, 61, 65
Schaopati, Brahman, 127
Schereschewsky, Bishop Isaac, 43
Schlegel, R., 208
Schleiermacher, Friedrich, 280
Schmidt, Pater W., 166
Schwarz-Bart, André, 34
Secularism, 190, 201
Secularisation, 190, 199, 217, 219
Sen, Keshub Chander, 98
Sen, P.K., 98
Senghor, Léopold, 177
Sengupta, S., 112, 114
Shari'ah, 70, 73
Smith, W. Cantwell, 57, 75, 80
South Africa, 278
Spain, 59, 60
Spear, Percival, 95
Sri Lanka, 132, 147, 148, 272
Stein, Gertrude, 223
Strato/Stratonican, 205
Strawson, P.F., 213
Sufis/Sufism, 73, 74
Sunna, 69
Süssman, Cornelia and Irving, 18
Suzuki, D.T., 151
Sweetman, J.W., 77

Tagore, Debendranāth, 97–8
Tagore, Dwarkanāth, 97
Tagore, Rabindranāth, 98
Taizé, 279
Talbu, Muhammad, 80
Talmud, 261
Tanzania, 62, 64
Taylor, Bishop John V., 182
Tempels, P., 168, 169

Temple, Archbishop William, 28, 198, 246
Tennyson, Hallam, 105
Thailand
Theravāda, 128, 131, 132, 138
Thils, G., 192
Thomson, Sir J.J., 204
Tillich, Paul, 221-4, 229, 230
Turkey/Turks, 59, 60, 64
Tylor, E.B., 10, 165-6, 168

U Nu, 132
Upaniṣads, 91, 94, 110, 120
U Tittila, 142, 151

Vatican II, 11, 48
Vedana, 137
Vedānta, 105, 108, 112
Vedas, 92, 95
Vermes, Geza, 50
Vicedom, G.F., 186, 286
Viññāna, 137
Vivekānanda, Swāmi, 99-101, 106

Von Rad, G., 264

Waardenburg, J., 89
Ward, Keith, 209
Webb, C.C.J., 114
Weinberg, S., 207
Weizmann, Chaim, 40
Welbourne, F.B., 185
Wheeler, J., 210
Whitehead, A.N., 29, 245-6
Wiley, Basil, 116
Wilson, Edmund, 160, 223
Winternitz, M., 154
Wittgenstein, Ludwig, 222-4
World Council of Churches, 79, 89, 268, 277, 283
World League of Muslims, 89
Wright, T., 55

Zaehner, R.C., 75, 81, 86, 115, 117
Zen, see Buddhism
Zionism, 39-40